PRAISE FOR *THE URBAN MONK*

"Written with page-turning verve, this book integrates ancient Taoist wisdom and modern brain science to offer hundreds of practical ways to feel better and do better right now. Funny, direct, and honest, Pedram Shojai feels like a trusted friend and teacher offering a full package of skillful means."
—Rick Hanson, PhD, author of *Hardwiring Happiness: The New Brain Science of Contentment, Calm, and Confidence*

"We know that the healthcare crisis in the West can't be fixed by pills. Lifestyle is the key. *The Urban Monk* elegantly lays out a balanced way of life that can not only bring us back to health, but help us relax and smile while we do it. I highly recommend this book to anyone trying to get healthy in our fast-paced world."
—Mark Hyman, MD, director, Cleveland Clinic Center for Functional Medicine, and author of the #1 *New York Times* bestseller *The Blood Sugar Solution*

"Knowing that meditation is good for us isn't enough. We need to practice it in our daily lives to actually benefit from it. *The Urban Monk* is a treasure, with many practical lifestyle hacks that can help you be happier and healthier."
—Daniel G. Amen, MD, founder, Amen Clinics, and author of *Change Your Brain, Change Your Life*

"Combining modern Western medicine and ancient Eastern wisdom, Dr. Pedram Shojai's cutting-edge, easy-to-implement program helps you burn fat, boost energy, and optimize your life to become an urban monk even in the most stressed-out environment. Can't recommend this one enough!"
—JJ Virgin, *New York Times* bestselling author of *The Virgin Diet* and *The Virgin Diet Cookbook*

"Pedram offers a fresh and unique perspective on life in the modern world. He truly is an Urban Monk and his friendly style takes us all along for the ride. If you deal with stress, time constraints, and the challenges of a busy life, this book is a must-read."

—Sara Gottfried, MD, author of *New York Times* bestseller
The Hormone Cure and *The Hormone Reset Diet*

"Being an Urban Monk is about facing every day with a sense of peace, focus, and drive, no matter what is coming at you. Pedram Shojai will put you on the right path to experience a clear mind and a total rejuvenation of your life."

—Mallika Chopra, author of *Living with Intent:*
My Somewhat Messy Journey to Purpose, Peace, and Joy

"*The Urban Monk* gives you the physical and mental hacks to take your life to the next level and feel better than you ever have. Pedram Shojai will heal your soul and kick your ass all the way to enlightenment."

—Dave Asprey, author of the *New York Times* bestseller
The Bulletproof Diet

"A fantastic book and an incredible resource for anyone looking to access the benefits of vibrant health and who lives a modern life where the conditions for that are less than ideal. *The Urban Monk* will be your guide into a new frontier of awakened living."

—Tiffany Cruikshank, LAc, MAOM,
founder of Yoga Medicine

THE
URBAN MONK

EASTERN WISDOM AND MODERN HACKS
TO STOP TIME AND FIND SUCCESS,
HAPPINESS, AND PEACE

PEDRAM SHOJAI, OMD
CREATOR OF WELL.ORG

RODALE

RODALE
wellness

Live happy. Be healthy. Get inspired.

Sign up today to get exclusive access to our authors, exclusive bonuses, and the most authoritative, useful, and cutting edge information on health, wellness, fitness, and living your life to the fullest.

Visit us online at RodaleWellness.com
Join us at RodaleWellness.com/Join

© 2016 by Pedram Shojai, OMD

Simultaneously published as a trade hardcover and international paperback by Rodale Inc.

Rodale books may be purchased for business or promotional use or for special sales. For information, please write to:
Special Markets Department, Rodale Inc., 733 Third Avenue, New York, NY 10017.

Printed in the United States of America

Rodale Inc. makes every effort to use acid-free ♾, recycled paper ♻.

Book design by Christina Gaugler

Chapter illustrations by Paige Vickers

Library of Congress Cataloging-in-Publication Data is on file with the publisher.

ISBN-13: 978–1–62336–615–5 hardcover
ISBN-13: 978–1–62336–734–3 paperback

Distributed to the trade by Macmillan

2 4 6 8 10 9 7 5 3   hardcover
2 4 6 8 10 9 7 5 3 1   paperback

RODALE.

We inspire and enable people to improve their lives and the world around them.

To the vision of a peaceful, sustainable, abundant future for our children's children. May we step in, step up, and make it happen for the future of all life.

CONTENTS

INTRODUCTION.....................................IX

CHAPTER 1: Stress:
How Do I Dodge the Bullets? 1

CHAPTER 2: Drinking from Infinity:
The Art of Mastering Time 27

CHAPTER 3: Energy:
Why Am I Always So Tired?...............49

CHAPTER 4:
What Happened to Sleep? 73

CHAPTER 5:
Stagnant Lifestyle................................97

CHAPTER 6: Weight Gain and
Negative Self-Image...........................119

CHAPTER 7: No Connection with
Nature or Things That Are Real 141

CHAPTER 8: Lonely despite Being
Surrounded by People........................165

CHAPTER 9: Never Enough
Money 187

CHAPTER 10: Living a Life with
Purpose 213

NEXT STEPS 237

RESOURCES 241

ACKNOWLEDGMENTS...........................259

ABOUT THE AUTHOR............................261

INDEX 263

INTRODUCTION

HAVE YOU EVER FELT guilty about missing a workout at the gym?

Ever felt guilty for missing yoga class?

Did you learn meditation at one point and then stop doing it?

Do you regret not spending enough quality time with your kids, spouse, friends, or aging parents?

Do you have a stack of books by your nightstand that you look at each night wondering when you'll get to them?

Have you ever come back from a vacation feeling drained and less ready to take on your life than when you started?

Are you stressed, tired, or just downright bored of the rut that you're in?

Welcome to the modern world.

Things were not always like this. Our ancestors had more time in life. They had more space. They walked to places and took in fresh air. They spent time preparing meals and enjoying them with loved ones, and they got more exposure to nature and the elements. Life was less stressful, less full. We were surrounded by family and belonged to an extended tribe.

Today, we've got bills. We've got millions of bits of information bombarding us every minute. News about militants trying to kill us is often served with reports about rising cancer rates and crashing economies. Our kids are being tugged on by commercial interests, and our ice caps are melting. Everything costs more money than we'd like, and we find ourselves running around like crazy people trying to keep the whole shitshow going.

All for what?

The crisis of the modern urban or suburban person is that we've got bullets flying at us, and we're ill equipped to deal with any of it.

We are stressed out, tired, out of energy, and lost. Some of us unwittingly bought into a narrative that the ancient secrets of the East were the answer to our problems. As the Beatles brought back the Maharishi and gurus started to journey over from Asia, we thought that yoga, meditation, fasting, tai chi, and Zen practices were going to save us. Now, we stand in the middle of a storm forgetting to ever call on those practices in our time of need. (?)

Others have hung on to religion and tried to stay active at church. For some, it's helped, but for many, there is disillusionment and disappointment. Many of the old institutions have not adapted to the changing times fast enough, and people feel that they're out of touch and don't understand our problems.

We read that exercise is good, so we tried our hand at the gym. We forced ourselves to deal with stinky, stale air and crowds of people admiring themselves in the mirror—yuck. We know we've got to keep moving, but just going there is an uphill battle for most of us. Moving? What's that? Most of us spend more than an hour a day commuting to work and then a good 8 hours sitting at a desk. By the time we get home, we're cranky, hungry, and not having it.

If any of this speaks to you, you're certainly in the right place. This book was written specifically with you in mind. Why? Because I traveled the world learning from spiritual masters, and I've learned healing techniques from some serious people. My training was to help me bring balance and peace to the world I had come from. When I came down from the Himalayas, it didn't take me long to realize that my patients, who were regular working people in Los Angeles, were not going to go do what I did. They weren't going to take the month-long meditation retreats, practice qigong for hours a day, or walk the earth anytime soon. They certainly were not going to move away and become monks. They couldn't shave their heads and journey up into the sacred mountains to find God. They had kids, bills, dogs, and shit going on in their daily lives, and this is where they needed help. They needed solutions down here.

I've spent my entire career working to bring the ancient wisdom of the East down to earth for regular people here in our towns and cities, and this book comes from thousands of successful encounters with patients in my practices. What I realized over the years was that there's been a terrible misunderstanding in the West, and countless millions are suffering because of it.

The problem is that the esoteric practices that have been brought over from China, Tibet, and India were mostly drawn from ascetic lineages but were being practiced by householders here in the West.

Ascetics have renounced the world. They've given up money, sex, family, and other worldly pursuits in search of a deeper connection with God the Divine, Tao, their Buddha Nature, or whatever lineage they draw from. They were given austerities and very specific practices, which keep them engaged for hours a day year after year. This is the path they chose, and, frankly, good for them.

What about the rest of us? Well, we feel guilty for missing our yoga class because our kid's soccer game went into overtime. We tell ourselves that we're going to meditate at night but keep nodding off because we've been crunching spreadsheets at a desk all day. We try to eat well, but airport food isn't quite what the monks were chowing on. We attempt to make the best of the crazy lives that we have, but there's a fundamental flaw in this interface. Ascetics have renounced the world. We have mortgages, leases, tuition, and cars to keep gassing up. We need a different set of guiding principles to help us navigate a world with money, with stress, with compressed time, and with lots of other people vying for our attention. The world we live in is not very quiet and is seldom peaceful. So how are we to find our serenity and keep our shit together down here where we live?

ENTER THE URBAN MONK

This book is filled with priceless practices that you can use in your daily life, right here and now, to find peace and have more energy. Instead of getting pissed at the lady in front of you at the grocery store for fumbling around with her clipped coupons, you could thank her because she's just given you the valuable gift of time. You now have 5 minutes to practice your breathing and tap back into the infinite source of energy and peace that is your birthright.

I was pre-med at UCLA and then I found tai chi. From there, I found a Taoist abbot who taught me kung fu and qigong. I became a Taoist monk and traveled the world, sitting with many masters, and have been a student of esoteric practices ever since. But I was raised in Los Angeles. I had normal friends and went to normal schools. I've partied with rockstars and sat in Amazonian huts with the best of them. I became a Doctor of Oriental Medicine and saw thousands of patients. This helped me understand human suffering. Not in an abstract New Age way, but in actual reality. I've helped normal people get through real life crises for years. Divorces happen. People die. Kids get into trouble with drugs. Couples have trouble getting pregnant. This is life down here in the cities, and this is where we need help. Let's forget the lofty spiritual stuff for a minute and get down to earth. Once we've gotten our shit together here at home, then yes, there's an amazing realm of mysticism to explore, but let's start where we stand . . . where we suffer.

I have a wife and kids. I'm a householder. I have dogs and a mortgage. I get where you're at. I'm the founder of Well.org and make movies and TV and have a large business that tugs on me all the time. I understand payroll is always around the corner and tax bills keep coming. It comes with the territory. A householder creates jobs and has the burden of taking care of lots of people in his or her universe. A householder makes shit happen month after month and doesn't cower when things get tough. A householder must be a survivor first and then learn to thrive.

Let's roll up our sleeves and get into it. I consider myself an Urban Monk and, by the end of this book, invite you to do the same. Why? Because the world needs you to step up and live your life fully. Our kids need you to help protect our environment and make better choices at the store. Your family needs you to be more aware, present, and loving when you are with them. Your business needs you to step in and bring more abundance to your world. And most importantly, you need you back.

Let's learn how to get out of our own way and be the people we're destined to be right here from our homes, offices, and even during our long commutes.

The book is organized into 10 chapters that each discuss a major life issue we have in the modern world: stress, time poverty, lack of energy, sleep issues, stagnant lifestyles, poor diets, disconnection with nature, loneliness, money issues, and lack of meaning and purpose. We

Organization of Book:

start each chapter with a little vignette from a patient encounter. These encounters come from the thousands of interactions I've had with regular people over the years as a physician and a priest. The names have been changed and the stories modified to protect identities; some have been slightly mixed and matched, but all of them are from real encounters and recommendations given to genuine people over the years. From there we get into the first section, titled "The Problem," where I help pick apart the issue at hand and look at it in a fresh way with you. This opens us up to the next section, "Urban Monk Wisdom," which draws from esoteric philosophy from the Eastern and shamanic cultures, giving us another way to look at our problems and see a way out. Then we drop into solutions. First up are the "Eastern Practices," which come from ancient wisdom and older traditions—tried-and-true stuff that's simple and elegant and has proven to work for people over the millennia. This is followed by "Modern Hacks," which are practical exercises, apps, and other techniques that I've found to be effective for contemporary problems we face. Each chapter is closed out with another vignette that rounds out the opening story with some resolution. In the end, I'll give you some recipes and an action plan that'll radically transform your life for the better. The practice is called a Gong, and I've been teaching it to students for years. It is a dedicated practice that you choose (based on the principles and lessons learned in this book) that actually gives you a plan, a road map, and a framework for success. I've helped thousands of people just like you with this model, and I'm confident it will help you, too.

You can pick and choose where you jump in, but I recommend reading the whole book through, as you'll likely think about many of the people in your life and be able to better identify with them once you can see how they, too, may be struggling. When you're ready to jump into your first Gong, you'll want to reference the practices in this book for years to come.

Enjoy the book and mark it up. Take notes in the margins and allow it to help you think about the aspects of your life where your energy is stuck. It will teach you to enjoy the ride and find your personal power along the way.

I'm excited you're here.

CHAPTER 1

Stress: How Do I Dodge the Bullets?

ROBERT IS FROM THE school of old. He was brought up in an era when there were three choices in life for young men: be a doctor, a lawyer, or an engineer. He studied law knowing it would be a stable job with good security. Long, hard hours of study, bar exam, 70-hour workweeks, lots of coffee, and dealing with difficult people were all bumps on his road to success. He fought and worked his way up the ladder and is now a junior partner in a pretty good firm. The days are still long and the stress is ridiculous. He's definitely got less hair.

His wife stopped working after their second child was born, so he now shoulders the entire financial burden for his family.

He lives in a pretty nice house in a good neighborhood. They have a pool and a Jacuzzi he hasn't been in since last year. They own a time-share condo that they stress about getting to. Health insurance prices go up each year, and his youngest kid has asthma and some crazy food allergies—all of which cost money and time and create more challenges around the house. Even with a part-time nanny, there seems to be no sleep to be had, and their last vacation to Maui was more trouble than it was worth. He came back exhausted and dejected.

Robert's life is filled with stress. Although he has a roof over his head, cars, and plenty of food, deep down, he's terrified. He knows he can't keep up at this pace. He feels like he's going to fall on his face one day, but he can't. After all, they all depend on him. He drinks coffee, goes to the gym, takes some multivitamins, and gets an occasional massage, but all the while his mind is filled with the pressures of keeping it all going.

A good lawyer needs to drive a Lexus.

Good parents send their kids to private school.

Gymnastics and piano lessons are a must.

The other parents are shipping their kids off to some fancy summer camp. Of course, we're in . . .

The joy is gone. The stress has tipped the scale, and he's constantly trying to keep his chin up. His dad taught him that "real men" never give up; they fight the good fight for their family and never show any weakness. He watches the morning news while eating his cereal with the kids. He feels like an absentee dad who didn't really see them grow up, and he mourns this fact. Robert feels the weakness is gaining momentum, and he is terrified that he's going to lose the battle. After all, with all the stuff he's constantly throwing money at, they barely have any savings, and if he stopped working, they'd be in real trouble within a few months. His life insurance would pay out a decent amount if he keeled over, and a couple of times already, he's thought about it, and this scared the hell out of him.

Robert is stuck. His adrenals are running on empty, and there's no end in sight. He can't see the way out, and each day, a silent desperation builds in the shadows of his psyche—a plight for the very survival of his family. Robert keeps fighting, but his doctor has warned that his blood pressure is getting too high. The stakes are high, and so are his numbers. What's a man to do?

THE PROBLEM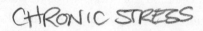

In a way, we all share Robert's problem. Our bodies developed and evolved over millions of years in response to some predictable stressors in our environment. "Fight or flight" is a beautiful system that helped us stay alive in a dangerous world filled with predators and scarcity. It evolved to help us get out of life-threatening situations by optimizing our metabolism to ramp up into crisis mode. When we're in danger, our cortisol and/or adrenaline levels surge to help divert bloodflow to the big muscles that will help us fight an opponent or flee from a predator. These are stress hormones that have top-down control over several systems in our bodies, and slight fluctuations in their levels move dials all over the place. They work in conjunction with an elegant switching mechanism in our nervous system. Our sympathetic nervous system drives the fight-or-flight reactions and quickly helps triage energy to where we need it in times of crisis. The opposite side of this switch is the parasympathetic nervous system, which can be considered the "rest and digest" mode where the body is free to heal, break down foods, and carry out detoxification and excretion. In times of danger, the body is designed to elegantly pull bloodflow from the internal organs, immune system, and parts of the brain that are associated with high cognition and drive that blood into the quadriceps so we can run like hell if we need to. It's great stuff when the shit hits the fan, but let's peel back Robert's life and see why this is bad news for a modern lawyer.

Robert's stress is not from an acute incident. Sure, occasionally the car in the next lane swerves over and gets his heart rate (and middle finger) up, but that's not what's killing him. It is the chronic stress. A wild impala in Africa doesn't think about the "what if" scenarios of a lion charging. He eats, cruises around, has plenty of sex, and if a threat shows up, he runs for it. If he survives, he shakes it out and goes back to his business. Not us. We keep replaying the event in our minds, bind it to emotions, and visualize it running in different ways; we don't drop it. The impala has moved on, but we're in therapy still talking about it or, worse, still bottling it up. We don't really get into "rest and digest" mode enough to balance these systems out, so we stay wound up.

Chronic stress is a killer.

Robert has mini "life or death" moments every time a client threatens to cancel or a judge throws out a case. His wife came home with a fancy purse the other day, and it turned his stomach. "How much did that cost?"

These modern stressors are basically death by a thousand cuts. Our abstract concept of money or currency is tied to our very survival and triggers the same circuitry. It messes with us and stresses us out. Money is tight, and deep down that means something that our bodies understand viscerally. Low levels of cortisol release over a sustained period of time have terrible consequences for the body. You can say that Robert lives in sympathetic overdrive and has forgotten how to switch back over and chill out. With the body constantly cutting bloodflow to vital systems, here's some of the predictable fallout.

Restricting Energy to the Immune System

A body that's under constant stress is like a country at war, and all the money, troops, and resources are being sent to the front lines (stressful fight-or-flight pathways). Who's left to police the streets? How do you deal with local gangs and terror cells? You can't. They sneak in, take hold, and then manifest as disease. By the time you call back troops from the front lines, the damage is done and you need to spend much more energy to fix it.

The problem is not one of poor design. The human immune system is amazing. It is an elaborate universe that helps us recognize objects that don't belong in our bodies and get rid of them. When things are running smoothly, it is a marvel to witness the precision and efficiency of our immune system. But most people in the modern world are suffering from the consequences of compromised immunity. The Centers for Disease Control and Prevention (CDC) attributes stress as the cause of 90 percent of chronic disease. This is huge. Robert is doomed to get some nasty chronic disease once his system gets weak enough. It is just a matter of time.

The problem is Robert's life.

Every day, Robert unwittingly does things that draw resources away from his immune system and make it more difficult for his body to maintain balance. After some time, things will break and he will get sick.

Cutting Energy to the Digestive System and Internal Organs

When the body gets a signal telling it that a lion is coming, it draws blood from the viscera (internal organs) and drives it to the muscles that can hopefully help us survive the "attack." When this happens, the organs take a hit. Bloodflow is diminished to the organs as it is shunted to the big "get me the hell out of here" muscles. This cuts the energy and nutrients delivered to the vital organs. Think of it like a wartime economy. There's no money left for school books, street repair, or food stamps.

When the digestive tract gets energy pulled from it regularly, we start to see issues with poor absorption, nutrient deficiencies, constipation or loose stools, indigestion, bloating, fatigue, and eventually leaky gut "syndrome." (I'll explain this later in the book.) "Rest and digest" is where we heal, but what happens when we don't allow ourselves to go there? Look around you. There's a trillion-dollar healthcare industry that makes money off of chronic diseases that stem from poor lifestyle and uncontrolled stress.

Causing a Blood Sugar Roller Coaster

When cortisol levels go up, all sorts of things happen. As mentioned earlier, bloodflow is directed to the "get me the hell out of here" muscles, but there's also a huge impact on blood sugar.

Cortisol is like a credit card.

In a crisis situation, the body needs energy immediately, so cortisol is like swiping a card to get instant gratification. It helps the body to draw energy from our glycogen reserves in the liver for our immediate needs, but that has some serious consequences. As blood sugar initially surges, the pancreas senses this and releases insulin to grab this sugar and shuttle it into the cells. This is all good, except when things start to fall off the tracks. After years of being on this cortisol energy roller coaster, the insulin spike often overshoots the sugar (energy) release, which then triggers us to get hungry and crave more sugar or carbs in order to balance it out. This can manifest in moodiness,

irritability, headaches, and general fatigue; it often <u>leaves us reaching</u>
<u>for some coffee to bail us out of an energy lull.</u> Maybe that muffin
will help . . . We'll discuss the role of adrenaline in this craziness later
in the sleep chapter.

Most people have so many <u>ups and downs with this</u> that they feel
like they're spent by midday Tuesday and are already dreaming of the
weekend.

Wreaking Havoc on the Endocrine System

I've had dozens of elite athletes come to my clinic and secretly admit
that they can't get erections anymore. Cortisol is often the reason
why. These athletes burn out their adrenals with chronic elevated
stress, and it eventually draws on their testosterone, estrogen, DHEA,
and several other hormonal pathways. Robbing Peter to pay Paul
seems to be the way of our modern era, and it is surely reflected in our
bodies. Today, guys like our friend Robert borrow energy from
tomorrow to get through today, but they don't look at the interest rate
on that kind of deal. It sucks. Maybe you can bang through your thirties, but then you hit a wall and your body goes on strike. Once our
hormones are off, we gain weight, drag around with fatigue, and take
a hit in the bedroom . . . sorry, sorry, give me a minute . . .

Of course, there are drugs we can take for all of these issues, but
the root is often bad energy economics stemming from our adrenal
burn rate. The drugs often have side effects, and the underlying problem tends to persist.

Taking a Hit to the Brain

Possibly the worst on the list of things that happen when we're chron-
ically stressed is the cutting off of bloodflow to the prefrontal cortex.
This is the part of our brains that separates us from the monkeys. It
helps us carry out abstract thinking, problem solving, higher cognition, and higher moral reasoning. It's the part of the brain that helps
with the negation of impulses. This area is called the third eye in the
ancient traditions and should be cultivated and cherished. The problem is that the body's switching system knows that this part of the
brain is not needed to scramble up a tree as a rhino is charging, so it

diverts blood and energy to the hindbrain, which helps with instant reflexive behavior. Again, the body's impulse is "get me out of here or tear through that guy who's trying to take my stuff."

On the off chance that you encounter a lion in Chicago, that's pretty handy. It also helps you to dive to a curb when a taxi doesn't see you crossing, but chronic misallocation of energy to the fight-or-flight brain keeps us reactive, distrustful, less empathic, and unable to

PERSONAL JOURNEYS

When I came back from the Himalayas, I decided to take on the health-care crisis with my exuberant energy and charged sense of mission. I thought that I could fix a broken system from within, so I started a medical group and quickly grew it to three offices. We were featured in journals for our innovations in complementary medicine and were getting cool accolades, but I knew it was bullshit. Essentially, my training was in the prevention and prediction of disease, and here I was in a business model that required me to wait for someone to break and come in with a diagnosable illness. I kept trying to find work-arounds within this messy system and constantly dealt with insurance companies holding our money. There was an immense amount of stress, and it really put my meditation skills to the test.

I was able to hold off for years, but then it dawned on me: No matter how good a fighter you are, if you stand in the ring long enough, you're going to get punched. This is when I realized that I could do far better and more meaningful work in wellness and media. I stepped out of the path of the stress bullets, and my life became very cool. The lesson? Sometimes we need to think outside the box we're stuck in and realize that the self-imposed stress can go away with a simple decision.

make long-term, thoughtful decisions. Higher moral reasoning is what really made us what we are. Religion, ethics, honor, and self-awareness all come from this good gray matter, and our inability to use it is a tragedy. Most people live in "survival mode" and can relate. It is also a reason why so many people do things that harm them despite knowing better. We know that smoking isn't good for us, but many still do it. We understand that the pie is fattening, yet we eat it anyway. We tell ourselves that our exes are trouble, yet we find ourselves calling them again. Without good access to the prefrontal cortex, we're not using the part of our brains that empowers us to suppress impulses that harm our bodies. Living in chronic stress keeps us locked out of this area of our brains and drives us to be more impulsive and unaware.

Vitality Is What Offsets the Damage

In my first movie, I spoke of the concept of vitality, the energy of life that feeds the organs, powers the cells, and fuels the brain. It is the common currency of life, and it is also the force field that protects us against disease and the harmful effects of stress. When Robert's stress outweighs his vitality, he's in trouble. Once the body passes the tipping point of sustained "fight or flight," trouble comes a-knocking, and it isn't pretty. When we've spent our "savings" and our energy levels drop to a level where the body can't make ends meet, we start having to sacrifice systems. That's when it gets ugly and we end up sitting in some waiting room until a white coat throws pills at us. That's when we panic and fear for our lives.

Mortality is always here, always reminding us that survival is not so far away. This is something we can use to our advantage.

URBAN MONK WISDOM

To merely survive is not enough. We want to thrive. The Urban Monk builds on a solid foundation and keeps moving up in conscious awareness. We learn to move out of "fight or flight" and up to the penthouse suite of the skyscraper that is the human body. What does this mean?

*Work to develop the prefrontal cortex.
Power up your third eye.*

Several studies show that even novice meditators develop increased density in the cortical neurons of the prefrontal cortex. That's good news. It means we can still actively develop this part of our brain. It helps us stay cool under pressure and makes it easier to navigate stressful situations. The arc of development from frenzied panic to calm and centered is the journey of the Urban Monk. Getting there is key, and we'll dance around the subject throughout this book because a lot of the foundational components involve a clean diet, good sleep, full spectrum movement, quiet time, and having a healthy mind-set.

The Master Remains Calm

The world is nuts. Our lives drive us toward panicked frenzy. If we don't hold the line, then we're lost. It's important to live in the eye of the hurricane, where things are calm and chaos isn't the law of the land.

Much of the wisdom of the ancient monasteries has been held for millennia in centers of excellence—temples, schools, caves, and academies that are not subjected to the fickle meanderings of the outside world. Our job is to bring that peace back into our cities and set the tone for a balanced life here and now.

In the West, we've fallen for the false assumption that meditation is something we need to do once we're already stressed out. That's like saying you need to stretch after you've pulled a muscle. Yeah, it may help, but it's a bit late.

Here's a way to look at it that can help:

Most people use meditation as an icon on their desktop. When they feel stressed out, they go double click on it, take some breaths, feel a little better, and then go back to the 12 open windows they have up and fall right back into the chaos.

*Try to use meditation as an
operating system instead.*

This means you constantly scan your consciousness and cue for calm. You can sense thoughts that make you reactive and uneasy, and you learn to let them pass. You don't let them knock you off your perch.

The mind is reactive.

We experience something and then we connect that experience with a past memory of something related; if there's an unreconciled emotional charge associated with that memory, we feel it all over again and start to get uneasy. That discomfort drives us to fidget, grab a smoke, abruptly change the subject, or whatever else we do to avert feeling crappy. All day long . . . this is what we do.

Learning to remain nonreactive is the name of the game. Does this mean living without passion? Absolutely not. Live, love, laugh, and learn—just don't be a sucker for drama. Live your life with enthusiasm and purpose, and don't be a pawn in someone else's vision for you. You drive. Better yet, let your Higher Self drive, and you relax.

Desire Is the Root of Suffering

The Buddha had a lot to say about this, and he's a guy who didn't talk very much. He traced human suffering back to two things: aversions and cravings. Either we dislike something and how it makes us feel, driving us to move away from it, or we like and crave it, making us long for more.

I spent a good part of my life studying Buddhism and walking the Himalayas before I came back and had to captain my own ship in business. In learning Marketing 101 and in the subsequent years of diving down that rabbit hole, I was aghast at how my two worlds were in conflict. As a Taoist priest and student of Buddhism, I was charged with alleviating human suffering; as a business owner, I was being taught to see desire as my strongest weapon in driving sales. It is an industry that feeds on people's weaknesses. You could become a parasite that lives off of hungry ghosts instead of saving them. Obviously, there are good people working within the system and doing their best, but the fundamental challenge remains how to coerce people and simultaneously help them. Fortunately, I found a healthy path and have used my drive for transformation to help awaken people to help themselves and the world, but the initial shock was hard to reconcile.

So what does this have to do with you? *Everything.*

All day, every day, we are bombarded with advertisements. It really has become a battle for the minds of humanity. From the sign at the bus stop to the text message spam you get, companies are vying for your attention and money all of the time. They are everywhere, and they won't stop. If you let down your guard, you may pick up a nasty mental virus (called a meme).

Mental virus?

Yeah, like "I need that truck because real men drive badass trucks."

Or how about "I need that purse because Suzy got a nice purse and she's getting all the attention."

Or "My kids need to wear this designer stuff so the other parents know we're also classy people."

The list goes on and on. We run and we hustle all day to make money, but then we often spend it on junk we don't actually need in accordance with the scripts and "necessities" embedded in our minds. Soon we find ourselves short on money and worried about making ends meet each month. Remember Robert? He makes good money, but he's still broke. That's the system we live in. Money is tied to survival. If you've got it, you're worried about losing it. And no matter what you have, there's never enough.

An Urban Monk doesn't worry about status; therefore, she is free.

Her sense of self is built on a strong inner foundation. She's cultivated her breath and tapped into her connection with the entire Universe. What accolades other people may give her do not matter. She is reinforced by life and nature as her exuberance and enthusiasm radiate from within.

Curate Your Information

There's a reason why the world's monasteries are usually tucked away on mountaintops and away from the craziness of the world. You are what you eat also applies to the information you ingest. Watching the daily news will convince you that the world is a dangerous place and that you need to stay stressed. It's a great way of thrashing your adrenals and working yourself into a doctor's office.

Following the "he said, she said" nonsense of daily life is a drama generator that pollutes the mind and robs us of our clarity. The Urban Monk works to become picky about what information he digests, and he engages in content that enriches his experience. There are amazing teachers, books, courses, and people out there to learn from. If we take the axiom "you are what you eat" to heart, then we look at everything we allow into our lives with a new filter. Learn, grow, thrive, and stay calm—this is the way forward.

Does this mean we shouldn't care about current events? No. I browse headlines in my news feed once a day and make sure I see the big stuff that I need to know. Every now and again I'll drill down on something that's interesting, but I *curate* the information that comes to me using tech as an ally. There are numerous readers out there; I use Google Alerts. I pick 5 to 10 subjects that I'm interested in staying up on and have only that content drip my way. That way I stay informed with relevant information. What the latest drunk celebrity did to embarrass himself has no bearing on my life and is a waste of brain space.

Care @ Subconscious, & what drops into it

Recalibrate Your Stress Bucket

Mortal combat used to be a way of life. Boys became men by facing death—looking it straight in the eyes. Little girls knew how to avoid predators and poisonous snakes. Lions came into villages, and bandits were all over the place. Life used to be a lot more dangerous, and death wore a different face. When I was learning to track lions in Africa, I had already done tens of thousands of hours of kung fu training and was accustomed to battle and the cost of coming in second place. Even that wasn't enough to prepare me for the feeling of coming up on a wild lion in its own habitat. There's something so primal about the feeling of being close to such an enormous and powerful predator, something that shocks you back into your body. I remember tracking a male lion across a valley and coming so dangerously close to it that we would have been in real trouble had the wind changed direction and he caught our scent. When it occurred to me that we were as close as we were and that the lion could be *anywhere* within 50 feet of us, every hair on my body felt electrified and each cell woke up suddenly. *Death is near. Wake up.*

I remember feeling transformed that day because none of the small stuff mattered anymore. We were alive, and that was pretty cool. I think that's why so many people do adventure sports and dangerous things—*to remember what it's like to be vibrantly alive.* There's a special feeling we've all become distant from, and it's the tragedy of the modern world: We don't feel alive. When we haven't calibrated or recalibrated our stress bucket in a while, then what Jenny said at the office sets the bar for what is going to stress and overwhelm our system that day.

We're playing small ball, and it is unbecoming.

Recalibrating your stress bucket can be as easy as doing something that scares you every day. It could be finally asking that coworker out, going to Peru alone, jumping out of that plane, or whatever pulls you out of the humdrum reality that's dulling your senses. In the old days, the monks would have to fend for themselves against wild animals, bandits, imperial soldiers, and whatever else came their way. If you think about it, our ancestors were filled with pioneering spirit and danger. You and your family were on your own, and your survival was in your hands. The nearest doctor was 2 days away by horse, so you'd better pay attention when crossing that river.

Stepping into your life really helps with stress management. If the small stuff is getting you down, then do greater things. Later in this chapter, we'll cover a variety of ways you can do this. The key is to elevate and look back so you can laugh at the stuff that used to bother you. There's nothing like feeling alive to reset your stress levels. Henry Ford once said, "Obstacles are the scary things we see when we take our eyes off our goal."

Learn to Listen

Millions of bits of information pass through your brain every second. From the position of your foot to the wind hitting your face, it's all data that reflects in the mind as noise. There's also a steady stream of past memories, trauma, emotions, and pain that your brain is constantly working to keep at arm's distance. It is loud up there. Most people first notice this when they try to meditate and panic when they realize it . . . *chaos is actually inside.* This is the curse and also the blessing of the human condition. Once we realize that peace is an inside game, we must learn to calm the chatter in our heads. We learn to be less reactive to the noise and become less impulsive. As we get better at it, we learn one of life's greatest miracles.

*The world outside us begins to change
as we shift our inner state.*

We begin to see the reflection of our newfound peace in the world around us as a powerful feedback loop emerges. The chaos comes to order. The drama resolves. Nicer people come our way. Nasty people go away.

"As above, so below, as within, so without,
as the universe, so the soul . . . "

—HERMES TRISMEGISTUS

The ancient Hermetic axiom sums it up perfectly. Basically, our outer world is a reflection of our inner one, and as we begin to find peace and change ourselves, we'll see that change reflected in the world around us. This is the original biofeedback. Let's dig in and look at some of the methods of getting there.

EASTERN PRACTICES
The Urban Monk Operating System

Learning to sit in equanimity is the way of the Urban Monk. This means a nonreactive state where we don't deny feelings of discomfort as they arise. We observe our thoughts as they come and go and learn not to cling. Attaching emotional qualities to thoughts as they pop up is the way of human suffering. Clinging to past memories keeps us out of the now. The Urban Monk learns to passively observe thoughts and emotions as they surface and *lets them be.* As we get better at this, we begin to perceive a deep sense of peace and well-being in life.

How do we do this? Enter the practice. The Urban Monk is constantly scanning his body for feelings and sensations. When discomfort arises, he breathes into it. He senses where this feeling is in his body and turns the light of his awareness on it—not away from it, as is the custom of our culture. This keeps our awareness on the present moment and brings us into the reality of our situation. Our minds are so amazing that they have an uncanny ability to float away into the abstract and out of this moment. This is great when we are trying to think, daydream, create, or wander, but when we're engaged in life's activities, it helps to show up. The Urban Monk is in the room. He's alive, aware, and attentive to the task at hand and handles his work with intent and purpose. Then he plays like a child and relaxes deeply.

Throughout this book, you'll receive several practices that will help you attain this state of mind. Practice them and find the value in each. In short order, you will get a sense of this state of consciousness. You'll wake up to a potent version of yourself who'll help you step through the cobwebs of bad habits and into a bright future.

Stress Relief Meditation

Learning to stop the insanity and calm your mind is the first step toward life mastery. If the turbulent waters of the choppy sea of insanity are left to their own devices, we start to feel more anxious, irritable, unfocused, and generally more run-down. Learning to calm our stress by using our breath is easy to do, but it requires practice.

To be an Urban Monk means you're
willing to do the work.

Getting good at meditation takes some practice and can be frustrating at first, but once you've turned that corner, the payout is immense and you reap the rewards for the rest of your life. It's a great investment.

The first principle we need to cover here is the Eastern understanding of the breath. The breath carries our life force. It is our connection with the essential nature of the Universe and our anchor into the Great Mystery itself. The expansion and contraction of the very Universe is mirrored in our breath. The inflow and outflow are cycles of life's circular nature, and the moments in between are particularly important. The top of the inhale and bottom of the exhale, just as we're about to switch—that's a great place to hang out and pay attention.

So what do we do with this? Let's train you on an exercise that'll get your foot in the door and build a framework for continued exploration into this amazing inner Universe. It'll quickly balance the right and left hemispheres of your brain and balance the energies of yin and yang.

Nada Shodharum
Alternate Nostril Breathing

Here's the exercise:

- Sit in a comfortable place where you can have your spine straight and limit the distractions around you (that means put your phone on airplane mode).

- Set a designated time to practice; 5 to 10 minutes is a good place to start.

- Now that your phone is off (for a change), set a timer for how long you'd like to practice and hit start. This way, you can relax into the meditation and not worry about losing track of time. It's important to give yourself *permission* to go here and not feel like you're late for anything. Open up the time and *dedicate it* to the practice.

Now for the practice.

- Breathing in and out of your nose, direct your breath down to your lower abdomen, about three fingers below the level of your navel. This will be the case for most of the exercises we do together.

- Place your left hand on your left knee with your palm facing up and your thumb and index finger touching.

- With your right hand, you are going to alternate the opening and closing of your nostrils. Put your thumb on your right nostril and have your ring finger ready to place over your left nostril.

○ Breathe out gently and fully from your left nostril as you cover the right one with your thumb, and then gently breathe back in through the same (left) nostril.

○ Now cover your left nostril with your ring finger (always using your right hand throughout the exercise) and exhale through your right nostril fully and then inhale again through the right.

○ Keep alternating and repeating this sequence until your alarm goes off.

○ When done, simply go through the exhale on whatever side you're on and then take a couple of normal breaths (no hand, both nostrils). Breathe in through your nose and out through your mouth just to clear the channels and come back into the room.

Shaking It Out

Clearing the body's channels and discharging stuck energy is the name of this game. If you look at what an impala does after it successfully gets away from a predator, you'll see it shake and tremble for a couple of seconds. This is the nervous system discharging all the stress energy (and hormones) from the event so it can reset and go back to "rest and digest" mode. But what do we do? We take arrows all day, watch some TV, and then go to bed all wired and jacked up and wonder why we can't sleep. Emotional and mental stagnation keeps us down. This exercise will kick up some dust, and if you breathe through it, you'll learn to just let things go without clinging to feelings as they arise; you'll feel lighter and have more freedom.

This practice comes from a powerful qigong tradition that helps clear blocked energy, discharge stagnation, relieve stress, and invigorate the system. You could do it for as long as you'd like. I recommend starting slowly and working up to longer bouts. Working through discomfort will be very therapeutic emotionally. If a joint hurts, take it easy and check with your doctor first.

You may want to be somewhere more private for this exercise because it'll look a bit weird when you're getting going. Here's the practice:

○ Stand with your feet shoulder-width apart, with your hands in front of your torso.

○ Turn your palms so they're facing your chest, as if you're holding a tree or beach ball in front of you.

○ Bend your knees slightly and curl your tongue so it's touching the roof of your mouth.

○ Breathe gently in through your nose and out through your nose to your lower abdomen.

○ Keep your shoulders, wrists—and your entire body—relaxed.

○ This is called Tree Pose or Tai Chi Post.

○ Let yourself relax into this stance and take a few breaths into your lower abdomen.

○ Allow your body to start subtly moving around within the confines of the stance. This means keeping your hands loosely in position and the stance intact.

○ Just start going with the movement. It may be side to side or front to back, or many people start with a gentle shaking or trembling motion.

○ However you start, the key is to start letting go and let the energy that's running through your body start to express itself. We spend so much time repressing the energy in our lives; this is your chance to let it go and move with the flow.

○ Try to maintain the slow breathing, but after a while, it's okay if your breathing also shifts with the shaking or moving, as long as you remember to come back to slower breathing if you feel uncomfortable or get overwhelmed.

○ Don't go for too long at first, maybe 3 to 5 minutes. You'll run the risk of not feeling anything at first, but start conservatively and you can always take a deeper dive as you establish more comfort.

○ Once you feel like you're done, start to slow your breath and gradually slow the movement or shaking until you come back to a still "Post" position after a few deceleration breaths.

○ Take five breaths, inhaling through your nose and exhaling through your mouth, before you let your arms relax down and get back into your day.

This exercise will kick your ass; be ready to feel old shit coming up and out. Your job is to keep breathing and let it flow through you. Stop trying to repress it and let it move; free yourself of all the restrictions you've imposed on yourself. Ease your way in so you don't overstep, but use this practice to really start clearing the cobwebs of your past. Use it to step out in front of your perceived limitations and into your power.

Over time, you'll find that this practice unlocks all kinds of blocked energy and helps with aches and pains in your body as well as mental blocks you may have. You'll run into places where you're uncomfortable emotionally at times. If you have a history here, work with your therapist to use this practice as a pressure release valve. Dig deep, but don't bite off more than you can chew—live to fight another day. I've included a video of this at theurbanmonk.com/resources/ch1.

Relaxing Herbs and Teas

An ancient and sophisticated tradition of herbology comes from the East. Plants have life force. They have consciousness. Plant spirit medicine is the original form of medicine on the planet. The shamans and medicine men of the past and present have a connection with the plants they harvest and use them as allies to help us get back on our paths.

Below are some powerful herbal remedies in the form of teas you can use to alleviate stress. I recommend having these teas around the house and using them as needed. A well-stocked cupboard of medicinal teas can really change your life.

Holy basil (Tulsi). This simple and elegant single herb has been proven to temper cortisol release and help curb the harmful effects of adrenal agitation. Many companies already offer it in tea bags, and it's an easy way to manage your stress while on the go. Drinking one to two cups per day can really help.

Kava. This traditional Polynesian herb has been used for millennia in ceremonies and is renowned for its mind-calming effects. Kava is best taken in the evening hours, as it can zonk you out in the middle of the day and your boss may not be into that. A cup of kava after dinner is a great way to wind down and chill out after a busy day.

Peppermint. Simple and elegant, a cup of peppermint tea can help calm the mind and ease the flow of energy. It helps move liver qi (energy) and break up stagnation in the body. In general, the mint family is good to drive the flow of smooth qi in your body and make you feel relaxed and mildly invigorated without having to juice up on coffee, which tends to make most people more anxious. Diffusing

peppermint essential oil in the house is also very calming.

Green tea. Although this tea does contain caffeine, the other main ingredient is L-theanine, which has been shown to effectively calm the mind. Green tea has been used by Zen monks for millennia to simultaneously stimulate and calm the mind—what a great combo! When the researchers got there, they isolated the L-theanine as the calming part and now sell that as a supplement as well (which works). A cup of green tea can give you a lift while maintaining your Zen, which makes it a great replacement for coffee.

Xiao Yao San. This classic herbal formula is a combination of a handful of Chinese herbs that, as a tea or in pill form, do wonders to calm stress and help the body function optimally. Traditional herbalism is very sophisticated, and most patients are given a custom formula based on their disposition and personal energetic signature, but this formula in particular addresses stress in a pretty universal way that helps most people stuck in the urban logjam. The gold standard is to work with an herbalist and go custom, but when push comes to shove, this formula is great for most people.

Note: Make sure you get Chinese herbs from a trusted organic source.

Morning Visualization

Most people start their day by smacking the snooze button before stumbling into their routine. A hot shower, coffee, the morning news, feed the kids—whatever the routine is, it usually spins into chaos pretty quickly. As you start to develop your skills as an Urban Monk, you're going to want to "ninja up" and take ownership of your mornings. This means having a plan the night before. Before going to bed, think about what you need to get done the following day and see it through. Visualize the day and see it flow with grace and ease in your visualization. Paint the picture in your mental canvas and tell your subconscious mind that you're embedding this image so that your mind can see it through for you as you sleep. When you wake up, run through your visualization again before you get out of bed, and then get up and start executing. In the next few chapters, you'll learn a handful of qigong practices that can jump-start your day. You want to step in and set the tone for the day with conscious awareness and focused intent. Nothing is better than qigong for this.

You rise, you visualize, you do your qigong, and then you engage in your morning while keeping your eyes on the prize and making sure you see through your big items for the day. As you get more adept at staying focused, the small stuff stops intercepting your consciousness and you get good at staying on track. Getting better at life starts in the morning, so make sure you take this seriously.

MODERN HACKS
Learn to Defend Yourself

Step out of your comfort zones

We used to fight for survival. We also used to run for our lives. The nights were cold and the winters harsh. Food was scarce, and sometimes we went hungry for longer than we'd like. In essence, we got tough by challenging our survival circuitry. *It made us stronger.*

Today, it's really easy to get fat and lazy in the city. We control the climate, and we eat before we're even hungry. The cops are here to defend us, and the lions are in the zoo. Modern society has come with all sorts of cool things, but it's also made us lazy and feeble. The Urban Monk steps out of this life of silent complacency and back into one of action, adventure, constant challenge, and general awesomeness.

You don't need to HALO jump into a Somalian pirate boat with a samurai sword and start slashing, but you do need to start stepping out of your comfort zones. Life is not a spectator sport, and that's why TV is poison.

Be the person an awesome TV show would want to feature.

What are your dreams and aspirations? What have you always wanted to do? What's it going to take to do it? Step up and start making a plan.

You won't be able to do so without a healthy mind and body, and that's usually the catch for most of us. We lack the *energy* to get going, and that's where survival training comes in. That's why rock climbing can help. That's how kung fu can save the day. As you start to follow the principles in this book, you'll start to get healthier and have more energy. You then take that energy and plug it into doing more awesome stuff so it wakes up your warrior and survivor genes. Once that happens, you have turned the corner and can start to feel the life coming back into your veins. The energy increases with your enthusiasm, and you start breaking out of your shell—you start coming back to life.

Find a good martial arts school and get to work. Man or woman, old or young, Urban Monks know how to defend themselves. Even if you're 90 years old, tai chi is awesome and will jump-start your flow. Grow or die: It is a necessity of life as dictated by nature and our survival genes. Stepping into this power is a critical piece of the puzzle. It helps you feel safe, alive, accomplished, and ready to take on greater challenges. In the Resources section, I've included a few exercises from the tai chi traditions I've trained in for you to try.

Caffeine Detox

Thousands of patients have come to me with anxiety, and a simple hack has sorted them out. A really easy one is cutting the caffeine. It takes a few days to pull out of the fog, but on the other end is clarity, focus, and lower stress levels. Caffeine tends to jack us up on borrowed energy. It's like turning up the volume on your music to quiet a screaming child—not the best play. Instead, we use our Urban Monk practices to move the energy and calm the nervous system to gain clarity and peace.

Many of my patients have shown tremendous success in bringing down their overall stress levels after 1 month off caffeine. You can start with a variety of coffee substitutes or simply switch over to a green smoothie and go for a run. It is all about swapping rituals and upgrading to better ones. We can stimulate the body with a cold shower, a brisk walk, some gym time, or preferably some of the qigong practices I'm sharing with you in this book. Try it in your first Gong. Chances are, you'll never look back.

Active Mental Scanning

Setting up a new mental "operating system" is the key to essential Buddhist meditation, but I'm bringing it back here because you don't need any of the flowery language to get the job done. Simply create an environment where you learn to "scan" your consciousness with a very simple question:

"What am I doing right now?"

    No matter what the answer is, simply *stop* doing that and relax. This exercise is designed to train your mind to get out of the habit of perpetually "doing" and get into a healthier state of simply "being." With practice, you'll find that almost every time you check in with yourself, you're doing something silly. For example, the answer might be "I was fretting over what would happen if my wife didn't get back in time from the gym and I'd be late for work."

This is a common type of thought that, in some form, is always running in the back of our minds. Usually, there's an if-then scenario . . . then drama or anxiety . . . worry . . . my response . . . I'm hungry . . . my leg itches . . . where's the kid? . . . blue balloon . . . where'd I leave my keys? . . . where the hell is she? . . . did I remember to e-mail that report? . . . oh, it's cloudy out . . . " Sound familiar? We all do it.

Learn to regularly scan your mind and check in to see what you're doing. Don't get mad at yourself for having a noisy head—we all do, even the Dalai Lama. The difference between the Master and the common person is that the Master learns to observe the noise and not react to it. Notice it and let it pass . . . don't jump in. Whenever you catch yourself tumbling down the rapids with your thoughts, simply acknowledge that this is happening and stop doing whatever you're doing mentally. This "tumbling" happens in the form of runaway thoughts, anxiety, restlessness, boredom, or anything else that pulls us out of the present moment.

Relax.

Learning to relax is the key to mastery. Living there is paradise. This is the abode of the Urban Monk—calm in the center of a chaotic world. Running to Maui doesn't fix anything. You can't go to peace; you find it within.

Exercise

Tried and true, exercise is an amazing way to bring down stress levels. It gets the blood pumping and the endorphins flowing. We evolved from an environment where we moved around pretty much all day. Fast-forward a few thousand years, and we go from bed to car to desk to car to sofa to bed. Still water breeds poison, and this is a huge reason why so many of the people around you are sick and miserable.

Start by simply walking. Stretch in the morning and do some work in the yard. Get going with a martial art and do your qigong daily. Go to the gym if you are into it, or find a way to swing some kettlebells at home. Learn how to dance. You've got to move, and a healthy physical fitness routine is the baseline for anybody who wants to live a happy and healthy life. None of this is new, but I'll stretch a bit and add that an Urban Monk strives for peak fitness. Can you climb a cliff? Can you jump a gorge? Can you carry buckets of water up a hill? Our ancestors used to do this stuff all the time. It was part of life. It's your birthright.

Heart Rate Variability

This simple calculation helps us monitor our stress response and our body's ability to recover from stressful events. More variability means greater resilience. Monitoring your heart rate variability has positive health outcomes and is being used all over the world as a modern hack to deal with stress. Check the Resources section for more on this.

ROBERT'S ACTION PLAN

Robert was a mess but totally fixable. He was leaking vitality at every stop, and the first task was to stop the bleeding. We turned off the TV and swapped out his breakfast cereal with some eggs and protein powders. We had him create a financial plan for retirement, which helped him see how much money he and his family squandered. He and his wife slowly scaled back on "keeping up with the Joneses," and it was great. They went on family camping trips, went fishing, and spent time at the park, and they stopped buying every new video game that came out. The kids were surprisingly *not* complaining about the lack of new toys because they were finally seeing their dad.

We swapped out Robert's coffee for green tea and taught him how to meditate. His phone would chime every 25 minutes and remind him to get up, stretch, and shake out his qi. He'd go outside and move or stand by the window and meditate for a couple minutes. A tall glass of water would follow this, and then he'd do a quick qigong exercise before jumping back into his work. He'd ask, "What am I doing right now?" and then think through his goals for the day. What was he working on? What needed to get finished, and what was the priority? He'd then jump back in (at his new standing desk) and bang out another solid 25 minutes of work. The 25 minutes on and 5 off really worked for him.

At first he was worried he'd never get anything done, but he hadn't factored in the added efficiency and clarity. He was actually finishing earlier, doing better work, and getting home sooner to hang with his family. With the TV off most of the time now, they'd walk the dogs and spend some quality time together each evening before the kids went back to their homework and Robert got to reconnect with his wife.

He directed his firm to start doing some pro bono work for a local cause, and he really brought up the morale at the office this way. All in, it took a few months to get things shaken up a bit, but now Robert's lab results are looking great and he has his glow back. He still often has to remember to breathe since his job is hectic by nature, but he's a transformed man and everyone can see it.

CHAPTER 2

Drinking from Infinity: The Art of Mastering Time

ASHLEY IS A MOTHER of two young children. She is working full-time again after her youngest started preschool and is trying to get into the swing of things. She never really recovered from all the sleep debt she accumulated with the two kids, and it's been an uphill battle for about 4 years. She never has time for anything.

Ashley studied tax planning in school and is happy to be back in her career, but the days are getting harder to handle. She's now waking at 5:30 a.m. in order to get about 25 minutes of treadmill time before the kids start waking up. From there it's all chaos: She needs to get them dressed and fed, in the car, and over to two different schools, and then fight traffic to get to work by 8:30. She's late often and can't remember the last time she sat down to have a decent breakfast for herself.

Work is hectic, and she's been drinking more coffee lately as she feels she's losing her mental edge. Guilt is setting in because she feels personally responsible for the advice she gives to people who trust her with their hard-earned money. Recently, she missed a detail on a document that nearly cost her client lots of money and earned her a stern reprimand from her supervisor.

Ashley's husband gets the kids from school now because she simply wasn't getting out on time. That's been a relief, but by the time she fights traffic to get home, it is already time to make dinner, bathe the kids, and get them to bed.

Exhausted, Ashley and her husband flop in front of the TV and watch a couple of their shows before going upstairs and going to bed. She tries to read in bed but is usually knocked out before she can get through five pages. There are 11 books stacked up on her nightstand, and they arrive faster than she reads them, leading to even more stress and guilt. She and her husband are both too tired for sex.

Ashley's dreams are active, and she's restless at night. She tries to make up some of her sleep debt on weekends, but there's always a game, event, or some relative popping in, so she's constantly entertaining and staying active.

Ashley doesn't have energy and is borrowing it (with coffee and stimulants) from tomorrow to get through today. She's "time poor" and suffering from not having the mental space to decompress and relax. Top it off with the guilt of knowing she wants to do more yoga, get that advanced certification at work, and call her girlfriends, and Ashley is at a loss for what to do, with no foreseeable end in sight.

THE PROBLEM

We're all overcommitted and have too many things to do in too little time. We suffer from Time Compression Syndrome. This is when we've committed more things to a given timeline than can reasonably be done. Time Compression Syndrome leads to stress and a strained consciousness, which bends under the weight of pressured time. It strains our soul. We've mastered the art of compressing so many items into our timeline that it now hurts to walk out the door.

Resting and relaxing are not acceptable in our society and are seen as a sign of laziness and weakness. Productivity is everything. Given no time to recover, we try to jam more things into our days as we stretch them to impossible timelines and are constantly stressed about being late and not having enough time to get it all done. We're gluttons for punishment; we dream that there will be some later time when we can catch up and finally slow down, but we don't make it happen.

Your "later" will always look the same
if your "now" is chaotic.

There's the old saying that how you do something is essentially how you do everything. If you can't relax and enjoy the present moment, you're in big trouble. Most people defer things in time so often that they will never stand a chance of catching up. This leads to

PERSONAL JOURNEYS

I was very excited when I first "found" tai chi. It became a part of my new identity: I got to become the spiritual guy, which was a cool rebranding in college. I often recall the one time when I was very late for class, zipping between traffic to get to my tai chi lesson. I was rolling through stop signs and cutting corners, in a major hurry to get to a class where I was learning to slow down. I was so caught up in the rush of getting there that I didn't see another college student trying to cross the street. I had to slam on my brakes to avoid hitting him. The tragedy was narrowly averted, and I apologized. Driving off, I had such a strong realization that I had to pull over. I went and sat under a tree in a local park and thought about what had just happened, and I realized that tai chi isn't a class. It is a way of life. I had gotten it all wrong and nearly killed somebody in the process. I learned a lot about tai chi that day, and it had little to do with movement. Stillness was the missing ingredient, and I got that piece loud and clear.

an uneasy feeling of being incomplete. It drives a baseline anxiety that we can't seem to shake.

Time is money, and time is running out.

Moms stress about playdates. Kids are given too much homework. Fathers are shaving while holding a baby. Dogs get really short walks. We then wonder why they chew our furniture . . .

Somehow the success metrics of industry and the innovations of the business world have us all believing that we need the same type of streamlined efficiencies built into how we run all facets of our lives. This has worked into dominant memes of our society and has done so at great cost. People have nervous breakdowns all the time. The anxiety pill business is booming. Drug companies are recording billions in profits annually and buying all the airwaves to keep dumping their dumb commercials on us.

What's the message? "You don't have time to stop, so take this shit and keep up, chump."

Time is quickening with technology, and we all feel like we're falling behind. There's always something new we have not heard of, new tech, a new restaurant, the latest trend in fashion, some new business competitor, altogether too many items in too little time. We've bought into a worldview where we need to look busy or else we're not important. We need to act and dress a certain way in order to belong.

The need to keep up is a very real thing. There's the Fear of Missing Out (FOMO), which is well understood in the blogosphere. We all feel it; some have taken a stance against it with movements like JOMO (the Joy of Missing Out). Simply being is not part of the mainstream dialogue anymore. With the advent of reality TV, it's not enough to keep up with our own reality anymore; now we need to keep up with the lives of multiple other characters unrelated to us in a never-ending stream of drama and events that our friends will be talking about.

These days, I know lots of people who dutifully follow their navigation systems everywhere, even to places they've been to several times before. This gets them to where they're going in a way that misses the environment they're driving through and deprives them of an essential part of human experience. What experience? The cou-

Losing experience @ nature & environment as silence too
we pass/drive through
GPS
DRINKING FROM INFINITY: THE ART OF MASTERING TIME   31

pling of time *with space.* Where we stand in Time/Space can be considered our Universal Coordinates, and now GPS has taken away our awareness of this. Being lost in both is a typical way of assuring that people are going to stumble through life and not have a clue how they got there. There may have been an amazing jasmine plant on that path, but they never smelled it. The giant oak tree wasn't mentioned by the navigation system, and neither was the amazing sunset we could have stopped to enjoy. We just rushed from airport to hotel, and now we can watch "reality" on TV.

Time can either be seen as our greatest gift or our biggest challenge.

To most busy urban people, time is viewed with dismay and seen as a problem of scarcity. We are dying to have more of it but then commit what we have to things that are not restorative or helpful in the long run. We complain about not having time but then squander what we do have on silly things that don't support our dreams or our vitality.

As humans, we average 2.5 billion heartbeats in a lifetime. That seems like a lot, but we run at around 100,000 beats per day. The question for us is to examine where it is we're spending that time. Is it moving us toward more happiness, enlightenment, better health, or adventure? The problem with most people is that those precious heartbeats are drumming in the wrong direction. Millions of people spend their days parked up in an office chair doing something they lack passion for. They gain weight, eat bad food, and look for mind-numbing distractions to pass the time.

Killing time is killing life.

We cannot get time back, and the way we spend it reflects on every aspect of our lives. We either move toward more awareness or fall further into a dreary sleep. Look around you. People like Ashley have become zombies because they've relinquished the most precious asset they have—time. Trading time for money is how the economy works, but that model is deeply flawed. Companies pay for work and results, not dead time. This misunderstanding has hurt the economy and has certainly dulled the minds of millions of people who simply clock in and check out. An Urban Monk wakes up from this dreary reality and takes her time back. She never wastes it and *invests* it intentionally to move forward in life and *grow as a person*.

URBAN MONK WISDOM

To the ancient monks of the East and West, time has always been considered one of life's great mysteries. What we consider "conventional time" is a linear and sequential construct that is very different from the "no time" of the monks.

We track conventional time on our watches. It is tied to the movement of the Earth around the sun, the rotation of the Earth, the phase of the moon, and our place in the solar system. It helps us have a common language and convention around how and when to assemble. This societal time helps airports run and schools operate. It works and is a wonderful tool we have to know "when" we stand in the Universe. It is a *convention* that is super useful in society and helps us all function together. Meeting a friend for tea is easier to organize around the notion of "4:45 p.m." versus "around sundown."

This conception of conventional time does not, however, speak to the *quality* of the time we experience. Time dilates. It goes faster or slower depending on the state of being or consciousness in which we are parked. When we're frantically engaged in our daily burn, time seems to fly and there's never enough of it. On a 2-week vacation in Hawaii, however, we allow it to stretch and find ourselves feeling restless, looking down at our watches and amazed that it's only 11:00 a.m. How does this happen?

When I go on vacation, I try to take at least 2 weeks. I give myself the first week to do only what I *feel like* doing, and that usually revolves around a whole lot of nothing. It kind of hurts at first—trying to slow down from all the insanity. The following week I'll go do some things if I feel like it. Why? Because *doing* is the disease of modernity, and *being* is a long-lost art. On vacation, I allow myself to be extra lazy. Nap when tired. Eat when hungry. Only do things that sound good to me.

In contrast, most people go on vacation and book activities so tight that it feels like a typical Tuesday juxtaposed on paradise. Tours, snorkeling, activities, driving around the island, museums, and going to shows all sound good if you're not exhausted and time compressed. Giving yourself permission to say "no" to more things and creating some mental and temporal *space* to unwind into is good medicine. Coming back tired from a vacation is insane. It's like running a marathon the night before your big race and wondering why your performance is hampered.

The ancients understood rest and recovery cycles well. First of all, they lived much closer to nature and the rhythms of the seasons. They also had a fundamentally different understanding of time. To an Urban Monk, time dilation is part of a living, breathing tradition that is still flourishing in monasteries around the world.

Time is also relative. It is infinite.

The Universe knows no time. Outside of our narrow band of self-conscious identity, time does what it likes. We recall events from our childhood that can make us moody by suddenly flooding our bloodstream with molecules, sparking emotions, and elevating our heart rate. We dream of an event in the future and are carried away to a fantasy realm where we happily reside and ponder things until the phone rings and brings us back to our desk.

We time travel all the time.

Our consciousness has access to things all over the timeline and often takes us out of the present moment. It pulls us into some "other time" where we can spend much of our energy. It can pull us away from "now" and keep us fixated on a traumatic event "then" or an anticipated event "soon." In fact, it seems that we've become quite adept at spending much of our actual time in "other time."

The key to being liberated from time is to understand this great Hermetic axiom: "All the Power that ever was or will be is here now."

The present moment is where we have full access to all of our faculties. It is where we can focus on the actual task *at hand* and perform it masterfully. It is where our bodies are relaxed and our minds are in healthier brainwave patterns. When we learn to come back to the present moment, we have greater mental acuity, a more relaxed nervous system, and better epigenetic expression of healthy genes, and we are capable of making far better decisions.

We can tap into the place of "no time" and "drink from Infinity" when we learn how to access certain parts of our consciousness. This is the *flow* state of athletes and the *Zen mind* of meditators. It effectively puts us back into the driver's seat and gives us the personal power to *choose* where we allocate our time. It also makes us much more efficient, so we can do more (and do it better) while staying calm. The professional athlete makes it look easy. The best martial artists look elegant. The most challenging ballet moves look so graceful, yet that ease comes from lots of practice and dedicated, focused intent. You must be present or you will falter in high-performance sports. Life is no different. Waking up means living life fully and being acutely present and aware; it means igniting your consciousness.

Taking Control of How We Engage with Time

We can slow the quality of time with our breath, with our mind, and by controlling our biorhythms. Taking time for ourselves is the most important thing we could do for our personal development and mental health. Our ability to choose wisely and spend our valuable time on our goals is the real sign of mastery.

Most people actively take on dozens of items at a time and wonder why they mostly falter. Each of these tasks takes mental time and energy. Most of us exhaust our vitality and willpower trying to feed too many ideas, gigs, social commitments, and projects because we've never really *stopped time* and taken a proper accounting of where we stand. Stop time? Yeah, an Urban Monk learns to step out of time and exist in a powerful timeless space.

In the modern world,
we don't have a center, so we spin.

When we learn to breathe down to our lower abdomen and calm the mind, we start to feel whole again. From this state, we can calmly examine our life and our commitments in time and ascertain where we are leaking too much energy. Without a calm perspective, our crazy monkey minds convince us that more is better and another espresso will handle this problem, layering on more insanity. Finding our center helps us control our perception of time and attain peace.

Tapping Into the Stillness Means Moving with the Universe

A critical misreading of ancient scriptures has many people trying to stop time and avoid all movement. This cannot be done. The entire Universe has moved on since you read the last sentence. Everything is moving and growing with each passing second. The Urban Monk understands this and relaxes into a *harmonic flow* with the Universe. By stopping time, we stop fighting the movement of Reality and we move *with it*. It looks like stillness, but it can be likened to sitting on a raft that's flowing down a river. You flow with it, and you do not fight the current.

Mastery Is in the Negation

This means learning to say "no."

Let's put it this way:

If the guys text me and ask that I meet them for a drink this evening, my impulse may be to immediately say "yes." After all, I don't see my friends enough, I'll be hungry by then, and I'm stressed out and have had a long week, so I *deserve* it and it'll be fun. Sounds reasonable, right?

But by saying "yes" to them, I've effectively said "no" to my children getting to spend time with their daddy, to my spouse who's also busy and whom I don't see enough, to my workout which was planned already and is supposed to be a priority, to my sleep which I'm always complaining about missing out on, to the reading I said I need to do to help get my career to the next level, and, of course, to my poor liver.

All of the important things that I had already committed to *in time* have now been compressed in my calendar because of this one impulsive decision. It sets off a cascade of events that further disrupt my timeline and compresses time itself within my psyche. This is classic Time Compression Syndrome, and we're all infected with it.

What would be the better way to handle this?

Stop and think about it. Take a few deep breaths down to your lower abdomen and look across the timeline and see what ripples this would make into your world. Can you afford another plant in your garden, or is this going to pull the water away from things that are more important to you?

The Urban Monk remains calm and collected.

Modern science has now caught up with what the ancient masters have been saying all along. Meditation helps us be less impulsive. Functional MRI studies show increased density of the cortical neurons in the brains of people who meditate. This is amazing because, as we learned in the last chapter, the prefrontal cortex is the part of our brain that is in charge of impulse control and higher moral reasoning. These are the very things that help us make better decisions and take control of our lives. This only happens when we can stop being reactive and understand the movement of time.

My fascination with this led me to build a brain lab in one of my clinics. We hired a genius doctor who was doing some cutting-edge research in quantitative EEG analysis of brainwaves associated with religious experience and flow states. I'd bring in meditators and study what "brain signature" they'd let off, taking lots of notes. Over time, we learned how to teach people how to "pop in the clutch" and get out of "high gear" when racing down Time's superhighway.

In the lab, we examined this wonderful concept of Universal "no time" that the meditators were entering. This stands in contrast to the idea of cultural time that is limited to the blocks on our calendars. We need to understand both, as they sit on opposite poles of a key realization. If we have access to experience time in these varying capacities, then it seems to be a key in the understanding of who we truly are.

Who we are *in time* is important to get. The Universe is moving, and we are moving with it. If we fixate on a particular point in time, the entire Universe has moved on and we're clinging to something that is no longer in that river of life. All the energy of the Universe moves with it, and that power resides in one particular point, and that is *now*.

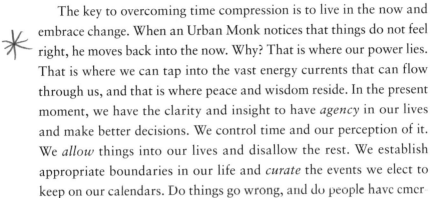

Change is the only constant in the Universe.

The key to overcoming time compression is to live in the now and embrace change. When an Urban Monk notices that things do not feel right, he moves back into the now. Why? That is where our power lies. That is where we can tap into the vast energy currents that can flow through us, and that is where peace and wisdom reside. In the present moment, we have the clarity and insight to have *agency* in our lives and make better decisions. We control time and our perception of it. We *allow* things into our lives and disallow the rest. We establish appropriate boundaries in our life and *curate* the events we elect to keep on our calendars. Do things go wrong, and do people have emergencies? Sure. We control what's in our hands and therefore have enough *agency* to move things around if big items surprise us.

The Master moves with time and adjusts constantly as a good surfer makes microadjustments in order to stay on a wave that is moving and crashing all around him.

Being rigid makes us fall.
Being afraid of change paralyzes us.

Thus the great paradox: To remain still means to *move* with time, to move with the Universe. Stillness is actually the state of moving with the Universe in unison.

I've done a good amount of backcountry backpacking in my days. I would hike into a remote mountain setting, find a meadow with a stream running through it, and make it my home for a few days. The goal is always to sit by the water and remain silent. Nothing says "change is constant" like a creek or a river. It acts as a constant reminder that the Universe flows and that time flows. When the sound of my racing thoughts is finally washed away by the gentle sound of the stream, I know I've "taken that sip" and am back in a sane place. This is when I return to the city and take the gift of nature with me. Stillness is our greatest asset, and those who walk with it live life with clarity and intention. I'll teach you this practice in more detail in Chapter 7.

In nature, things move with the sunlight and with the seasons. In society, none of that seems to matter anymore. In a world filled with artificial constructs and compressed time, the only way to stay sane is to take control of our personal time. Tapping into timelessness connects us with all Life around us and helps us feel a part of the fabric of the Universe. It connects us and helps us whistle while we work. It stops the walls from caving in. We are in stride with the life flowing around us and don't get knocked off our perch every time someone else's frequency or "time stamp" invades our space. I like to call these interruptions time pollution. That's when someone who's running at a different frequency infects your space and agitates your state of mind. An Urban Monk stays anchored in her own time—one that is intentionally throttled for the activity at hand—and remains immune to any infiltrating frequencies that don't serve her.

We can elect to stay in the central timeless space and be a source of solace and inspiration for all those around us. From this place, we gain insight into our Eternal Self and are freed from the bondage of time.

Being a slave to time is the ultimate failure in trying to understand who we are.

EASTERN PRACTICES
Four-Count Breathing Meditation

This is the essential Urban Monk meditation practice that helps calm the mind and hone our focus. It is designed to give us an "anchor" for our consciousness: something real to focus in on, like the breath. The essential design is a repetitive practice of counting the breath and pausing between the inflow and outflow. When you catch yourself drifting off and being distracted (and you will), simply return to the practice and keep going. Over time, it helps calm the mind, decrease reactivity, and power the frontal lobes of the brain, which will help you think before you commit to items on your calendar. This is an essential mindfulness meditation practice and is designed for people just getting in. That being said, seasoned masters practice this daily, so don't let its simplicity fool you. Tapping into Universal time can be achieved by first tapping into your breath. You can effectively practice time dilation once you learn to control and understand your breathing.

○ Sit in a comfortable position with your spine straight.

○ Touch the tip of your tongue to the roof of your mouth.

○ Gently start breathing in and out through your nose with your mouth closed.

○ Breathe to a spot about 3 inches below your navel called the lower dantian. (We'll be breathing to this place in all of our qigong [energy work] and many of our meditation practices throughout the book. It is essentially three fingers below the navel, deep in the center of your body. It is an empty space where we can breathe and cultivate energy and settle our minds.)

○ Inflate (on inhale) and deflate (on exhale) this area with each passing breath.

○ On your next inhale, slowly breathe down to your lower abdomen for a count of 4, counting slowly and evenly.

○ Hold your breath when full for a count of 2.

○ Slowly exhale for a count of 4; be fully empty by the end of it, and time it so you can do so.

○ Hold your breath for a count of 2.

○ Back to the inhale for 4 . . .

○ Keep following this basic pattern for as long as is comfortable (or desired).

○ Make sure your in and out breaths keep the same cadence with the count. Be particularly aware of the space at the top of the in breath and bottom of the out breath.

That's it. I recommend doing this practice for at least 10 minutes a day. Set the timer on your phone, put it on airplane mode, and go in to nourish your time-compressed brain. Step out of societal time by syncing with your breath. Balancing the breath is key, so make sure the inhale and exhale are the same duration. This will do wonders for your mind.

Moving Qigong with Time Dilation Practice

This exercise is designed to help break our fixation on time and shift our consciousness. It takes a bit of practice but is well worth the effort. The basic design is a simple movement with breath that we connect up with. From there, we start to adjust our speed of movement in our hands while keeping our breath nice and slow. Doing this for a few minutes can really cause a pattern interrupt, help the mind break free from the drudgery of compressed time, and help us jump out into the living, breathing, present moment, which is full of potential and energy.

○ Stand with your feet shoulder-width apart and your arms at your sides.

○ Breathe in and out of your nose with your tongue touching the roof of your mouth.

○ Slowly breathe down to your lower abdomen (to the area known as the lower dantian, as in the previous exercise).

○ Once you've connected with your breath and slowed it, move your palms to touch the front of your thighs on the next EXHALE.

○ From here, slowly lift your arms, shoulder-width apart, up in front of you to the height of your shoulders ON THE INHALE.

○ Then slowly let your arms coast back down to where your palms touch the top of your thighs ON THE EXHALE.

○ Gently repeat this practice for about 10 repetitions, going nice and slowly.

○ Look at the space between your hands with a soft gaze.

○ Now keep the breath going at the same pace and DISCONNECT the arm movements from it by picking up the pace of your arms to 2 times the speed.

○ Do this for about 10 to 20 repetitions and notice how you feel.

○ Now start moving your arms at 4 times the speed while keeping your breath slow and low (and disconnected from the arm movements).

○ Do this about another 10 to 20 times and see how you feel.

○ Go back to the original pace where your arm movements and your breath are connected (a slow rhythmic movement tied to your breath).

○ Go back to a basic standing posture and slowly breathe to the lower dantian for about 10 to 20 more breaths.

Candle Meditation

This practice is designed to help connect our consciousness with the primordial "element" of fire. Practiced for thousands of years in Taoist monasteries, candle meditation helps nourish the spirit and center the attention in the heart. Bringing our awareness to the flame of a candle helps "stop time" and sever our fixation on the minutiae.

○ Set up a quiet room with no draft where you can be alone for a few minutes.

○ Make sure the room can be fully dark—the darker the better, so unplug electronic devices or at least cover them.

○ Get a single candle and position it so it is about 3 feet in front of you and just at about chin height from where you plan to sit.

○ Turn off the lights.

○ Sit in a comfortable position with your spine straight (facing the candle).

○ Breathe in and out of your nose to the lower dantian.

○ The tip of your tongue should touch the roof of your mouth.

○ Gently gaze at the blue part of the flame.

○ Keep breathing to your lower abdomen, but move your attention to the flame.

○ Soften your gaze and allow your eyes to take in the flame fully.

○ Try not to blink, but don't hurt yourself either.

○ Take several breaths while relaxing into this; 5 to 10 minutes should suffice.

○ When ready to end it, breathe out of your mouth on the exhale and take both palms and cover your temples.

○ Take 10 more breaths down to the lower dantian from here and then slowly open your eyes and come back to the room.

○ Try to sit in quiet meditation for a few minutes after this. Four-Count Breathing would be ideal.

This is a powerful practice that helps shift our consciousness and brings us back to the moment.

MODERN HACKS
Media Fast

That whole business of leveraging us on our desires and unfulfilled longings has no better home than TV. The news media constantly batter us with stories about how scary and unsafe the world is. This hits us on a primitive level and pokes at our fear for survival. This is why Urban Monks learn to protect themselves and their loved ones. Having the police and the Army around is great, but handing over all our civil liberties in exchange for "security" is a slippery slope that some darker elements in our society are eager to exploit.

The news can quickly poison your mind.

TV programming is also a race to the bottom for the most part. Drama, intrigue, infidelity, violence, murder, and avarice are what sell. Sociopaths are made out to be the heroes, and after enough "downtime" watching this stuff, subtle memes start to embed our psyche and we fall for it. Fall for what? A worldview that is inaccurate and dark, which drives us to feel unsafe, unloved, alone, and unattractive. This is the perfect formula for the mindless consumer, and it drives the global economic machine—millions of people buying bullshit they don't need in order to feel better or fit in.

An Urban Monk categorically rejects this. Choose your media and curate it. The Internet is perfect for this. Watch what enriches you and learn. There's nothing wrong with entertainment, and some great programs are being produced now, but the point is, if you're sitting there mindlessly watching a network show and all the commercials in between, you're in trouble. Pick the good stuff, and know that "you are what you eat" also applies to the media you consume.

Garbage in = Garbage out
(tech wisdom about database architecture)

A great exercise here is to spend *1 month* avoiding all TV and social media. See what happens to your time. On average, an American will watch more than 5 hours of live television per day and spend more than 3 hours a day using social media. That's more than 8 hours! So assuming we work 8 hours and sleep another 8 (as we should), then according to these 2014 stats, we spend almost the entirety of the rest of our time either watching TV or goofing off on social media. Is it any wonder why most people never realize their dreams or aspirations? Maybe you can argue that people browse social media *while* watching TV . . . okay, touché . . . welcome to more attention deficit disorder.

"Downtime" is a farce. You are not really resting, and peering into the lives of others is mostly a waste of time. Reabsorb it. Time is bound to your life force. Taking it back gives you the energy and the clarity to direct your power toward things that matter to you. At first, it may feel frustrating, and you may be bored, not knowing what to do. That's all the momentum of bad habits drawing you into unhealthy behavior. As you reabsorb it, you'll notice how much you've squandered, but instead of crying over spilled milk, enjoy what you've liberated and move on.

The Urban Monk takes her time back. Time is the most precious treasure we've got. Squandering it on TV and social media is insane. Take a month off and see what happens. At first, you won't know what to do with yourself. That's fine. You'll figure it out. Hiking, the gym, time with the kids, reading books, doing night school to get out of that shit job, connecting with friends, and whatever else that's awesome are all options that await. Life awaits.

Scheduled Breaks: How to Use Your Calendar Correctly

When I speak with people and ask them about their priorities, most of them mainly talk about their families, their health, and travel. That's when I ask them to show me their schedules on their phones. There's *seldom* any time allotted that hints at any of the above-mentioned priorities. Most people *say* they care about certain things, but because those things don't make it to their calendars, little to no time is spent on them.

We vote with our time, and by not putting our priorities into our calendars, we are effectively saying to the Universe that we don't really care about them. I book my walk time with my wife, the kids, and the dogs every morning. Unless I'm out of town, my calendar tells me that's where I am committed, and I seldom let anything (unless crazy urgent and time-zone sensitive) draw me away from this valuable time. I also book in "recovery" blocks on certain days so I can recharge. That means no intruders: Leave me be and let me rest.

Your task here is to do the same: Take your top priorities and block them out in your calendar. If you mean it, stand by it. You'll be surprised at how well this works and how it'll challenge your bad habits.

E-Mail Chunk Time

Constantly changing channels every time an e-mail comes in is terrible for our focus and makes us sadly inefficient. It pulls us off the activity at hand and drives us to be more distracted, stressed, and generally less effective. An Urban Monk takes control of matters in this department by choosing when to engage in communication with the outside world. This means checking e-mail only at designated times during the day. On creative days, I do not check e-mail until 11:00 a.m. That gives me 3 solid hours of uninterrupted time to get my work done before the world comes knocking with demands that were not on my schedule. Most people who successfully practice this will set two or three designated chunks of time (30 to 60 minutes should be enough) to jam through and handle e-mail communications.

Most e-mail programs now have great tools like labeling, starring, and categorizing to help us triage e-mail as it comes in. The general rule is that if you could answer and handle an e-mail in less than 5 minutes, just do it right then. If longer, star, forward, or schedule to deal with it at a later time. This way, we don't fall behind in communications and also leave appropriate time to handle important issues via e-mail.

Having good spam filters and learning to unsubscribe to feeds that don't serve you are also key. One way to do this is to use a secondary e-mail address for random stuff online and have all mail from those ventures dump into that bucket. You can always go back and check out that inbox should you choose, but those promotional or noncritical e-mails won't distract you from your day.

Over time, you will learn to be better at this, and your productivity will increase. This doesn't necessarily mean that you should do more work. It can, if that's what you choose, but the added efficiency can also buy you time to go for a run, go home an hour early and see your kids, or take night classes and move your career forward. Maybe a nap . . .

Again, time is incredibly valuable, and an Urban Monk does not squander it. Do things intentionally, and don't let the constant barrage of e-mails distract you from your goals for the day.

Brainwave Meditation Tracks

Over the years, I've looked at a number of different technologies that can help with stress and time compression, and I've found some to be amazing. I used to own a brain lab and have watched thousands of hours of EEG data on meditators and yogis going into altered states. I've found certain brainwave tracks to be particularly useful in helping people snap out of time compression, so I do recommend them. Why? Because labs have been studying the human brain in these altered states, and some interesting data supports it. The brain functions in many different brainwave states, and at any given time, one is usually more dominant than the others. When stressed and time compressed, we are usually in Beta (12 to 19 hertz) or High Beta (19 to 26 hertz). Getting the brain to drop into Alpha (7.5 to 12.5 hertz) and then further into Theta (6 to 10 hertz) can be very therapeutic and relaxing. We find seasoned meditators are capable of dropping into the Alpha state very readily, and others can drop down lower into Theta and even Delta (1 to 3 hertz) while in altered states. Some of these new technologies can serve as a tool to entrain the brain to drop into these states faster with fewer years of "cushion time."

There are some links to tracks I've created in the Resources section.

ASHLEY'S ACTION PLAN

When we looked at Ashley's life and thought about where we could get the quickest results with minimal effort, we realized that the first stop was her TV time. What a waste of life force! We got her to unplug from all "push" media, like TV and traditional radio, so she could handpick the information and content that came into her life. The result: far more time every day to walk with her family, garden, and do some yoga in the evenings. She started doing some reading for work in the evenings as well, and the anxiety of always being behind quickly started to fade.

Ashley and I worked on her morning routine next. Running on the treadmill wasn't a great idea for someone like her. Her adrenal profile showed a real challenge here, and running was making it worse. She began doing some burst training and some full-body activity during the time she previously spent running. We've coupled this with dedicated recovery time. The result: more energy, better mood, and a tighter, toned body. We also added a 10-minute qigong set in the mornings, which has really helped her center up and get clear in her mind. She was always trying to "catch her breath" in life, and this practice helps her drink from the Source before starting her day.

Ashley learned to put her priorities into her phone calendar and also schedule regular breaks throughout her workday. At first this freaked her out, so she didn't take long ones, fearing reprimand from her superiors. Taking 5 minutes to breathe to her lower belly proved to be huge for her. As she started to realize how much better she was and how much more clarity she worked with after these breaks, something magical happened. She became more efficient. She started to get ahead of the curve and, within a couple of months, was *done* with work by 5:00 p.m. and getting home sooner. This meant more time with her family and time for herself. Her work quality was also better, and she received a promotion a few months later.

Another major piece for Ashley was learning how to shut down at night. She was so used to spinning all day that the momentum led her to stay crazy after hours. She and her husband started hanging out in candlelight a couple of nights a week, and she put her tablet away at night in favor of a good old-fashioned book. Over the course of a couple of months, her energy levels were better and more sustained. She was complaining less of fatigue and making huge strides in checking items off her list. Some romantic time under candlelight also triggered the return of her long-lost sex drive.

It simply took a few adjustments to her lifestyle and a shift in her *orientation* to really make a difference. When Ashley took control of her time, she got her life back.

CHAPTER 3

Energy: Why Am I Always So Tired?

JESSICA DIDN'T SEE IT coming. She was living her life like any normal person would, and, slowly but noticeably, she started to run out of gas. At first it was fine. She'd meet her friends for an afternoon coffee and talk about life. In the evenings, she'd grab a drink and some dinner with her regular crew, and it usually didn't get out of hand. She was in her late twenties and living in New York. That's what you do.

Mornings started to get harder. She used to jam on the bike before lifting some weights at the gym, but her enthusiasm was dwindling. Everything was getting to be too much work. For a while, she took some "skinny" pills that someone had recommended; they worked but made her really agitated and restless. Eventually, she fell off that wagon and put the pounds back on—not many, but enough to make her feel "fat" all the time.

Her last vacation was to Europe. She and a girlfriend went to 12 cities in 14 days. Museums, nightclubs, river boats, walking all day, and more museums—she got a healthy dose of culture, lots of pictures, and a cough that accompanied her home.

Jessica's career has been rough. She got her degree in journalism and has tried her hand at a number of gigs. From PR to investigative reporting, she hasn't quite found her passion yet. The money sucks, and it's almost impossible to make ends meet in the big city. She skimps on all she can but still manages to maintain her social life, which is meaningful to her. It seems that all she orders are salads, so she can't figure out why she is always so tired while eating this healthy. After all, she's doing everything right. Why is she so exhausted?

THE PROBLEM

Jessica isn't alone. The number one complaint at the doctor's office today is fatigue. Everyone is tired, and it's becoming an epidemic. Our bodies are telling us something is wrong, but we're too busy to listen.

Energy is like cash. In the East, we call it *qi*. It is a *currency* that flows. It needs to move through us in a cycle of abundance. If we stay balanced, our energy will be healthy and flow as it should. There's a lot dedicated to this later in the chapter, but let's start painting a picture here.

You are at the store, and you see something that you want. You reach into your pocket for some money and realize that you spent the last of it this morning. In the old days, you'd walk away without the item, possibly learning better cash management along the way. Today, we don't need to face that reality at all—we've got credit! You pull a card from your wallet and swipe that sucker. Bam! The thing's in the bag, and you're smiling on your way home—smiling until you get the bill and realize you need to come up with the money. Sound familiar? That's what we do with our energy every day.

Jessica could have gone to a mountain retreat and read a book, taken multiple naps, done some yoga, and sat by a nice fire for a week and totally recharged her batteries, but, instead, she spent all her money *and energy* parading around Europe. She actually swiped most of the trip on a card and is super stressed about her bills now.

Now she's tired and more agitated.
She's blown out her qi and feels depleted.

Because she doesn't rest, she doesn't recover. It's a basic principle: What goes up must come down. Yin and yang must always find balance for energy to flow.

Jessica does find balance, but it doesn't come in a friendly manner.

She pushes and pushes until her body gives out and is then flat on her back recovering for a week—no dinners, can't talk, taking flu medicine, and watching reruns of *Friends*.

Caffeine Is Like an Energy Credit Card

In a capitalistic society, debt is used to leverage growth and generate wealth. It can be useful if you borrow money to flip a house and then bank some nice profit. Your line of credit can help with cash flow woes when your business has some bumps—that's all fine.

The problem here is with bad Energy Economics.

You can't spend more energy than you can produce. This used to be simple math and most people understood it, but there's a monkey wrench in the gears now. Life is fast and hectic. There's never enough time (refer back to the previous chapter on Time Compression Syndrome), so stopping to rest and breathe sounds crazy. *I must keep going*, we think. *I'll drink coffee and grab a bite . . .*

Since time is so short in our perception, stopping to eat is so inconvenient and burdensome. It's an enormous contemporary problem that affects most of us, and it is derailing people's lives: Life and rituals used to be assembled around meals, but now we don't have time to sit down for one. The act has become meaningless, so *what* we eat is also of little consequence; we just choke down that protein bar and keep going. Problem: That shit isn't food.

Food Isn't the Same Anymore

Food is where we derive our energy, and now we've screwed it all up. We've poked, prodded, genetically modified, and artificially enhanced so much of what we eat that our bodies are having trouble recognizing stuff as food. What this does is confuse the immune system into not knowing "friend" from "foe" and mounting an attack on food particles along our gut lining. This leaks a tremendous amount of energy and keeps us tired, inflamed, and foggy in the head. Chapters 6 and 7 dive into much more detail on this, but for now, know that the moral of the story is to eat *real food,* which comes organically from the earth and hasn't been tampered with. It is the best bet for health, nutrition, and our overall well-being.

Toxins Are Smothering Us

Seventy-four billion pounds of chemicals are being added to our environment daily, and many of these are harmful to our mitochondria, which are extremely susceptible to damage. The mitochondria are tiny organelles in our cells that help us produce energy. When they are damaged or compromised, our energy output is dampened and we complain of listlessness and fatigue.

We are living in an epidemic of toxicity that is pounding us from all sides. As our bodies lose resilience, the mitochondria are harmed, and we have less energy for our immune systems, our detoxification pathways, and excretion. In essence, it is a downward spiral of toxicity and fatigue. When the light starts to flicker, our brains get foggy and we get moody and irritable, reaching for a pill or a cup of coffee. This isn't the answer. It lies in the household products, the processed food, the polluted air and water, and the cosmetics we subject ourselves to daily. My second movie, *Origins,* took a deep dive into this subject and showed the negative health effects of this chemical experiment we've all become a part of. Looking away from this scary stuff doesn't resolve it. The Urban Monk cleans up his food supply and realizes that "you are what you eat" applies to much more than just food.

There is also a problem with toxic mold, which is a silent energy zapper in our society. Mold triggers the immune system and can give us a slew of symptoms from brain fog to autoimmune reactions. You don't always see it, and its effects can be cumulatively harmful. If you feel you may have sensitivity to mold, check the Resources section for some tools that can help you.

The Body Is Designed to Move

A major piece of the low-energy puzzle is the stagnation we've adopted in modern life. In Chapter 5, we'll go further into this matter and explore the nuances. What we need to understand is that our bodies are electrical in nature and that movement generates charge. Moving legs drive blood and ions to power the nervous system, helping it to communicate appropriately with the brain. Our endorphins kick in, and our senses are working in three dimensions. This is who we are:

vibrant and powerful beings who can scale rock walls and jump ravines.

Fast-forward to today, and we find ourselves parked behind desks or in cars hoping to get some treadmill time after work. We are sitting instead of standing and are driving instead of walking. This shuts off the natural cycle of energy flow that the body knows and flows with. We then begin to stagnate and fall asleep. Our genes stop coding for optimal performance, and we gain weight. We begin to age and fall apart because a robust, healthy system is one that moves and explodes with bursts of energy.

Energy Needs Somewhere to Go

We talk about energy as if it fills a bank account, and that's why we've gotten fat. Remember: Energy needs to move. It cannot stay in one place, and storing it happens in the form of fat, which is something we don't necessarily want in our bodies. So how do we reconcile this?

Always give energy an outlet.

An Urban Monk stays plugged into things that require energy in our world. From causes we support to intellectual pursuits, we constantly need more and more energy to feed the demands of our personal growth. We move more energy *through us* as our signature grows. This means being a conduit for power in our world. From the work that we do to the dirt that we move in our gardens, we drive power. From the books that we read to the lectures that we give, that's energy. From the people that we serve to the self-care that we practice, there's an energy requirement. The more we learn to get out of the way and become efficient, the more force we can run through us.

The problem with modern lifestyles is that watching life on TV doesn't demand any energy. Eating food you didn't grow or hunt doesn't carry any direct exchange. Getting across town in a car consumes petroleum, not love handles. Life has become abstract, and our separation from the basic needs for output of energy has drawn us away from the source of our real power. Let's step back into our bodies.

URBAN MONK WISDOM

Everything carries a life force. Everything is imbued with Spirit and consciousness. Life and sentience are all around us, and the natural world is teeming with it. We live in a great web of life, and the matrix of energy is like a delicious soup we swim in. We feed off of this power, and we breathe energy back into it. It's a beautiful and powerful system of interconnected life and energy transfer bound by a common consciousness—a Universal mind or spirit *of which we are all a part.*

When we eat foods that are full of life force, we gain energy. The *quality* of the food we eat determines the quality and volume of our qi. Things that are close to nature have a high vibration and carry more nutrients and life force. Manufactured foods are mostly devoid of this. No life in the food means no life in us. Is it any wonder why everyone is so tired? Again, we get much more from food than just calories. Sure, there are nutrients, minerals, and cofactors, but what about qi? We extract all forms of subtle energy from food aside from just calories to break down. The connectedness of all life is always a transfer of energy and consciousness. We feed off of the people we are around, the books that we read, the shows that we watch, and the environments we rest in. We're all part of a Universal intelligence that helps us feel connected and vibrantly alive. Everything is alive and imbued with consciousness.

Consume Life

We share the eternal energy of the Universe with all other life, and the act of eating is sacred. We are transferring energy from one life form to another. It is to be done with reverence and respect. An Urban Monk eats *consciously* and gives thanks for every meal, every bite. It is an attitude of inclusion and respect that sits atop all strategies and tactics we can talk about with diet. Everything else is secondary.

From here, we ingest only foods that are alive or were recently alive. Organic vegetables are key. If you eat meat, make sure it was grass-fed, pastured, and loved. The toxic burden we pick up from eating conventional meats is tremendous. It activates our immune systems and detox pathways and generally makes us more tired and lethargic.

One step further would be to say that if you eat meat, then you *need* to go hunting and *kill* whatever it is you're eating. You need to see what goes into taking a life and do so reverently. Hours of hiking up and down ridges and braving the elements gets our blood pumping. It's a big deal, and once imprinted in your consciousness, you'll never blindly scarf down another chicken sandwich again.

Avoid anything that comes in a box or even needs a label. Vegetables come from the ground. Get close to that. Start a garden and grow some or all of your own food if possible. *Touch life.* Know where it comes from and develop a deep respect for it. This is what's missing in the West. We blindly consume foodlike products that are devoid of qi and wonder why we're tired, sick, fat, and depressed. If you want to feel alive, step back into the cycle of life and eat only real food that's supercharged with natural energy. This way, you'll get your nutrients, feel better, lose those horrible cravings, and simply start feeling more energized.

Fetch Water, Chop Wood

In the monasteries, the old saying went:

> *Before Zen, fetch water, chop wood.*
>
> *After Zen, fetch water, chop wood.*

Work is great. The Hindus call it Karma Yoga, and it is good for us. Just because you may have a desk job, that doesn't mean you shouldn't move around. A standing desk, office workouts, daily walks, and many other strategies are covered later in this book. Getting moving is a critical piece to feeling better and having more energy.

Putting the "work" back into *workout* is an important Urban Monk ethic. Getting out there and getting dirty is good for us. Somehow society decided that it isn't classy to work outside because that's for a labor class and rich people watch TV at the gym on treadmills.

Bullshit.

Build a shed, bail some hay, break some rocks, plant a tree, and clean out that attic. In the old days, we moved around, and that kept us charged with energy. We got hungry because we were moving all day, not because the clock struck 6:00 p.m.

Rest When You're Tired

The human body has circadian rhythms that have an ebb and a flow of energy. Understanding how to surf these is critical for the Urban Monk. Simply closing our eyes for 5 to 10 minutes can help us power

PERSONAL JOURNEYS

After the birth of my first child, I had no idea what hit me. I had always slept well and never really suffered from insomnia. With the new baby crying and waking us all the time, the disrupted sleep patterns I was experiencing started to take a toll. Work was busier than ever with a movie launch, and I was running with less fuel in the tank daily. I was tired, my sex drive was lower, my digestion was not as great, and I generally lacked enthusiasm. In fact, I felt like I was heading for "enthusiasm bankruptcy." I drew some blood and found that my adrenals were exhausted, so I went on a program where I took some supplements for adrenal support as well as some tonic herbs, and I changed my diet around to only consume carbs at night. This kept me burning fat and protein during the day, and the carbs at night helped trigger an insulin spike that helped lower my cortisol levels. By layering in some meditation and taking turns with my wife to support the baby, we were able to turn it around quickly. I realized that most people never really recover from these events and then carry that fatigue into everything they do in life. This book will help you erase that energy debt.

down and recharge in the middle of the day. Oftentimes, that's all we really need to get going and have sustained energy, but the problem is that we don't allow it. Giving yourself permission to relax is very hard for the Western mind. After all, our culture came from Anglo-Saxon and Germanic roots, which emphasized hard work and persistence. That has helped us build a huge economy and fleets of aircraft carriers, but it has also put us on drugs for everything.

You have permission to chill.

There, I just gave it to you. One day, you'll be able to give it to yourself, but until then, you can use my pass. The Urban Monk learns to work smarter, not harder. Looking busy just to please the people around us is foolish, yet we all do it from time to time. Take the time to recharge your batteries, and you'll see a profound difference in your energy levels, performance, and health. It'll lead to lower caffeine consumption and probably lower carbohydrate consumption. When we get the right amount of rest, the leptin (a satiety hormone) levels in our brains are balanced and we don't get into harmful fits of food cravings.

Sense the Force

Although we derive our calories from food, we take in all sorts of other subtle energy from the life all around us. Everything that's alive is radiating with energy, and our bodies perceive this intrinsically. Learning to feel the energy of a room, a valley, a forest, or a meadow is a skill our ancestors innately had. I'm sure you can remember an experience of being somewhere in nature and marveling at how nice it felt there. That's the good stuff right there. An Urban Monk doesn't dismiss that and move back to the land of lost souls. *That's* where we regain our vitality and tap into the energy fields of plants and animals all around us.

Before we surrounded ourselves with walls, carpets, gadgets, and furniture, we had a lot more access to nature all around us and were able to "drink" this energy through every pore. We were surrounded by it and bathed in it. Now, we've lost the connection and feel like something is missing. It is.

The Urban Monk spends as much time as possible in nature

around pure living things and is better for it. He connects with the life force in the trees, the air, and the water to restore his vitality and be a part of the ecosystem. You know that you've arrived when you don't sense that your energy is the dirty stuff that's polluting the pure nature around you. As we clean up our lifestyle and learn to throttle our energy in a sustainable and sane way, we stop exuding chaos and become reconnected with the fabric of life all around us. When this happens, the feeling is undeniable and pure. This feeling is your birthright.

Know of the Shadow

There's also a dark side. There are parasitic elements in society that have a vested interest in having us disconnected from our natural vitality. They feed off of life and need us to stay asleep and disconnected so we unwittingly leak our vitality away.

The ancient Gnostics called this shady nonphysical element the *Archons,* which were disembodied entities known to practice "counter-mimicry," a practice of emulating something good and coming close enough to resemble it so you can fool people into trusting you. They are energy vampires, and they permeate all elements of society. They are everywhere and have infected much. It is a form of consciousness that is predatory, pervasive, and perverse. Many are infected by it.

> ### "The greatest trick the Devil ever pulled is convincing people he doesn't exist."
>
> —KEYSER SÖZE, *THE USUAL SUSPECTS*

We see this in religion. We see it with drug companies and the business of medicine. We see this with politicians, and we see it with companies that use "green washing" to pretend they're being clean and eco-friendly. It's so common that we've come to accept that this is simply the way of the world, although, deep down, we know there's something wrong.

A Taoist priest spends a fair amount of his time performing exorcisms, and I've seen some crazy things, so let's hash this out. There are people who do bad things, and they want to stay in control. That we can all see clearly. What most people don't see is the infectious mental virus that infects and permeates among these people.

Let's tease this out with some real-world examples of "counter-mimicry."

Religion: "We represent God and all that is good."

- ✦ "God is okay with us slaughtering your tribe because you're heathen and we're chosen."

- ✦ "I am a man of the cloth, so it's okay for me to touch you there, son."

- ✦ "We love everyone and don't judge, but black people ride in the back of this bus."

- ✦ "God is on our side, and we will win the Holy War" (insert any country or religion here).

Politics: "We represent the people and are working for the greater good."

- ✦ "I am a champion of the people; I would have never signed a law like that . . . but I did . . . sorry."

- ✦ "We value freedom of speech and civil liberties but just vote against those things because our patrons don't agree."

- ✦ "I've taken an oath to serve my country but take money from special interests because that's how the system works. We're all bought, so it's just the way of politics."

Medicine: "We're here to heal the ailments of humanity and do no harm."

- ✦ "We understand that diet and exercise will resolve most chronic disease, but there's no money in that, so let's change the dialogue and push our pills and procedures, regardless of any side effects."

+ "Sure, that herb works, but we can't patent nature, so let's discredit that study and keep pushing shit that rings our cash register."

+ "I can't possibly keep up with all the new data out there but am going to be arrogant and dismissive of your question because it challenges my authority and I won't be able to charge the big bucks if you don't buy into this game. I'm the doctor, bitch."

Corporate: "We bring you what you want and are good global citizens."

+ "We are totally green because we have a picture of a barn on our cereal box, although we didn't do anything else to make our ingredients more healthful."

+ "Let's buy that eco-friendly brand and keep its image to help us look good while swapping out cheaper GMO ingredients. Those idiots won't know the difference."

+ "We can sell our conventional apples at the farmers' market and call them organic, which is awesome because customers will just pay more for the same shit. What a great deal!"

Media: "We are fair and unbiased, and we love to share art, culture, and entertainment with you."

+ "Pay me a cut or join my church and I'll get you the role in the movie. You know the drill—this is how it works."

+ "We tell the news like it is and never have an opinion or interest in the story—although we're owned by an interested party."

+ "I don't care how well they sing; are they willing to smoke cigarettes in front of our teen audience? We want a 'bad boy' image and can find another kid easily. Musicians are a dime a dozen."

The list could go on and on, but you get the story—people pretending to be who they're not, people gaming systems and being douchebags. Gatekeepers are everywhere, and we've all been led to believe that you need to do a deal with the devil in order to get ahead in this world. Money is evil, and we need to dance because everybody does it . . .

Bullshit.

An Urban Monk categorically rejects this premise and understands it comes from parasitic elements that have been pushing this meme for millennia. We have the technology to convert completely to solar energy right now, yet we fight wars for oil. Arms dealers push for constant wars in the Middle East, and soda manufacturers add "natural" flavors to make us think their products are healthy. We don't need to get dirty in order to make money. We can produce products and render services with integrity and honesty. The Buddhist precept of "Right Livelihood" is alive and well, and the good people of the world need to live by it and defend it. Namely, what you do shouldn't harm the planet or other people.

We are to defend what's right and beautiful.

So what does this have to do with low energy? A lot. We've been bred to be zombies. We've been bred to not think for ourselves and to follow. We need to be told what to do: Vote red or blue, eat burgers and fries with a Coke, accept reality as it is, and frankly, shut up and keep paying taxes and buying shoes. *How exhausting.* Maybe we're tired because we are subdued and unconscious. Maybe we've been so lulled to sleep that the "spark" of life is the real missing ingredient.

There is no qi flow without healthy Shen.

Shen loosely translates as "Spirit." The parasites distract us and keep us disconnected from Spirit, which is our ultimate source of infinite energy. They make us feel that we're nobody without that car, purse, degree, or ideal mate. They drive us to desire an impossible life filled with a false promise so we'll readily part with our money and feed the parasitic beast. They make us believe in scarcity and the incessant struggle of human life—the story that bad people are out to get you and the world is not safe.

The good news is that Spirit is infinite and eternal. Once we connect back up, we laugh at the silly distractions and are back in our power—a *personal power* that comes from within and radiates outward, a personal power that we understand is much greater than us, a channel for the Source energy that is common in all life. It drives the sprout to break through a concrete sidewalk and also drives a penguin to stand in the freezing cold sheltering its young for months on end.

An Urban Monk wakes up to her potential and becomes a beacon of light in her community. She stands up for justice and does the right thing. She thinks through her decisions and challenges memes that don't serve her. She doesn't roll over when a sociopath tries to push a jaded worldview on her, and she certainly doesn't try to fit in with the zombies. She awakens them. She is free in Spirit, and this liberates her energy. She is vibrantly alive and is filled with qi.

Energy is qi, and it needs to flow.

It comes from our food and builds our Vital Essence. It is fueled by our Spirit. Squandering our Essence is also an easy way to crash the system. Learning to cultivate our Essence and move our qi is a critical practice in restoring our energy. We need to learn to rest when tired, eat good food when hungry, move around and use our bodies, and (here's the missing ingredient) *cultivate* our *qi* so we can glow and be vibrantly alive. This is your next step in becoming an Urban Monk. It's time to learn to use "The Force."

EASTERN PRACTICES
Qigong

If I were to tell you that there's a practice that can help you feel better, have more energy, gain more clarity, become more flexible, build better immunity, and increase vitality, would you do it? Well, here you go!

The literal translation of *qigong* is "energy work," and it's the foundation of an Urban Monk's practice. Given the fact that we live in such amazing times, it is so much better to *show* you this practice instead of trying to have you make sense of it in this book. Simply go to theurbanmonk.com/resources/ch3, and you'll have free access to the Urban Monk Qigong Practices (Levels 1 and 2). Here, you can either download the videos onto your phone, tablet, or PC, or stream to your TV or device. Basically, I've made it easy to learn however you need to access the information. If you're a step-by-step book person, I've also included those instructions there (no need to make this a 500-page book).

Start with Level 1 in the mornings and, if you're able, do Level 2 in the evenings. Together, you'll cultivate yang in the morning and yin in the evening and find balance in life. Expect more energy, but note that for some people whose adrenals are shot, it takes a little while for energy to return. This is *your* practice, so treat it accordingly. Do it consciously. Block off the time and see how much better it makes you. As you gain more vitality, you'll see what a great investment it is.

Tonic Herbs

A very well-developed tradition of tonic herbalism has helped people regain their vitality and boost qi for millennia. Below is a list of herbs that have adaptogenic qualities. This means they help regulate the body and give it what it needs; they'll give you a boost where you need it or sedate you when necessary. This class of herbs is extremely interesting and a testament to the genius of the natural intelligence we find in plants. All of them can be taken in tea form. Many companies sell them as powders that are simply stirred into hot water. The traditional method is to boil the herbs together in a clay pot for a few hours and pour off the liquid as your medicinal tea.

Ginseng. Considered the "emperor" of tonic herbs, ginseng has powerful qi-building properties. It helps restore vitality and build Essence. There are different types that you can use according to your disposition. The red ginsengs are more yang in nature and stimulate excitatory pathways, while American ginseng tends to be more yin and restorative. Many master herbalists use combinations of different roots to create a custom formula for an individual. An interesting side note is that the active ingredients we've learned have the most medicinal properties are the ginsenosides of the ginseng root. The more a plant struggles to grow and the harsher the conditions it has to fight through, the higher the content of these and the more potent the medicine. This will be a recurring theme (kung fu) for you as an Urban Monk.

Ashwagandha. One of the most powerful herbs in Indian Ayurvedic healing, ashwagandha has been used since ancient times for a wide variety of conditions and is most well known for its restorative benefits. It, too, is an adaptogen and helps ease stress, boost immunity, restore vigor, and stabilize blood sugar.

Reishi. This mushroom is a powerful immune booster that's been used in tonic herbalism for millennia. It has been well researched and has been shown to stimulate brain neurons, destroy cancer cells, and prevent the development of fat in obese people. It protects mitochondrial DNA and helps a key longevity gene express.

Astragalus. Often combined with ginseng, astragalus is also a mainstay of Chinese tonic herbalism. It helps boost immunity, raise qi, increase stamina, and aid digestion. It has recently been effectively used for heart disease as a diuretic. Work with a good doctor if you want to go there, though.

Rhodiola. This herb grows at high altitudes in arctic areas of Europe and Asia. It's been used as a tonic adaptogen in Russia and Scandinavia for years. It helps prevent fatigue, stress, and the damaging effects of oxygen deprivation. I took it in Nepal, and it helped boost my energy and helped me avoid altitude sickness.

Custom formulas. Much of tonic herbalism comes from an individualized approach to health. If you know where you need help, what energies are imbalanced in your body, and what you can handle, you can create a custom blend of herbs to suit your needs. The adaptogens are easy to work with, as they are versatile and most people can take them, but when you get into medicinal herbs, you want to know what you're doing or work with someone who does. Check the Resources section for at-home herbalism tips.

Drink Your Food

The diet of a monk was mainly vegetables, rice, and lean meats (if any). Modern food doesn't resemble what people ate hundreds of years ago, and the way back is simplicity. Two of the major problems with modern diets are poor food quality and excessive *quantity*. We eat till we're stuffed and don't rest to digest.

> Eat till you're halfway full and then wait 5 to 10 minutes.

Usually, this will be enough time to trigger satiety, and you can be done with the meal. This alone can help you shed lots of unwanted pounds. It allows the body the time to secrete the right volume of digestive enzymes, get your stomach acid working, and also move things along without undue burden to your digestive system. Learning to chew thoroughly is also an amazing way to break down a meal, unlock more nutrition, and get more intimate with your food. An easy way to do this is to count how many times you chew each bite or morsel of food. A good number to start with is 10. I know people who chew each bite 20 or even 36 times.

In many traditions, soups, stews, or congees (rice-based porridges) are a major part of how the monks are fed. These are made with lots of wonderful ingredients and are slow cooked together for a good amount of time over low heat to help extract vital nutrients and break down the food better. In his groundbreaking book, *Catching Fire: How Cooking Made Us Human*, Richard Wrangham describes how the advent of using fire to cook helped our species unlock vital nutrients and get more calories out of our food so we could be more adaptive, become more agile, and grow bigger brains.

So the nutrients and calories in the meals of Urban Monks are made more readily available, and the meals are light, energizing, and simple. They help nourish us and avoid saddling us with a high digestive burden, which slows our systems down and makes our minds foggy. After all, if the goal is to sit and contemplate life and the nature of our existence, scarfing down a cheese burrito can assure one thing: a sleepy monk with a foggy brain.

When else do we eat soup? Often when we're sick. Grandma's chicken soup helps because some of the food has been "predigested" for you, which makes it easier to get better. In other words, the heat has helped break down the food and lessen the burden on our bodies.

If your troops are off at the front lines fighting an infection, you want them focused there. You don't want to pull energy away from the immune system when there's a fight, and that's why soup is great medicine. So why not eat like that more often? Why not use soups to help ease the burden on our tired and ailing bodies so we can liberate some energy and start feeling better?

Eat like a sick person once a week.

Eating soups once a week is a form of fasting—call it Digestive Fasting. It gives your stomach, pancreas, and intestines a little break so they can catch their breath and function better. Replacing solid meals with liquid ones once a week really gives the body the break it needs to recover and heal the gut lining. I like to add bone broth, tonic herbs, and medicinal plants to my soups and make them work for me. This is an amazing way to practice using food as medicine, and it's still a living tradition in Asia. There are two great recipes in the Resources section in the back of this book for you to try.

Start using soups as a part of your life and see how much it helps you unlock your energy. Using food as medicine and information is the key to unlocking your energy flow.

Rejuvenation Practice

Something we keep coming back to is the need for us all to chill out. We do too much. Even when we come home at night, we have a million things to do and spin our way into bed wondering why we can't sleep. This doesn't build qi. An Urban Monk pulls it in and learns to *gather qi in the evenings*. Better yet, he learns to do so all day, so he's never spent or exhausted. Let's assume we're not there yet. Here are some great practices to help you get your mojo back and start feeling some life pulsing through your veins again.

Salt baths with essential oils. This is a great way to decompress in the evenings. A nice hot bath with Epsom salts and a few drops of some essential oils can really calm the nervous system and chill you out. I like lavender, frankincense, and peppermint for this. The added benefit of using Epsom salts is that the magnesium soaks through your skin, calming your mind and helping out your mitochondria. As you may recall, the mitochondria help us produce energy, and they are super vulnerable to environmental toxins. They need all the help we can give them, and a nice boost of magnesium really helps this along. What a great Taoist practice—powering up your qi while helping you relax.

Vow of silence. Taking a vow of silence once a month goes a long way toward restoring our vital energy. We flow off so much qi talking bullshit all day, so cutting off that flow can be extremely beneficial. One translation of the word *Genesis* is "As I speak, I Create." Think about this and ask yourself how you may be responsible for the life you have. It may not be a fun exercise, but it's an important one. We live in a culture that thinks it needs to fill the silence. Silence is where all the energy is. Learn to listen to it and drink from Infinity.

Drinking from Infinity is the
Way of the Urban Monk.

I routinely take 1 day a month to simply not speak. It usually falls on a Sunday, and I tell my world that I won't be responding. Some people find it odd, but the Urban Monk doesn't care. Do what's good for you and have them notice your benefits. It helps to create some separation so that you have space to contemplate, meditate, and actually *enjoy* the silence. Do it from waking one day until waking the next morning. In times of greater introspection, I'll do this for a 5- to 10-day retreat or once a week if I'm stuck in town having to run my life. It is powerful stuff. It'll make you uncomfortable and help you grow with a tremendous amount of power awaiting on the other side.

MODERN HACKS

Detoxification

One of the best things you can do for yourself to gain more energy is to clean out your system. As I mentioned earlier in this chapter, toxic chemicals, heavy metals, and food allergies are major culprits in what drags us down. As with any protocol, rule Number One is to stop the bleeding. By this I mean, stop eating processed junk. Stop using chemicals that harm you. Become an informed consumer and make sure you guard the gates. There's no point in *detox* if your life is all about *retox*. Welcome to Hollywood. Most "detox" fads don't work except to line the pockets of bad doctors all over the place.

Detoxification has become a fad—really, another word for *diet.* "Oh, I'm detoxing" means very little if taken out of context. The question is "What are you detoxing?" Are you handling Phase I and Phase II liver pathways? Are you chelating out heavy metals? Do you know that's your problem? Have you cleared out toxins in the right order and helped restore your gut lining? What about floral reinoculation?

The moral of this story is *it's complicated,* and you can really hurt yourself by doing it wrong. You can zap your energy further and dig yourself into a hole. Worse, you can release toxins from fat or bone and have them accumulate in the brain.

Some people may need to work with a qualified health-care practitioner on this, and others can run it on their own. Know the deal and go in with your head in it to win it. The gold standard is to have lab data that you can test against. You'll want to check heavy metals, liver function, kidney function, blood sugar, triglycerides, and cholesterol levels. This way, it's not another dart thrown but part of a comprehensive plan to clean up your system, rebuild energy production pathways, fix the gut, and get things firing again. This doesn't mean you have to do it this way. Millions of people benefit from self-administered detoxes. Essentially they take herbs and supplements that help support liver function, rebuild the gut lining, and support better bowel movements. Again, your doctor can help determine what course would be best for you, but be careful with the commercialized fad products that keep springing up out there.

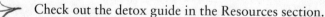 Check out the detox guide in the Resources section.

Adrenal Reset

With our bodies, most of us are guilty of borrowing energy from "the bank" and forgetting to pay it back. Society makes it hard to do otherwise, and we have to learn to fight for a new way of life that helps us rejuvenate. How do we restore energy to balance out what we expend?

Helping reset your adrenals is key. You can slowly pay off that high-interest debt. For some, it can take 6 or more months, but *it has to be done* or you're likely screwed in the future. Here are a few things you can do *right now* to get started on this.

+ Sleep more, stress less. I've been saying this throughout the chapter and will keep layering on more nuggets throughout the book. Suffice it to say that this is a big one.

+ Bring down your caffeine intake, especially after noon.

+ Practice qigong regularly and meditate. I cannot overemphasize how effective this is.

+ Mellow out your exercise. If your adrenals are burned out, too much exercise may be harming you. Tai chi and qigong are great for helping with this. Once you're feeling better, you can go back to that exercise class you love, but some of us may need to slow down before hitting it hard again. We'll cover this in more detail in Chapter 5.

+ Eat soups, chew your food, remove toxic foods from your diet, and do a smart detox.

+ Go by candlelight at night.

+ Take adaptogens and tonics to boost your vitality and restore adrenal function.

It is really important to know where you stand when it comes to your adrenal health, and there's a great and relatively inexpensive way of learning about it with a simple saliva test (diagnostechs.com). You need to see what your numbers are at four time stamps throughout the day so you can see the phasing of cortisol. I highly recommend you find a physician who's been trained in functional medicine to help you go through this. Once you have a plan, most of it will be in your hands with lifestyle measures and supplements. Just stick to the plan and you should see great results, but be aware that it may take a while. Check the Resources section for a link to a qualified practitioner who is trained in this form of medicine.

Lift Some Weights

Muscle tissue is dense in mitochondria, as is heart tissue. Getting fit and firm helps us have greater density and size of our mitochondria, which, in turn, help produce more energy for us. The added muscle tissue helps raise our metabolic rate and also helps us against insulin resistance. This gives us more cushion to get away with eating carbohydrates and sending the fuel somewhere we can use it. As mentioned before, energy needs an outlet, and the muscles are a great place for this. Sure, we spend lots of energy noodling things around our brains, but a balanced body that is functionally fit and muscular creates a healthy channel for energy flow and pays us back in kind. In Chapter 5, we'll discuss functional fitness and some of the sane ways of going about working out. Just pushing dumb weights to develop "beach muscles" won't serve you in the long run, and it'll create body imbalances that can lead to injuries. In anything and everything, the Urban Monk is committed to doing things the right way so he can have longevity with his vitality.

JESSICA'S ACTION PLAN

Jessica was a tough nut to crack. She really wanted to cling to some of her ways, so we started off with some small moves. A hard-boiled egg in the morning with 2 grams of fish oil was the first concession. Within a couple of weeks she noticed more energy and needed less coffee before noon. Awesome.

From there, we started to deal with the evening wine. Her blood sugar wasn't stable, so she started to have sparkling water with a lime wedge when out with the girls. Her new drink had no calories, so that made it a sellable swap for the wine, which she knew was fattening. It took no time at all for her to notice more energy in the mornings and, again, less need for coffee. She was getting to bed a bit sooner, and we were able to hack her social routine to get her girlfriends to meet at the Jacuzzi in one of their buildings two nights a week instead of some restaurant. This both saved money and helped them relax and get some quality time without the hectic noise and marauding men.

Next up, we started to deal with the salads. She was eating all kinds of traditional shit that was sprayed with pesticides and had no real nutritional value. She started going to the local farmers' market twice a week and buying organic produce. It cost a bit more, but we easily carved it out of her restaurant budget, which was *way more* money than she had originally thought. No wonder she was broke. She began to eat more soups and warmer food that was easier on her digestion, and that also helped. We also got her to cut her cable TV, which was $80 per month, so she now had plenty of money to get the best ingredients for her salads and, most importantly, *pack her lunches* during the week. Now, she had access to delicious organic food that was nourishing her and feeding her cells. "Grabbing" lunch usually took an extra 40 minutes, so she started going to the gym during lunch and eating back at the office.

She and her friends identified one girl who was the "drama generator" of the group and realized that most of the friction in their social life came from this one person. They started to uninvite her from certain events, and this helped to drive better behavior. All of a sudden, there was oxygen in the room, and they all felt uplifted.

Finally, we got her back into yoga. She started with a restorative class that wasn't too hard-core and eventually phased back into normal flow classes. With the qigong breathing she had learned, Jessica was learning to conserve and gather energy at every stop. Yoga and breathing became a part of her life. She was eating quality food, taking in more healthy fat and protein, and not spending her money like a fool. Her glow came back, and, surprisingly, she found that she didn't even need much of the new nontoxic makeup we'd gotten for her.

Jessica was back and feeling great. She was in a good place and found a career path that made her happy. There she met a man, and the story continues soon with a child to come.

CHAPTER 4

What Happened to Sleep?

JAMES CAN'T REMEMBER THE last time he felt refreshed. Even when he tries to get to bed early, he has trouble falling asleep. The racing thoughts seem to boot up as soon as he hits the lights. He's tried meditation but couldn't figure it out. He's taken kava, St. John's wort, chamomile, herbal sleep aids, and anything else he thought might help. Nothing.

His doctor threw some pills at him, but they make him really drowsy the next day. On top of that, he simply feels like he's cheating by taking that stuff.

James thinks there must be another way to fix his sleep problems, but he's at a loss for what it would be. He's tried everything from relaxation CDs to reading comic books in bed, yet he still can't get his mind to settle down. The fatigue is starting to build up, and it shows. He gets sick more often and recovers slower. Last year he was sick on and off for almost 2 months. The dark circles under his eyes have been there for a couple of years. The expensive eye cream he's used hasn't done a thing. He knows it's not a skin problem.

He sits in his bed and reads on his iPad into the night. At first he'd look into sleep solutions, but since nothing has worked, he now plays video games and hangs on social media.

James is at an impasse. This sleep thing is starting to really impact his performance at work. Ever since his divorce, he's had a tough time bouncing back financially. Now he stays up worrying about money, which certainly doesn't help him make any more of it. He has resorted to taking a "natural" energy drink that used to work great, but its effects are starting to diminish. He calls it crack in a can and knows that it can't actually be good for him, but what's he to do? The show must go on, and James is stuck having to push forward at all costs. He can rest when he's dead, right?

THE PROBLEM

James has to share the midnight oil. According to the National Institutes of Health, roughly 30 percent of Americans suffer from insomnia, and about 10 percent of them report daytime impairment of their activities because of this. The others are kidding themselves.

Losing sleep sucks. Sleep is when our bodies detoxify themselves. It's where we process thoughts and clear chemicals that act as brain toxins from the long day we just had. It is also where we build new tissue and restore balance to our nervous systems. As if that isn't enough, sleep is also where we modulate our immune systems.

What does all this mean? Losing sleep makes you age faster, hang on to toxins, stay stressed out (causing anxiety or depression), get sick more often, and have a higher likelihood of developing a major chronic disease like arthritis, cancer, heart failure, lung disease, gastroesophageal reflux disease (GERD), overactive thyroid, stroke, Parkinson's disease, and Alzheimer's disease.

It is not pretty, and neither are we when we don't sleep.

We become cranky bitches who are much more likely to snap at people, make bad decisions, eat the wrong foods (poor sleep messes with satiety hormones that keep us from pigging out), and generally want to kill someone.

Our complexion goes to hell, and our energy levels hit the floor. In essence, we feel like shit, look like shit, and can't function *for shit*. We stumble through our days and look for a chance to pull over and pant, but we all know that there's seldom time for breaks in the modern world.

So why is sleep such a big problem in the modern world?

The simple answer is:
We're out of sync with nature.

Our brains have a tiny light-sensitive gland in them called the pineal gland. This is a master gland that helps control a major switch in our physiology by secreting melatonin. Now before you go off and say "I've already tried that shit," let's back up. We are not good at knowing how to dose melatonin for insomnia; just 1 to 3 milligrams (a common dose) can boost your blood melatonin levels by up to 20 times. Not only is this overkill, but it's also oftentimes ineffective. In fact, it's been shown to work better for jetlag by resetting the circadian rhythm than for insomnia.

So back to the glands . . .

When light hits the eyes, it triggers a nerve pathway in the eye to an area in the brain called the hypothalamus. There, a special center called the suprachiasmatic nucleus (SCN) initiates signals to other parts of the brain that control hormones, body temperature, and other functions that play a role in making us feel tired or awake. This is where the pineal gland comes in, as it is "turned on" by the SCN and begins to actively produce melatonin, which is released into the blood. When this happens in the evening, we begin to naturally fade and eventually go to sleep. It's part of the natural shutdown process of the body and physiology.

The problem with today's world is that there's light everywhere; it's constantly bombarding us and triggering our brains to think it's daytime. This, in turn, revs up the brain's machinery, causing hormones to be pumped that keep us warm, alert, and eager to keep sweating our bills.

Think of it this way: Ten thousand years ago, we'd go hunting and gathering all day and then huddle up around a fire to eat, tell stories, and go to sleep. When the sun went down, it meant we needed to shut down, too. We didn't stand a chance against nighttime predators so we had no choice but to hunker down. The darkness helped cap off our days and set the tone for evening time, which was chill, social, and relaxing. Nights were typically cold, so we'd huddle up next to each other to stay warm. Tell some stories . . . make some love . . . fall asleep.

Today, that seems like a caveman fantasy. We watch idiots on TV and call *that* "reality." We play on our tablets in bed, keep the lights burning bright, and work into the night. There's no allowance for slowing down, and doing so is almost seen as a sign of weakness.

Slow is stupid. The world is fast,
and we've got to keep up.

We see this on another level as well. If you look at the brainwave frequency pattern that correlates with sleep, it's around 1 to 3 hertz. That's 1 to 3 cycles per second. Even the faster brainwave patterns that are associated with super-alert and tense and anxious states range between 22 and 38 hertz. Your average lightbulb runs at 60 hertz, which is 20 to 60 times faster. That's the frequency we're bathing in at night—a constant trigger of light energy competing to speed up our physiology. Now if you think that's fast, a typical wireless home phone is often 2.4 *gigahertz*. Coming down from there is a huge challenge on its own, but trying to do so with tablets blazing, phone calls happening, a TV in the background, and buzzing wires in the wall is insane. We have no idea what that super-speed frequency does to the brain, but we're happy to slap that thing right up there and talk for hours.

Yup, news flash: All the electronics around us may be fucking us up.

When an electric charge is generated, a field is created around it called an electromagnetic field (EMF). It is a natural reflection of the electrical (stationary charges) and magnetic (moving currents), and together we call the combined forces electromagnetic. Over the past couple of decades, we've started to see a surge of health-related issues emerge around EMFs, and, as we keep juicing up our gadgets with more power, it is becoming a serious matter we need to look into.

We're not sure what these energy fluctuations do to our physiology. Although initial tests have not found conclusive evidence of harm, the fact remains that our cells all respond to subtle shifts in electrical gradients. We may learn several years from now that these EMFs were causing all kinds of mischief. Thousands of people claim that they are bothered by them, and it seems sane to allow the science to play out but avoid unnecessary exposure for now.

Crack Kills

The majority of insomnia patients I've helped in the past decade or so have had terrible caffeine consumption habits. They would rely on coffee or an energy drink later in the day to keep going and stay alert, but didn't realize that the stuff was still cranking in their systems well into the evening.

Caffeine takes a certain amount of time to work through your system. One study some years ago showed that the half-life of caffeine in healthy adults is 5.7 hours. This means that if you consume 200 milligrams of caffeine (about the amount in one to two cups of coffee) at midday, you will still have 100 milligrams in your body at around 5:45 p.m. So slap another 5 hours on to move through the remainder, and you're cranked up till almost 11:00 p.m.

Most people need to cut the caffeine after noon (or 2:00 p.m. latest) This gives ample time for the body to get the drug (yes, caffeine is a drug) out of your system so you can slow down. I recommend *no caffeine* for insomniacs—get over it. The slow deceleration process that's needed to actually get some good sleep is biological and subtle. Using different chemicals to hit it from one side or another is challenging. A glass of wine may seem to help after a long day, but alcohol is also a stimulant and will tamper with your sleep cycle.

Coffee has some great health benefits for sure, but we're talking about insomnia and sleep problems here. If you're in this category, consider cutting the caffeine. I'll show you some tricks in the Resources section. The moral of the story is that sleep is delicate, and the use of chemicals to nudge us up or down has a taxing impact on our bodies. An Urban Monk steps through this addiction and needs nothing to come to balance because she lives there.

Blood Sugar and Adrenals

Another major piece to this equation is blood sugar levels. When they're out of balance, we typically draw on our adrenals for help, and this dramatically impacts our sleep. Basically, we're back to the cash and credit example again.

Environmental Toxin Mitsochondria

Blood sugar is like cash in the pocket. During the day, when we've got enough, we're good to go. When the brain is getting low on sugar (energy, really), it makes us anxious and we get brain fog. It calls for an immediate fix. Usually the brain looks for food to fix the problem. What happens when it runs out, however, is that we can tap into a hormone called cortisol, which is produced in the adrenal glands, to help make up that gap. It's like a line of energy credit where cortisol induces cells to release glycogen reserves, so sugar is released into the bloodstream and keeps us going. When we don't listen to the body's needs—when we ignore the call for an energy injection through good food and skip the meal—we force the body to "borrow" on the cortisol card. Eventually, the adrenal bank gets tired of lending us our daily juice and stops issuing notes. That's when the shit hits the fan.

At night, since we're not awake to go grab a bite, the body usually depends on the cortisol credit line to drip energy to the brain and keep it happy. But when the adrenals start to flicker and fade, they can't supply cortisol every time we need it, so they resort to a fallback position and instead release adrenaline. Now, instead of the generalized uneasy "I can't fall asleep" feeling we face with low cortisol, we may fall asleep but then—BAM!—we wake up with our heart racing and sweating in our sheets. This is because the adrenaline is screaming, "Wake up and get some food, asshole."

This is a sign that we've gone way too far. The body loves sleep. If we can't go there, then looking at blood sugar and adrenal health is key. Taking caffeine to get through the day also messes with our blood sugar levels, making us a hot mess by nightfall. Eating complex carbohydrates with healthy fats and adequate protein is the short answer here. The long one is slowing down, taking adrenal support, and learning how to chill out.

I don't make the rules: Sleep is an enigma for many because we insist on looking at it as a process. You can't "do" sleep. It is a state of "being," which makes the Western mind super uncomfortable. We *fix* things . . . we tinker . . . we are industrious and resourceful . . . and yet we're still up tossing and turning.

URBAN MONK WISDOM

Think of bad sleep patterns like the classic male/female sex mishap story. Guy wants to get in there, bang away for a few minutes, move on, and eat some food, while, in contrast, Girl needs romance, sensuality, and a slow deepening into the experience. Our world is overly yang and masculine. We *force* things in time. We tear through the earth and mine her for resources. We push our bodies to keep marching when tired, and we try to force sleep to come quickly after racing all day. We bang too hard and wonder why slamming on the brakes doesn't work so well.

Sleep is yin. It is a passive process of allowing and being, totally different from the "masculine" go-go-go way of our world and daytime craziness. It is the opposite of "doing." We *fall* asleep. We let go. We release and get out of the driver's seat, and boy is that hard for lots of people. After all, our entire culture is shifted toward accomplishment, doing more things, and keeping score.

> *To the busy person, sleep can seem like such a waste of time.*

In Chinese medicine, sleep is when our *Hun,* or ethereal soul, travels and connects with the life around us. It is when we dock our conscious minds and allow the subconscious to communicate with the Superconscious Mind. This is where we download wisdom, heal the body, and do our soul work. Sleep time is as important as our waking hours. We do a lot of heavy lifting on the soul and spirit planes in our sleep, which is why we feel so hollow when we've lost it.

The body needs to be in balance and the blood needs to be pure for deep, meaningful soul work to happen. When we're toxic, manic, time compressed, and wound up, we can't drop into the unconscious mind. The self-conscious aspect of us fights to keep pushing.

> *The ego feels like it is dying when we need it to disengage.*

This is where the real work comes in, and this is where we can use sleep as a wonderful spiritual accelerator in our lives. When the self-conscious mind doesn't want to let go, that's a good indicator that we're trying to run our lives and are not *allowing* our higher self, Divinity, the Great Tao (whatever you want to call it) to drive. The ego is trying to dominate. All the great spiritual disciplines out there teach us to get out of the way and let Spirit guide us. In fact, the great spiritual delusion is that our personal will *even exists*. All the great mystical traditions lead to the same conclusion: Namely, that the Universal Will to Good is running the show, and the *delusion* of separation is what keeps us suffering.

Fearing the Noise

Most people are terrified to hear the noise right under the radar. That's why people fear meditation. "Holy shit, it's so loud up there!"

We live in a culture where the norm has become aversion to pain. We don't like feeling uncomfortable, and our whole culture is oriented toward helping us move away from pain. Medicine throws pills at our discomfort. A nightcap helps ease the stress. Meaningless sex helps distract us from the lonely nights.

This is also why most people are afraid of the dark. The yucky undercurrents of our shadows come out in the dark, quiet nights. The mind starts to race, and we can't deal with what's coming up.

We toss.

We turn.

We move to distract.

Maybe it is just temporary financial stress. Maybe it's the person you lie next to. Should you file for that divorce? Maybe it's all the missed opportunities in your life or perhaps the trouble your kids are in. Maybe it's a deeper, darker secret you have never dealt with. What to do? How are you going to make it? So many worries . . .

Don't trip; we've all got this shit going on. It is right under the surface but gets way louder when everything else starts to calm down.

As the silence begins to take hold,
our inner noise magnifies.

Take all the stuff you've been processing over all these years, don't get to it, and then lie down and try to sleep. That's the problem.

That's a big reason why we don't sleep. Thoughts and emotions start popping up and stimulating us when we're trying to go down. We can run all day, but in the quiet stillness of the night, it's all there in front of us.

The Urban Monk takes on his weaknesses. He deals with the unturned stones and looks under the rug. This is the way of the warrior, and the fact is that there's no other game in town.

*We must reconcile our lives
and come clean with ourselves.*

In a way, losing sleep is a good thing because it highlights all the shit we drag around all day. Just because the perpetual motion, noise, TV, and other life activities drown these undercurrents out when the sun is up, it doesn't mean that they're not there. The need for sleep helps us see them. Sleep is when we become aware of our personal spiritual work and see what it is we need to do to heal.

Face your demons and you'll sleep better. I've seen people come back from the darkest of places and shine in their lives. I've seen people with gut-wrenching histories work through their trauma, accept, forgive, heal, and move on. I certainly am a fan of working with a good therapist if your demons are pretty hard-core; that's fine. The amount of power and liberation on the other side of that is immense, and I cannot overemphasize how valuable that work is.

Small Death

We have important start and stop cycles in our lives, and there's a reason why the ancients called sleep the small death. We allow ourselves to fall and die to the day. We prepare to be reborn to the next day, which is filled with our dreams, plans, and aspirations. Shutting down helps us learn to get out of gear so the innate wisdom of our bodies (and souls) can take over. The better we get at this, the better we heal. The more we learn to let go, the deeper we sleep and more rested we are.

We can also practice this in mini-cycles during the day. A power nap goes a long way. A 5-minute meditation break can tap into the same energy. The goal is to learn to unplug and drop down into a deep, relaxed place for a designated amount of time. Maybe you can sneak a 10-minute nap at work; set your alarm and go for it. At night, you should have a whole shutdown ritual that prepares you for slumber. Taking sleep seriously is the first step to making it a priority. We grew up around rituals. Our brains understand rituals. Set one up for your sleep shutdown process and make it a nightly habit. It'll help direct your psyche to go there, and it'll cue your physiology to follow suit.

This shouldn't be mistaken with the other "small death" that happens with sleep apnea, however. This is when your airway is obstructed by your tongue or throat, and you struggle for air at night. The brain freaks out when oxygen levels drop and cues us to wake up so we don't die. There's also a nervous system version of this which is rarer, but sleep apnea is serious business. If you or your bedmate snores like a busted chainsaw and complains of fatigue all the time, go see your doctor. People die from this stuff.

Sleep for Enlightenment

The ancient sages placed the third eye right in the center of our forehead where we have our pineal gland, and they knew the importance of this tiny part of the brain. In fact, this is really where much of the magic happens. The chemistry of the pineal gland is particularly interesting for an Urban Monk. Serotonin is the neurotransmitter that helps us stay happy and powers the prefrontal cortex, the part of the brain that allows for higher moral reasoning, complex thought, and the negation of impulses. It's the part of the brain that has been shown to grow in functional MRI studies performed on meditators. A healthy diet rich in tryptophan (an amino acid we get through various foods) helps keep our serotonin levels high. Serotonin converts into melatonin in the pineal gland. Melatonin, as we've discussed, helps us sleep. It's also a potent immune modulator that helps our bodies boost our natural defenses and fight off disease. This is important because sleep is when we shut down and scavenge for cancer cells, move out toxins, flush the brain, and restore healthy tissue. Melatonin helps us sleep and heal.

There's something interesting that also happens in the pineal gland. Our melatonin is converted into dimethyltryptamine (DMT), which has been described as the "Spirit Molecule." DMT is released in bursts in people who've had near-death experiences and is an active ingredient in *ayahuasca,* which is a psychotropic plant medicine used by Amazonian shamans to communicate with Great Spirit. Rick Strassman, MD, has done some groundbreaking research on this subject, and I encourage you to check it out. For our purposes here, a really important axis for personal growth seems to happen in the pineal gland, and that subtle neurochemistry gets all messy if we're not sleeping. People who don't sleep well seem to have a critical roadblock to personal growth and happiness, and this is likely a reason.

Later in this book, we'll learn to cultivate this area and wake up our "spiritual eye." For now, the take-home message is that you've got to sleep if you want to break free and live a fulfilled spiritual life. Let's get into the hacks.

EASTERN PRACTICES
The Ritual of the Moon

Shutting down today for a good night's sleep is the name of the game, and developing a ritual to do this is important. We evolved around rituals. Our brains understand these and use them to change states. They help us "close the windows" of mental apps we have running all day and clear the "desktop" for the night. The sacred is the door to transformation. Since we departed from this perspective, we've gotten lost and people are all tripped out.

The Ritual of the Moon (originally taught by the great Swami Kriyananda) is a powerful way to "close those windows" and prepare for sleep. Have a notebook by your bedside and use it nightly to dump your excess thoughts. The goal is to get all of the "to-dos" and "don't-forgets" out of your head and onto paper, where you can schedule them for the next day. The really valuable part of this exercise is creating a *plan* for your next day that you can *execute* before the next bedtime. This keeps you honest in a couple of ways. First off, it makes you do what you say and really hold yourself accountable to your word. This is obviously really difficult for people and the reason why New Year's resolutions are a joke. That's why the second reason is key. The Ritual of the Moon forces us to consider how much we're trying to bite off each day. Are we pushing unreasonable expectations on ourselves? Do we commit to building an Eiffel Tower each day and then kick ourselves for not getting it done? Is *that* how you roll?

It could also be the opposite. Maybe you genuinely do suck at getting things done. Whether it's too much time around the water cooler, reading e-mails instead of getting work done, talking on the phone, or simply the brain fog that won't let you focus, maybe you are just plain old inefficient and need some help there. You're not alone.

At the end of this book, I'm going to teach you the powerful practice of the Gong, which will help increase your focus, build your willpower, and help you better triage your time and goals. In fact, we're working up to that with each chapter here by dissecting out all the areas where we trip up.

For now, start practicing the Ritual of the Moon. Start taking note of what's still on your plate by day's end, and you'll know what's jamming up your mind at night. Commit to finishing what you set out to do each day, and if you find that's not happening, cut back on what you commit to until you find an activity level that works. Prove to yourself that you can make a plan and stick to it. Get some wins under your belt. This is going to set up a new culture of success and inspired planning that will help you master life. Reconciling each day and making sure you're on track is an enormous step in that direction.

Take Pause

Phasing in rest periods based on circadian rhythms is a wonderful way to run your day. Generally, you want your greatest energy output in the morning and want to phase things down as it gets darker. By nighttime, you want to chill out and relax. That's the basic cycle of life, and it simply works for most people.

Within a given day, though, there's a golden opportunity to take some mini breaks. The Chinese medical system tracks the maximum expression of an organ's energy throughout the day. This gives us an opportunity to work on healing this organ when it is fully powered, essentially giving us an edge on getting better faster. Here's a chart of the times each organ is at its highest expression of energy.

Much of the ancient systems revolves around a profound understanding of these rhythms. Let's look at a couple of lifestyle strategies one can take based on this chart.

The highest expression of the Large Intestine is from 5:00 to 7:00 a.m., so that's the ideal time to evacuate the bowels. From there, the Stomach and Spleen (which includes the function of the pancreas) go into expression, so that's an important time to eat and take on fuel. The kidneys are at their highest from 5:00 to 7:00 p.m., so that's a great time to restore the adrenals, and the Liver best detoxes from 1:00 to 3:00 a.m., so it's really important to be asleep then so the body can do its thing.

The information in this chart is also diagnostic. When a patient tells me they wake up at 2:00 a.m. each night, I look at blood sugar and adrenal levels but will usually suspect toxicity.

*Interesting
Natalya*

Don't take what some ancient Chinese doctors said at face value, though. What does your body tell you? What's your best nap time? When are you at your best? Where do you begin to fade? Begin to chart a deeper understanding of your personal rhythms so you can plan your life and activities around them. We can then look at where we can improve your health and vitality, but let's work with what we've got first.

Kick It Old School

The cavemen had a lot of good things going for them. Sure, hot showers are great, but a life of simplicity and connection with nature is also pretty cool. There are several techniques you can employ to get back to our most basic, ancestral rhythms. Start by purging your tech at nights. That means, after 7:00 or 8:00 p.m., no more TV or computer time. I know it's hard, but if you're not sleeping well, *life* is certainly harder. The tech slams our subtle biology and makes everything get a bit edgy. Think of a deer in headlights. His nervous system has no frame of reference for a light so bright, so he's just stunned into a stupor. Our brains feel the same way around artificial lights at night. Just try it for a month and see what happens. I think you'll be pleasantly surprised with the results. It is simple, so it seems ineffective because *we're complicated,* and we assume we need elaborate solutions to our twisted lives. Nope. Chill the fuck out and chances are you'll sleep better within a couple of weeks.

As you work to cut out the tech, consider replacing your nightly wind-down with something else a little more ancient and natural. Going by candlelight at night is an amazing practice. People notice a difference almost immediately. You calm down. You have a different tone of conversation. You ease into your body. It makes us less insane.

I like to have insomniacs go by candlelight and passively stretch and hang out on the floor for a while. Relax into your body. Relax into some downtime. It'll feel odd at first, but that's just your crazy talking. Let the chatter settle, and start to enjoy some quiet time with yourself or your loved ones.

Another key piece to the mythic caveman life (and no, a majority of our ancestors didn't live in caves because there simply aren't enough of them around) is the actual idea of a cave. Rock helps shield us from electromagnetic energies. Although our ancestors didn't have too much to worry about there, we certainly do. Learning to unplug all the unneeded electronics in your bedroom can go a long way. Make it a tech-free zone and see how you feel. We need to feel safe and secure in order to let go and sleep. Locking the doors and windows in urban environments helps us feel the safety we need in many ways. Let's face it: Some of us live in areas where people do break in and it may not be safe; I get it. Lock down and let your mind comfortably settle into "safety" for sleep. If you had a bad break-in experience in your past, make sure your house is locked down, but then do some work to fix your heightened fear response to that shit. Enough is enough. I've

PERSONAL JOURNEYS

I learned the story of a modern Taoist master who had gone into the woods on sabbatical and was inspired to follow suit. His covenant was to do only that which felt natural with his time. Having been a busy Westerner in his past life, he found that he was simply tired all the time, so he kept wanting to nap. Holding himself to his deal, that's what he did, and 3 weeks later, he woke up after yet another awesome nap and felt like he had caught up. I was so inspired by this that I committed my winter break (I was still in school) to follow this. I slept a lot and felt guilty about it. I kept it up and, just like him, woke up one day and felt my batteries were back to full.

Now, I make it a theme every winter to hibernate. I have to allow myself to sleep in more and nap when tired. Work, family, and e-mails are relentless, so I build a culture around it in my companies, home, and with e-mail auto-responders. The result is more energy, creativity, and enthusiasm all year-round.

included some information in the Resources section for you on wall shielding.

Starlight

Another powerful play is to spend time under the stars. Again, this used to be a common thing, but now we're always inside. Looking up at the stars is like looking into the depths of our inner selves. There's just as much space between the electrons of our cells (to scale) as there is between the stars in the sky. Marveling at the magnitude of the Universe we live in is part of understanding who we are. Lying there and asking the big questions keeps us sane and grounded. Who the hell are we in all of this anyhow? How did we get here? Where did the Big Bang come from? This is the stuff our ancestors tripped on. This is how we developed art, culture, religion, and philosophy. We thought and we pondered. We examined reality and contemplated it, and didn't just watch some idiotic version of it on TV and call it entertainment. Make stargazing a nightly ritual, and if the weather permits, try to sleep under the stars a few times a year.

Calming Meditation

Learning to bring down the velocity of the day and ease into the evening can take a little while, as we're creatures of habit who don't shift modes instantaneously. A powerful way to ease those transitions is to learn to meditate. Using our breath to slow down our metabolism can really help in a safe and natural way. This is an ancient practice that's worked for millions before us.

I've created a bonus meditation track for you to use in the evenings, which you can get through the Resources section. It'll help calm your mind and settle you in for a good night's sleep by slowing down the breath and clearing your thoughts.

The Art of Making Love

The forgotten nightly pastime of making love can also be an amazing way of getting sleep harmonized. How? Turn it into an event. Make love and take your time. That obviously means getting to bed sooner in order to enjoy each other's company. Caress and be tender. Make love and connect. Once done, it can really help calm the mind and ease you into a peaceful night's sleep. After all, it'll push serotonin, which makes us happy and (as we recently learned) is what converts to melatonin as well.

Instead of thinking of it as a chore or a quick release, look at the art of making love as a better way to spend your evenings with your lover than watching bullshit on TV. You'll connect better, boost your healthy hormones, and fall into a deeper sleep once satisfied. If you don't know how to satisfy the one you're with, then get to work. *Ask.* It's usually not that hard if you're willing to be of service. Selfless acts can go a long way here, and the result can be a magical release of stagnant energy in your life and relationship.

Herbs and Minerals That Help with Sleep

If you have blood sugar issues or caffeine in your system, these remedies won't be nearly as effective. You need to break your addictions to the substances that mess with your internal rhythms; don't think that pounding down a few cups of tea or some supplements will be an instant fix for the damage you've done to your body's cycles. You shouldn't be looking at herbs as if they're miracle drugs; they are a part of a comprehensive strategy to get better sleep and, in that light, can be very powerful adjuncts to lifestyle modifications.

Chamomile. This stuff works to mellow you out. A nice cup of chamomile tea will take the edge off.

Kava This herb has been used for millennia in Polynesia for ceremony and peaceful altered states. Drinking kava tea can help you shut down some windows.

Magnesium. Taking an Epsom salt bath is powerful stuff. It has the dual action of juicing up the mitochondria (which power up our cells) and also calming the nervous system and muscles. It is very relaxing and can be used as part of a strategy to nudge the mind into slower patterns in the evenings. A salt bath with candles and some deep breathing is my drug of choice when the bullets are flying and life is crazy busy.

5-HTP (5-hydroxytryptophan). A precursor to seratonin, this stuff works great for most. Check with your doctor if you're on SSRI drugs, though.

Suan Zao Ren Wan. This traditional Chinese formula helps calm the mind and nourish the blood. It really has helped thousands of my patients get better sleep. It usually comes in pill form and should be taken 1 hour before bed with a tall glass of water. Taken as part of an overall lifestyle shift, it can help you get to sleep more easily and rest throughout the night.

I've got a great source for this at theurbanmonk.com/resources/ch4.

MODERN HACKS

The basics of sleep hygiene should be taught in every grade school. Following is the information patients got coming into my clinics, and usually it resolved most of their problems. Here we go:

+ No TV at night (hit that already).

+ No caffeine after noon (or 2 p.m. latest).

+ No bills or stressful activities in the bedroom.

+ The bedroom is for sleep and making love; leave all else out of there.

+ Keep your bedroom cool and dark.

+ Stay hydrated, but don't overdo it so that you have to pee all night.

+ Have some protein and some healthy fat an hour before bed if your blood sugar level isn't stable. I like a 4- to 6-ounce chicken breast with some olive or coconut oil here. I also like turkey breast with some hummus.

Warm Body, Cold Head

The way we used to sleep and wake was also pretty much tied to our environment. There was no heating or AC to speak of. Our ancestors would light a fire, huddle around it, and usually wake up in the early morning hours freezing their asses off. Think of your last camping trip.

According to most studies, the ideal room temperature for sleeping is 68°F. That helps us go down. Keeping the head a little cooler (out of the blankets) also helps drop us into delta waves.

This is how we've adapted to sleep for millennia, so instead of trying to reinvent the wheel right now, maybe we should just get some sleep and move on with our dreams and aspirations. Why fight nature?

Blood Sugar Management

Keeping blood sugar levels stable is a critical piece of the puzzle, as we've discussed already. Getting some slow-burning fuel on board (fat and protein) about an hour before bed can help deliver slow and steady energy to your brain and keep it from freaking out when your sugar levels plummet in the middle of the night. This is obviously a temporary fix while you work to restore your adrenal health and balance your diet, but it's a key strategy that will help you out of this mess and allow you to get some sleep while you're on the mend.

Note

Caffeine Detox

Here I go again, grabbing at the mug you keep clutching.

If you're having trouble sleeping, it's time to deal with your caffeine intake. It's time to stop living on borrowed energy. Balancing your blood sugar will help you feel more energized and, in doing so, will allow you to need less and less caffeine. Working to decrease your dependency on caffeine will help your adrenals come back to health and optimize your metabolism.

You'll find that it's not the lack of energy we feel at times but more the chaotic flow of energy. We often mistake brain fog for fatigue, and the cause is not usually a lack of adenosine triphosphate (ATP), or energy output, but a frivolous expense of energy in the gut or immune system. Cleaning all that up makes us need less caffeine. Taking less caffeine helps us not lose sleep. Getting more sleep helps us heal and improves our mood. It gives us energy the next day.

Get on the right side of this equation. Cut caffeine out if you have trouble sleeping. Getting out of debt is not easy. Some people go cold turkey and have headaches and withdrawal symptoms. Nothing says "I'm a serious drug" louder than that. You can go that way, but I recommend a slow easing down with better blood sugar management and stress management. Switch to decaf later in the day and start to phase out. You'll have a bumpy week and then be well on your way to independence. Decaf teas and coffees can help, as can herbal teas. I like a Chinese herb called gynostemma, which helps boost energy naturally without caffeine. Brew it into a tea and sip on it throughout the day to get moving. You'll be happy you did.

Brainwave Tracks

In recent years, I've done a lot of work with companies that have been pushing the envelope in brain science. There's a lot of hokey shit out there, and also some stuff that works great. There are technologies out there designed to help with delta wave activity training. Essentially, they help entrain our brains to slow down and, if used correctly, can really help influence our sleep patterns. Many seasoned meditators claim to have experienced impressive results working with these technologies, and in some cases, they may help accelerate the learning curve for people wanting to learn meditation. Think of it like resonant tuning. Once you have an experience of a brainwave state, you can find your way back there naturally with your own consciousness.

Of course, you can't be an idiot and think you can slam coffee, watch TV, do bills in bed, and then cheat your way into sleep with this stuff, but, as part of an overall strategy to resolve insomnia, it's pretty cool.

I've listed some I like in the Resources section for Chapter 2.

Time Management

Learning how to segment your day into chunks of activities that serve your needs and overall goals is key to success. If you plan things into the evening hours, you're going to press up against your sleep. If you're thinking, "Yeah, but that's my life," let's discuss how to make you more efficient during the day so you get more done and don't have to schedule work into your leisure or family hours. That's the way of the Urban Monk.

The mark of the new economy is going to be ethical business coupled with work-life balance. Don't let your boss argue with me. Get good and get better results *while there* and then come home. The model we've just snapped out of is a shadow of the 1950s, when they were trying to cast a worldview of society that was paternalistic and just fucked up. Don't buy into that anymore.

Pareto's Principle states that 80 percent of our positive output comes from 20 percent of our time and effort, and the flipside is that 80 percent of our time goes to bullshit. Find where you're best and engage there. Do more to enhance your superpower and delegate or punt the rest. Getting efficient means getting results. Time spent and quality work done are not the same.

Don't trade time for life anymore.

Create amazing things (whatever you do) and be excellent at it. Get good and call the shots at work. Get good and liberate yourself from the insanity.

Here's a framework for time and event management that can really help you look at your life in a different light:

Workdays: Take 5-minute restroom and exercise breaks every half hour. Stretch, do some squats, close your eyes, and move around to keep your mind fresh and your body activated.

Take at least a half hour of personal development time every morning and another 30 minutes at night when things have settled and the house is calm. Read for pleasure in bed and take back your time from the TV.

Weekends: Try to avoid any plans that don't serve you. Sure, there are things we have to go to and stuff that our partners need us to participate in, but the Urban Monk makes a habit of allowing his free time to serve him. Make sure you drink from the eternal fountain on weekends and get some more vitality.

Sleep when tired and get outside if the weather permits. The ideal is to work hard during the week so the weekend remains as play time. Outdoor gear is so awesome now that you can even get outside on rainy days by wearing a light jacket that is warm and waterproof and do all sorts of things without getting soggy. Life is better when you've taken the time to play. Also for weekends, take at least a dedicated hour a day to do your personal practice and sit in meditation for at least 30 minutes uninterrupted.

> *Do not stay up late on a Sunday night.*
> *This is suicide.*

Spend some time thinking about where you're efficient and where you need to cut back. Working into the night creates a fundamental imbalance in our lives, and it's not sustainable. If this is why you're losing sleep, wake up and smell that shitty job you've got.

Hacking Your Environment

So we don't live in a cave anymore, and that comes with benefits and disadvantages. Our walls are buzzing with electricity and our Wi-Fi may be frying our brains, but at least we don't need to fetch firewood in the middle of the night (well, at least most of us don't).

If you have a relatively modern thermostat, you can set the nighttime temperature to be around 68°F. This means maybe using a heavier blanket if you run cold and only a top sheet (or an even lower thermostat) if you run hot. Control the temperature to tell your body it needs to slow down and conserve heat. This helps you slow down.

Blackout shades are amazing. Las Vegas totally gets this. Keep the light out and you can sleep way better. If you have flashing lights from clocks or other electronic displays in the room, get rid of them. Learn to enjoy the darkness and let your poor pineal gland thrive. Once you've cleared the room, make sure the window dressings are adequate so outside light (especially if you have street lights right out there) doesn't penetrate. The darker the better.

If you feel you have a sensitivity to the EMFs in your house, the Resources section has some information on this.

Sound can also be an issue in many areas, so fortunately there are cheap and easy ways to soundproof a room. Moving blankets do well, but they're ugly. Egg crates are amazing, and you can get the black ones and be artistic. However, the egg crates are better for bouncing noise from inside. If you have loud neighbors or cars down there, a double-paned window can change your life. Acoustic ceilings are also nice.

The moral of the story? Do what it takes to make your bedroom cool, dark, and quiet, and for God's sake, get the stupid TV out of there.

JAMES'S ACTION PLAN

James was a hot mess, but his resolution was remarkably simple. He planned his day like a fool, leaving the intense stuff for last. Upon reflection, he realized that it was the remnant behavior of a college kid who crammed all night to get a paper done. He never really lost that momentum. When something was important, James would leave it for last and handle it at night. This happened for years, and after his divorce, it was so easy to keep himself occupied with work at night. Who's lonely? I'm busy . . .

He was never really finished with work but would give up when his brain got too foggy. He'd then watch an hour or so of TV to decompress before going to bed. His dinner was usually a bowl of cereal while sitting on the sofa.

We changed that straightaway. We cut the sugar and got some slow carbs like broccoli, squash, and zucchini along with some protein in at dinner. We cut caffeine after noon and got him eating regularly throughout the day. His adrenals couldn't take the hit, so we created a program to protect him from himself.

It took a month or so for him to get used to handling the important work stuff in the mornings. It felt very unnatural at first, but as he started to get it, a lightbulb went off and he finally got how insane his old rhythm was. I got him reading books and stretching at night. Once we cleaned up his work inefficiencies, he had leisure time in the evenings that opened up. At first it was awkward and uncomfortable—too quiet and lonely. We got him out dating, and he met a nice woman who had a couple of kids from a previous marriage. Bedtime was serious around her house, and that worked perfectly for our friend James. In fact, I asked him to mimic the sleep cycles of the kids for a few months. It changed his life.

How is it that we demand our kids get to bed on time and follow all sorts of good advice, but we can't do it for ourselves? James started to come back to life. His sleep quality and duration started to increase, and his energy came back. It took a few months to round it all out, but what a worthwhile pursuit. Once he let go of the quick-fix mentality and returned to some good old-fashioned clean living, there was no turning back.

James loves his sleep and is very grateful for it now. He doesn't allow much to get in the way of it. *Making room* for sleep made all the difference.

CHAPTER 5

Stagnant Lifestyle

STACY HAS BEEN STRUGGLING with her weight for as long as she can remember. She's tried hundreds of diets, done exercise programs, fasted, cleansed, and starved herself. She feels like she has lost and gained back thousands of pounds. She always seems to fall back to a heavier weight than she'd like, and despite her best intentions, she can't stop repeating this cycle.

Stacy's life is monotonous. She works in HR at a medium-size company. Her mornings consist of a hot shower, blow-drying her hair, putting on makeup, and then dressing up in her corporate armor. Her cleanly pressed suits rotate through the dry cleaner's weekly, and she owns more uncomfortable shoes than she cares to count.

Her drive takes just over an hour, so she eats some oatmeal in the car with a mug of coffee. Some days she finishes her makeup on the drive when she's running late. The drives are long and stressful. She's tried listening to NPR, but the news is so depressing nowadays. Audiobooks have been a good substitute, and classical music has helped keep her calm, but she's still aggravated and stiff by the time she arrives at work.

Her desk is comfy, but she sits too much. Dealing with e-mails and meetings all day keeps her stuck in an assortment of chairs. She and her coworkers often cater lunch in so they can have meetings and talk about the other meetings they just had. Her entire life is a chain of meetings about meetings, and she hardly gets to see the sun.

Her drive back home usually takes even longer, and she uses the time to call her friends and family to catch up. It helps her blow off some steam and feel like she has some semblance of a life. By the time she's home, she microwaves a meal, watches a couple of her shows, and goes to bed.

This is her life 5 days a week, and she can't figure out where she can sneak the gym in there. On weekends, she tries to get outside when the weather doesn't suck. She'll go for a long walk with a girl-friend or hang out with a guy she's dating, but there's always a heap of laundry, a trip to the cleaner's, groceries, bills, and other errands that stack up for weekends.

In all, Stacy hardly moves around all week and gets only minimal activity on weekends. When she does get some workouts in, it happens in spurts because getting up at 4:00 a.m. is unsustainable for her, and she's too hungry and tired to do anything after work. Stacy is stuck.

THE PROBLEM

For thousands of years, life was about movement. We'd hunt and gather for hours a day under the sun. We'd brave the cold and rest in the sweltering heat—it was the only option. We'd fight for our lives and sometimes run like hell to save them. Life was busy and life was active. Thorns were sharp, and a broken bone could mean your life. The stakes were high, and we were not always at the top of the food chain.

Our activity was multidirectional, and we spent a lot of time on the ground sitting and holding ourselves upright without furniture to prop us up. Our cores were engaged, and our bodies were fit, limber, and primed to explode with burst activity when needed. Jogging wasn't a thing because we worked all day and didn't need it. When we ran, it was usually for a very good reason. Getting that food meant your family got to eat and survive. Becoming food meant the obvious . . .

Our vision was sharp, and our sense of smell was acute. After all, our very survival depended on it. The birdcall helped us know if a predator was around, and our sense of "spatial" awareness was tightly bound to our survival instinct. Death was potentially around every corner, and we needed to be ready for it. If you didn't pick up the scent of a predator, chances were that you'd be lunch. Predators could see and smell better than us, so we had to be doubly careful and alert.

After the advent of agriculture, we'd still move and haul stuff all day. We chopped wood, fetched water, carried babies, and walked to most places. Life was a lot of work and was filled with strife. After all, not having rain meant not having food. Shit was real.

All that has changed today: We are stuck in offices with artificial light, recirculating air, toxic carpets and cleaning products, unnatural sitting positions, electromagnetic fields (EMFs), toxic people, and unnatural rest and recovery cycles. We live like Stacy and go from a seated position in a car to a desk and back again. We lie down in bed, toss and turn, and then get up and go back to sitting around all day.

The average American commutes just under an hour per day and typically sits on a sofa watching 19.6 hours of TV per week. This is after a typical 8 hours per day (or 40 hours per week) of sitting at the office. Is it any wonder why we are gaining weight and stagnating?

Today we are a shadow of our former selves and perform so little activity that we have a 48 percent greater risk of premature death and disease. Stacy is not just holding on to the weight. Her inactivity is negatively impacting her heart, her hormones, her mood, and her lower back. She's crunching her hip flexors, compressing her lumbar discs, letting her back muscles atrophy, and destroying her knees with the heels she wears.

The surgeon general recommends a *minimum* of 1 hour of cardio exercise per day, but fewer than 5 percent of Americans get even 30 minutes of daily physical activity. Stacy may get a couple hours per *week*, and that's if life doesn't get in the way. By all accounts, she's in trouble, and deep down, she knows it. She's lost her sparkle. She looks forward to the weekends and is disappointed when they don't nourish her. She reads about the lives of others that are interesting and filled with adventure, because her life sucks right now.

Stacy has fallen prey to the governing principle of pathology in natural systems, namely: "Still water breeds poison."

URBAN MONK WISDOM

The literal translation of the words "kung fu" is "hard work." Life is hard work, and mastering this makes you *good at life*. As mentioned earlier, tasks such as fetching water and chopping wood were a daily routine in monastic life. This is the great secret of the ancient East that didn't quite make it over to our modern translations. We all run from the world thinking the lofty "spiritual" realms mean freedom from pain, stress, and reality.

The exact opposite is true. We *master* our understanding of reality so that the profane becomes sacred. We feel the ups and downs of life without attachment and develop *resilience*. This taps into our survivor genes, helps us put on lean muscle mass, keeps our brains active and alert, and also boosts our immunity. It helps calibrate our stress response so that only real emergencies constitute a crisis and the "he said, she said" bullshit doesn't even faze us.

Between chores, farming, foraging, hunting, and the martial arts, the daily life of the monks was a lot of work and a lot of activity. It kept their minds active and senses sharp. It helped flush their detox pathways and kept them out in the sun. Fresh air, cold rain, hot days, and steep mountains kept their bodies strong and clear. Again, they built resilience and resolve. Life was hard, and so were the monks. When you step into your body and master the daily rituals, the rest of the social drama means little.

There were no office chairs; if you sat, you did so on the floor or on a rock. Cushions were a luxury and were the only props you got. The unnatural seated position we've adopted for chairs and cars is relatively new to our bodies. Elbows on the table or hands on the steering wheel help prop us up and disengage critical core muscles. It keeps us lazy and makes us weak.

> *Sitting on the floor helps us develop postural strength.*

Look at how babies develop. They go from rolling around, to creeping, then crawling, to pulling themselves up, standing, falling (a lot), and then eventually walking.

Much of our whole-brain coordination comes from postural and positional information, and our dexterity and balance work with this. Staying active along three dimensions works this part of the brain, and this body-brain balance helps us thrive and be robust. There's some great research being done now that shows how kids who skip the crawling stage and stand too soon or, worse yet, get propped up in baby jumpers are more prone to learning and developmental disorders. We need to engage all the primitive parts of our brains in order to fully develop as the badasses that we are. This means spending time on the floor crawling around like a lizard and going from a seated position to standing without needing a hand.

The ancient monks knew this, and their strength came from the ground up. The fundamental kung fu stance called Square Horse is all about rooting down into the ground with your feet and "grabbing" the earth with your feet. We use our connection with the earth to draw power and drive force. This comes from a fundamental and deep *connection* with the earth that is born from *sitting on it*. That's where a lot of Western martial art students get stuck in their training. They don't have a relationship with the ground and are unrooted.

What about Stacy? Well, she's not even in the ballpark. Think of a stagnant creek late in the season when the rains have stopped. The water stops flowing, and little pools start to develop along the sides. In those pools we get moss, bugs, gunk, and unhealthy water. This is what happens in our bodies. This is what is happening in Stacy's life.

Staying active and fit *throughout* the day is key. We can adjust our environment to help us stay alive with standing desks, floor stations, stretches, exercises during breaks, and primal workouts that engage our brain-body connection. We'll get into this in the hacks soon, but the key to understanding how to get out of our stagnant lifestyles is to realize that there is very little time for dedicated fitness compared to the multiple hours we spend getting crunchy all day. This means learning how to hack our environment to stay active and moving during our busy, hectic lives. The monks had this and we've lost it. Bringing it back is the way of the Urban Monk.

The Earth Is Round; Now the Earth Is Flat?

Paving over the earth, we've taken *dimensionality* out from under us. The contour of the earth under our feet gives us information and drives our brains to work correctly. But in a few generations, we've managed to "flatten" the earth along our thoroughfares and homes in order to simplify transportation. Think of the last bumpy dirt road you drove down. It sucked. It made you slow down and drive differently. Our modernization has created a need for fast and efficient transportation corridors, which have now become the norm for all city streets and sidewalks. Forget about cobblestone, just go flat concrete and move on. No bumps or someone may trip and sue the city . . .

The valuable information stream that comes from contours in the earth under our feet constantly sends information to our brains to process. Subtle nuances in the terrain send millions of postural signals to our brains, which are equipped to compute and adapt to this world we evolved in. Because we live in three dimensions, our brains need this constant flow of postural information from the periphery so they can keep our heads up straight and maintain balance. This data to our brains and the processing of this information via the sensory motor strip keep our brains activated and alive. After all, this is how we did it for millennia, so it's what we're used to. Our brains built on the foundation of this multidimensional processing and went to higher cognition from there. Now, take an entire dimension out of the equation, and we're really fucking with our brains. We've pulled the rug out. Since the earth now is almost always flat under our feet, all of that complex data flow about posture is limited, and that part of our brains becomes underactive. With the rise of anxiety, depression, learning and behavioral disorders, dementia, and more, many scientists are now looking at these correlations. Movement ignites a healthy fire for our brains to process, and the lack thereof is causing problems.

The Earth Has Qi

The earth is the greatest electron donor we have, capable of providing a seemingly endless supply of electrons that can flow through our bodies and help us combat oxidative stress. When we have tissue damage or inflammation in our bodies, the tissue holds a positive charge and acts as a free radical in our bodies. This further damages other tissue and can set off a chain reaction that leads to more inflammation and disease. Clint Ober, Stephen Sinatra, MD, and Martin Zucker have highlighted this phenomenon in their book, *Earthing*. According to them, our ancestors used to draw on electrons from the earth, and this flow of negative ions would help neutralize the positive charge of inflamed tissue and help us heal. This happened through connection with the earth through our feet, and through our spines

PERSONAL JOURNEYS

One of my favorite pastimes has always been bouldering, which is climbing up a riverbed or a creek. The routes are seldom the same, depending on the time of year and water flow. It gets me to use all four limbs, test my balance, leap across distances and land lightly, and use my strength to pull up my body weight. Not only is it an amazing form of outdoor exercise, but it also has an incredible effect of calming the mind and making me happy. As I do it, it almost feels like I'm coming whole, connecting up disparate parts of my splintered self back into a cohesive being who is vibrantly alive.

I used to own a summer camp for children, and I led hundreds of guided journeys through creeks with them. It helped build their confidence, test their courage, teach them to face fear, and activate their mind-body circuitry. I used to take this stuff for granted because I lived and breathed it. Once I got into medicine, I became accustomed to seeing mediocre results with patients. I had a moment where I was falling asleep to it, and then I snapped . . . fuck this. Take people to where they can come to life and help them feel the life coursing through their veins. That's the real medicine.

when we sat. Now, we hardly ever sit on the ground, and we walk around with rubber soles that act as a perfect insulator for electrons. This cuts off that vital flow and keeps us spiraling out of control. Our ancestors were either barefoot or walked around with leather soles that were still conducting charge. Today—well, look all around you. The connection is lost.

So when we take a super-stagnant lifestyle, cut off our connection with earth, prop ourselves up with furniture, and work under fake lights in stagnant air all day, is it any wonder why we're not thriving? An Urban Monk unleashes her power by freeing up movement. She uses her body every day in a variety of ways and connects with the earth by stretching, sitting on the ground, and hanging out with bare feet. She doesn't go from zero to hero on weekends and play an intense tennis match after sitting all week because she understands that she'll get injured.

Learning to move functionally is key, and that comes with whole-body movements and the intelligent use of the core muscles. An Urban Monk brings back the fundamental principles of movement into her daily life and builds back a foundation of strength, flexibility, stability, and *flow*. Life needs to move or it stagnates. Life flows, and so should we.

Move It or Lose It

Kung fu is known for its five animal styles. This comes from careful observation of the behavior of different animals in nature and the mimicking of their primal movements. In the context of battle, it offers deep insight into body mechanics and battle tactics. In terms of health, it opens up the joints, keeps the blood flowing, and keeps us moving in a multidirectional way. An attack could come from any direction, and that's how our bodies evolved to stay vigilant, relaxed, and yet alert. Using fast-twitch muscles in the martial arts helps enliven that circuitry and wake us up to this again.

Much of the exercise trend that's rapidly been proven wrong in the past couple of decades has been inspired by trainers pushing single vectors of force. An example of this would be the bench press. This helps linemen push opponents aside in football. It also helps us look good at the beach, but aside from those two things, the bench press has very little functional use for the body. In fact, most bodybuilders who work out this way have overdeveloped front side muscles and a weak posterior chain (the complex of muscles on the back of the body that help pull us back, maintain our posture, and balance out our physique). The muscles of the body are designed to complement and support each other. They strike a dynamic balance and keep us agile and strong when working correctly. An overemphasis on certain muscle groups at the cost of others leads to injury. Foundation Training, taught by Eric Goodman, DC, is a powerful tool that specifically targets the posterior chain and helps wake the whole body up. I've seen this training resolve serious orthopedic problems in patients over the years and can't say enough about it. A weak posterior chain in the upper body leads to shoulder injuries, and when the core is weak in three dimensions, lower backs and knees go out. (Consult the Resources section for a link to learn more about Foundation Training.)

Here's a key concept: The core isn't just your abs. It runs from the tip of your sternum to your pubic bone and wraps all the way around your body in three dimensions. When we begin to see it that way, we start to train differently. We understand how rotation is a huge part of functional movement and how certain injuries are bound to happen when we sit around all the time. We stand on wobbly surfaces, jump, do lots of planks, and generally build our strength from the ground up using our own body weight at first.

The multiplanar rotational movements in kung fu, dance, yoga, and Foundation Training are powerful tools to stay functionally fit. Once you have a baseline of true functional fitness, then playing basketball, surfing, skiing, and all the other stuff you used to do can happen with less likelihood for injuries that sideline you. One of my good buddies, Dr. Tim Brown, always tells his elite athletes, "You train to play, not play to train." This essentially means that we need to get functionally fit *before* we can play sports. This is fundamentally different from how most busy people do it, which is sit around all week and then lace up their sneakers for a once-a-week pickup game, pull a hamstring, and wonder why they are so "unlucky."

Another aspect of functional movement has to do with the activation of the brain. Using both hands, driving balance, coordinating eyes with hand movements, lateral slides, rotation, and whatever else you're doing in 3D really help light up the brain and balance it. After all, we evolved doing all this stuff and then suddenly stopped. Going back to using the whole body is a welcome change for the brain.

Life Isn't a Spectator Sport

When the hell did we all get sidelined from life's adventures? At what point does throwing around a football with the boys downgrade to watching the big game on a sofa with chips and beer? What ever happened to jumping rope and climbing trees?

Our society happened. When you take active creatures and subject them to unnatural postures and lock them away at desks all day, the biomechanical function of the body begins to falter. One by one, we fall prey to injuries or simply gain too much weight to be able to run up and down that court. One injury puts us out for a few weeks, so we gain some weight, and coming back too soon without proper rehab or functional training sets us up for the next. Whether we turn the same ankle or that weakness leads to another joint failing, we keep taking hits until watching sports and kids' soccer games is all we're left with.

Getting sidelined sucks. It's like having a flat tire on the road trip of life: We're frustrated that we can't cruise and upset that we're on the side of the road. The problem here is that so many people are in the same dilemma that the side of the road looks more like a parking lot. A huge crowd sits on the sides and watches the few fast cars whiz by. We drink beer and jeer, unaware that we could get back in the game and taste life again. Let's show you how.

EASTERN PRACTICES
Stand to Live

I've been consulting with large companies for years and showing them how to offset huge health-care costs. One of the key pieces in this is liberating their employees from their chairs. Standing desks and workstations are the way of the future. You burn calories, move more blood, stay alert, avoid crunching your back, and use postural muscles all day.

In fact, when I first transferred to a standing desk myself, I was shocked at how sore my core was for a couple of days. It didn't occur to me how much core engagement was needed to simply stand upright.

Over time, standing at your workstation will really help boost your energy, mood, and performance. I've recommended this for individual patients as well as for large corporations, who started to see a return on their investment. Sitting kills. According to a 2010 American Cancer Society study, women who sit more than 6 hours a day were 94 percent more likely to die prematurely than those who were physically active and sat less than 3 hours. No shit. For men, it was 48 percent. Sitting slows down calorie burning and increases our risk of diabetes. After 2 hours of sitting, good cholesterol drops by 20 percent.

One powerful hack I like to implement when working at my desk is to do kung fu stances. These help develop the leg muscles, which give us more balance and are dense in mitochondria. More energy can thus be produced and be available for you in your life. I switch up my kung fu stances throughout the day and rest when I'm tired. After a few hours, I feel like I've gotten a decent workout *and* I've gotten my work done.

Go to theurbanmonk.com/resources/ch5 for a link to a video with some kung fu stances you can start incorporating into your day.

Qigong Breaks

Qigong is the practice of moving stuck energy in the body through breathwork. Staying under your breath can help you go all day, whereas getting ahead of yourself will leave you panting by the side of the road. Sip and stay steady. It's the perfect thing to do during your breaks. Taking 5 to 10 minutes each hour and working some vital breath into your limbs will supercharge your day and your life. After all, the stagnation of energy and blood is the problem with modern life. In Chinese medicine, we say the blood is the mother of qi and the qi is the commander of the blood. This means that as the qi flows, so does the blood.

Moving qi is easy. It means coordinating the eyes, the mind, the body, and the breath. This is the magic formula for success. It links up the consciousness with your activity and anchors it in deep breathing. It lights up the sensory motor strip of the brain and helps balance us out. Just a few minutes of qigong daily can really boost your energy and mood. Do not wait till the end of the day to mop yourself up and recover. Take little sips of vitality throughout your day and avoid getting exhausted.

There are a couple powerful (and quick) exercises you can do while at work to power up your qi and stay vibrant. I've posted them in the Resources section.

Go Barefoot

Cutting off the flow of vital qi to your body is a bad idea. This happens as we cut off our contact with the natural world. We all get stuck doing it at times, and too much of it makes us weak and sick. Taking some time to reconnect with the planet and its free flow of limitless electrons is key. Take off your shoes and touch the earth. Doing so on raw earth is best. Grass, gravel, sand, and seawater are powerful ways to connect back into the "life soup" and let your body heal through the vital exchange of energy it needs (and direly misses) with the earth. The more the merrier on this. Some people take it to the extreme and go barefoot everywhere; I don't advise this simply because walking around in urban environments subjects us to a barrage of petrochemicals and nasty agents that are *not* natural and have negative health impacts on us. We absorb things through our skin. We drag things into our homes with our feet. That's why in traditional Asian cultures, shoes are left at the door and the house is to remain pure and clean. I'd say use shoes (with leather soles if you can) while walking the streets and go barefoot in nature, your yard, and your own house all the time.

Eyes, Mind, Body, and Breath

Earlier, I mentioned this as the secret sauce to qigong and want to take a minute to spell it out a bit more here. Deep breathing is the hallmark of most yogic work. The slow, methodical, and intentional movements of qigong and tai chi are linked with this deep breathing, and this activates the brain. The final piece is the eyes, which usually track the yang, or active hand, in qigong. When all this is linked up, it has a deeply relaxing effect on the body and mind. When we do this, we start to feel connected and more coordinated.

The mark of our culture is fragmentation and discombobulation. We've separated everything much like Adam and Eve started to name things in the Garden when they had fallen and were no longer whole. Learning to integrate our vision with our movements and breath is a way back. Applying this magic formula of coordinating eyes, mind, body, and breath to your exercise is a powerful way to connect mind, body, and spirit back up. Do *everything* intentionally, and watch the world around you light up with life and energy.

Slow Walking Meditation

A really nice practice that can help you connect back up and settle your mind when you're feeling stagnant is the walking meditation. This basically starts with the standing posture of *Wu Chi* and has you take the show on the road. Remember, *Wu Chi* is the stance where your feet are shoulder-width apart. You inhale as you raise the knee (leading with the knee) of one leg all the way up and slowly exhale as you step it forward and roll from heel to toe. You then repeat this movement on the other side and keep walking for as long as you deem fit. The lesson is to slow down and find balance. Shoot for 30 seconds per step and then try to slow it down even further once you have enough balance. The slow, methodical steps help calm the mind and really fire up the postural muscles, which light up the brain. Over time, you'll have better balance and feel more alive.

This can be done everywhere, and, yeah, it looks a bit weird, but so do your officemates. Stop worrying about what people think of you, and get to work doing stuff that really helps you.

MODERN HACKS
Get Up, Stand Up . . . or Hit the Deck

We already talked about how standing desks are revolutionizing our work environments. Standing up will change your life, but so can sitting down—way down. Another concept I've played with recently that's been fun and invigorating for people trying to part with the office chair is setting up a floor space for productivity. This is an area where shoes come off and people can work while sitting on the floor. Millennials are great at this, but older folks have lots of trouble with it at first. Why? Because we've been sitting in those fucking chairs for way longer . . .

The key is to use your muscles to prop up your body weight and get comfortable on the ground again. With my corporate wellness clients, we've used Japanese dining tables, which are low to the ground. They work great. Pillows and cushions help soften the hit, and meditation cushions are useful.

The key is to stay active, change positions, and keep your body engaged all day. This concept is a philosophical stance and can be applied to all facets of the workday. Either work while standing or gain flexibility and core strength by sitting on the ground. Whatever you do, don't collapse into that damn office chair at any cost.

Workout Toys

One way to keep your workday engaging is to have workout tools all over the place. I set up little exercise stations around offices with a ground mat, a couple kettlebells, and maybe a jump rope. Pullup bars are awesome, as are exercise balls.

The opposite of gravity is *levity*. Working out and keeping active all day helps boost your levity. The rule in my office is to stop at the workout station every time you walk by and do 10 reps of *something*. Mix it up all day, but keep doing stuff. Don't let yourself collapse under the weight of the day. Having different tools to access at the office or around your house will hack your environment and remind you to use these things. The opposite is also true. A soda machine also sends a signal—one you don't want to be getting.

What's it going to be: a cheese pizza or a treadmill desk? Will you surround yourself with poison or life medicine?

My good buddy, Abel James, speaks of environmental design and has great advice on how to adjust your world to reflect your stated goals. When we hack our environment to show us only the things we elect to adopt in our lives, it becomes easy. The simple first step here is at the grocery store. If you buy bullshit, you'll have it in the house and eat it. From there, look at household cleaners and chemical poisons; get them out of sight. You can extend this to having weights around and incense burning. You can lock the doors to keep out unwanted friends or family, or you can have musical instruments around with an open door/open jam policy. The question is: What do you want? Create a world that codes for that dream and you'll get it.

Barefoot Shoes

A major piece to the maintenance of our overall balance is posture, and as with any skyscraper, the foundation is the most important. This puts all eyes on our feet. This is where all the delicate balance and calculations happen that drive information to the brain and nervous system.

The human foot has 26 bones, 33 joints, 107 ligaments, and 19 muscles and tendons. The 52 bones in your two feet make up about 25 percent of all the bones in your body. This is a big deal biologically because it points to the overall importance of our feet and how critical it is to take care of them.

With the flattening of our world, we've changed the game. As mentioned earlier, we've gone from barefoot or soft moccasins that gave us a feel for the earth (and conducted electrons) to thick rubber soles on flat concrete roads. This has taken away the need for all the elaborate biomechanical sophistication we have in our feet and basically flattened us out, too.

Our arches are collapsing, so we go to the foot doctor and get orthotics, which can be likened to wearing a tight corset to fake strong abs. It's a crutch.

Walking barefoot is a challenge with all the shit out there on the roads (glass, gas, and cancer-causing pollutants), so going bare skin is not recommended on city streets. There are a variety of barefoot shoes out there now that are amazing. They are best worn on softer terrain and not for long distances; I've had to deal with several patients who bought a new pair, ran 10 miles, and really messed up their feet. Like anything else, ease into it and break them in. Chances are, you've gone a few decades wearing normal shoes that have made your feet and arches lazy. Slowly work into building arch strength, and you'll find that your feet can take you farther.

There's also a secondary win that is really cool. Because the feet are the foundation of all our body, strengthening them changes the whole kinetic chain downstream (which is actually up the body). I've had people with chronic knee, hip, shoulder, and even neck problems report amazing recovery once we began to sort out their foot issues. This makes total sense, but recovery takes some time, so be patient and start working your way back to your primal badass state.

You can't get moving and break through the stagnation if you hurt yourself at every turn. Get your feet right, and you're well on your way to flowing again.

Functional Movement Training

It's amazing how many random vectors of force have impacted our balance and how much noise our nervous systems are dealing with just trying to get us from the house to the car. No wonder we're all so tired. The cerebellum is where more than 50 percent of our brain's neurons are, and this is where we deal with motor function and balance. When we're off in this category, we're spending an exorbitant amount of energy just trying to keep our heads up and wondering why we keep forgetting where the car keys are. It is time to get that energy back.

Sometimes this means getting back on the floor and crawling like a lizard and then on all fours—whatever it takes to trigger the nervous system to help your body work correctly again. Once you crack this, your life will change and you can move freely and feel young again. I've seen amazing things happen in this realm, and I encourage you to start looking into it immediately.

There's a strong movement out there now led by some leading orthopedic surgeons and very intelligent physical therapists and fitness trainers that is helping people get functionally fit and ready for sports. It starts with balance, flexibility, and posture. Certain muscle groups need to fire correctly, and certain muscle chains need to activate. When our bodies are doing this, we're far less likely to get injured and can enjoy exercise again. Much of this is developed by watching the movement of small children before they get tortured by the desks at school. Watch a kid go from a seated squat to standing with total ease. Watch how they move and see where we come from.

One great exercise is standing on a Bosu ball (a half ball with a solid platform to stand on) with your feet shoulder-width apart. The exercise is to put both arms out to your sides and then close your eyes. Careful! Most people will lose balance and fall over at first. Do this until your brain can integrate and balance, and then try it with your hands in front of you, hands above you, and hands behind you, and then with trunk rotation. Do it all with your eyes open and then slowly close your eyes and try to find your balance.

Use Your Phone for Reminders

Just because we're busy doesn't mean we have an excuse to forget to take care of ourselves. The Urban Monk uses her tech to hack her life and make it better. Set reminders for every 25 minutes to get up and stretch. Maybe do 10 squats or pushups—whatever you need for your own personal growth. Book it in and value it. If it doesn't make your calendar, it's not important enough for you. Establish your movement goals for the day, and *plan* to do them daily. Completing 10 reps of a given exercise will take all of 30 seconds, and you'll feel better, think better, look better, and do better at work. It's a no-brainer. I like to do sets of five exercises of 10 reps each on my breaks.

Another great hack I use for my corporate clients is to set reminders (on employees' phones or desktops) to drink a sip of water every 10 or 15 minutes. This has the double effect of keeping them hydrated and also triggering an old biofeedback loop that's totally effective: It fills the bladder and gets us to check into our bodies and think, "Hey, I've gotta pee." You get up, walk to the bathroom, do your thing, walk back, refill your water, do 10 reps of something, stretch for a minute (or more), and then go back to work. It helps keep you hydrated, moving, and limber all day.

You won't remember to do it, so *use your phone or desktop* to remind you until it becomes a habit.

Telecommuting

Maybe the mark of the future economy is people working out of their homes more and driving less. Think about it. If you could do your job from home, you wouldn't need the 2 hours you currently spend on the road driving to and from work. You would save on gas and maybe even share a single car with your spouse. You wouldn't crush your spine with all of the sitting while driving, and you'd free up the roads and pollute less. Maybe the future for people who don't work in manufacturing jobs will be a way healthier version of work-life balance and the only people on the road will be delivery trucks and people going to the park or to visit grandma.

Lots of successful tech companies allow their employees to work from home, and they simply track accountability. If we could be adults and do what we say we're doing, it's all good. Be excellent at work and nobody cares where you do it from. If they still do, prove to them that you could be better. They pay for a job to get done, not to watch you sit there and look miserable. That model from the 1950s is dead; it's bullshit, and innovative companies are reexamining it so people can live happier and healthier lives. We used to need to be by our desk phone. Now we're mobile. Work shouldn't suck. Make them see that you can be trusted and that you will be a more valuable employee if you can work where you want.

An Urban Monk takes control of his life and drives outcomes with excellence and clarity. Take back your commute, and you'll gain the time you want to work out and hang with the kids or dogs. Free yourself from that stagnation and have more energy to get your work done and enjoy life during the week. Freedom is yours to be had. Stake your claim.

Alternative Transportation

Walking to work is a dream. Riding your bike is awesome. If your work is too far away for that, is there a train, ride share, or other way to get there other than driving? You can read or nap on the train but not at the wheel. Obviously, if you could make your transportation become your recreation and exercise, then you win.

If you're stuck having to drive to work, here's a tip that'll literally save your ass. Most people drive automatic cars now, which means the right foot is doing all the work while the left one just hangs out. What this does is slowly nudge the right hip into an anterior tilt, meaning it basically rotates forward over time, as that leg is getting all the action. If you're driving an hour a day, 5 days a week, 50 weeks per year, for the past several years, well, you get how this could be a problem. I've seen thousands of patients with this issue. It causes back pain, knee problems, weird postural issues, and, of course, hip issues. The way to correct this if you're stuck having to drive is to push your left foot against the little footpad off to the left side of the floor. Yes, it's there in almost every car: Just to the left of all the pedals, there's a little landing pad for your left foot. Push against that so your hips balance out and don't rotate forward and right anymore. Over time, you'll start to sort out the imbalance here and take less of a hit when driving.

Take the Show on the Road

Unless I have to be watching a webinar or going over a document on my computer, my new personal rule for phone calls is to take a walk while I talk. I qualify this with the people I speak with all the time. Basically, I tell them, "Look, I spend thousands of hours a month on the phone, and if I were to do it at my desk, my back would hurt and I'd gain weight, so if you don't mind, I'm going to take this call on a walk, and I recommend you do the same." For me, it's easier as the founder of Well.org because we're a health and wellness company, and I simply state that I need to walk the walk (nice accidental pun). You may need other calculus to make it fly, but, nonetheless, figure out a way. Maybe if it's the president of a huge company, you stand at your desk rather than hit the road, but how many bullshit calls do you take daily? You could get a treadmill desk and still burn the calories without the fresh air, but at least you're moving. How many interoffice colleagues do you speak with who wouldn't care if you were taking a walk? Start there.

I do the same thing with meetings. We used to have roundtable meetings with our partners a couple mornings a week, and we'd cater in food and coffee for the group . . . yawn. I switched it up so we all went on a hike. We'd move some qi, have someone record the conversation and transcribe it, and have notes and a recap on our desks by that afternoon. We'd see a couple of bunnies and some flowering plants, get some fresh air, and burn 500 calories *all while working.*

That's the take-home message here: Don't allow those 8 work hours to get you stagnant. Find a way to activate your body and mind throughout the course of the day and build resilience. Burn calories. Get sunlight and fresh air. That's the way of the Urban Monk. Don't let the outside world bully you around.

Find a way and you'll start coming back to life. With that, you'll have more vitality to do better and make cooler shit happen. You will look back one day and wonder, "What the hell was I thinking?" Life can be very grand; step into it and then *keep stepping.*

STACY'S ACTION PLAN

People hardly recognize Stacy anymore. She was able to negotiate working from home 2 days a week, which opened up all kinds of drive/shower/dressing time for her. It took some coaxing, but she had her bosses track her productivity for a quarter and showed improvement on all fronts. Once they saw this, she was free to come and go as she pleased. She did some functional fitness exercises until the trainer cleared her, and then she began a hip-hop class on the two mornings she didn't have to drive. It helped her unlock her spirit and feel so much better. The other mornings, she was throwing some quality vegetarian protein into a blender with some organic greens and still hitting it in the car to save time. Audiobooks to help her get ahead in her career became the listening of choice for the morning drive.

She completely transformed her workstation. She got a standing extension for her conventional desk and started an initiative to wear comfortable shoes at work. Upper management went for it because enough female employees signed a petition to demonize the heels. She would take regular breaks and do something active all day. She rearranged midday meeting times to never run through lunch. That became personal time again. She'd batch cook on Sunday and Wednesday nights and have healthy lunches daily. She'd eat in the break room and then go for a walk with a couple of colleagues. They slowly added some velocity and were getting about 3 miles in daily.

Being in HR, she was able to wrestle a room away from another department and turn it into a relaxation room. Anybody can go in there and chill out, nap, or meditate when they feel inclined, and at first, the management was freaked out about this. Within 3 months, however, the writing was on the wall. Employee morale and productivity started to go up, while absenteeism and sick days started to go down. It was totally working. Because she spearheaded the effort, she was able to ride on that win and get some more healthy programs implemented at work. A mini gym, healthier snacks in the kitchen, and a walking club were among the new ones.

In the evenings, Stacy cut out the TV and got a dog. This meant daily walks and time running around in the park. It helped her meet a nice guy at the dog park. He is a rock climber and loves to camp. Stacy doesn't like the heights, but she goes along on the trips and spends some quality time barefoot in nature. She reads a book, stretches, or goes hiking with the dog.

The sunshine, fresh air, and "me" time really helped her start feeling alive again. She slowly lost 3 to 4 pounds a month for a few months straight, and her weight plateaued at a nice number. She's been able to keep the pounds off because, unlike with all of her other attempts, this wasn't about losing weight. It was about getting her life back.

It all started with her hacking her workday and led to some pretty cool places.

CHAPTER 6

Weight Gain and Negative Self-Image

ANN HAS NEVER BEEN comfortable in her own skin. She was a little heavyset in junior high and became very self-conscious of it. By high school, she mustered up all her will to make a change. She dieted and exercised obsessively. It worked. She was thin and people noticed. She became a cheerleader and carried that on into college. On the outside, she was in an enviable position. Girls wanted to be like her. Guys were attracted to her. She was popular. She was also miserable.

Ann always felt fat and unattractive. No matter what people said, she felt as if· they were humoring her, lying to her. Spring break required a long series of pep talks with herself. Being in front of people in her bikini was her idea of hell. They will see. They'll know. She skipped out on a couple of big trips because she simply couldn't deal.

She struggled with this through college and as she started her adult life. Two kids and a nice husband later, Ann had put on a good 30 pounds. She was never able to shake off the extra weight after the first child despite ceaseless efforts to do so. In fact, she dieted so hard that her milk ran dry and she had to switch the baby to formula— something she still feels guilty about. From cleanses to juices to boot camps, Ann spent a small fortune trying to find the "one thing" that would work for her. After her second kid, she basically gave up. What was the point? She was in her late thirties and nothing was working.

Ann hated how she looked and found herself making excuses to miss parties and other social events because they caused so much anxiety and grief. They reminded her that she was fat, that she was ugly. Everyone on the outside saw her as a pleasant, attractive, and kind person, but Ann couldn't see that girl. All she saw was the failure . . . the love handles and the hips.

Her husband's work required her to show up and hang out at various mixers and galas. She hated it. They fought over it. He couldn't understand why she was being so selfish and unreasonable. She kept making excuses and putting it on people she didn't like there. She was too ashamed to tell him the real reason—too ashamed of herself overall.

Her marriage was in trouble. Her social life was nonexistent. Her kids were feeling the bad vibes, and Ann simply couldn't help herself. Her negative self-image was derailing her life.

Ann's problems didn't start in junior high. That's just when her body started to show signs that it wasn't able to compensate anymore. She grew up eating sugary cereal, milk pumped with hormones and antibiotics, pastries, pastas, cheese pizzas, and candies as treats. Her mom would park her and her brother in front of the TV while she did stuff around the house, giving them each a box of crackers and a fruit juice. Ann would go to ballet in the afternoons and come home starving. She would try not to eat because her teacher was really particular about how Ann's body looked in tights. It turns out that having a person with an eating disorder influence a young girl's self-image is a bad idea. Ann and her parents had no idea how much drama this teacher's influence would later bring.

But the problems could be traced back even further. Ann was born a C-section baby. This means she wasn't exposed to the vital mix of good bacteria that was supposed to be transferred by mom's vaginal canal. The standard practice with this procedure is to put mom and baby on antibiotics for safety. What this did was create an environment where the wrong types of bacteria took hold in Ann's gut. She was a colicky baby who hardly slept. Mom didn't breastfeed because her doctor convinced her that formula was better. The formula she had, in some form of infinite wisdom on the part of the manufacturer, was shit. The first few ingredients were maltodextrin, corn syrup, and more sugar. This fed the bad bacteria in Ann's gut and created an environment where she dealt with constipation, indigestion, and picky food aversions her whole life. It also made her a sugar addict from day one. Get 'em while they're young—*real* young.

THE PROBLEM

With obesity, diabetes, and heart disease on the rise, we obviously have a big problem on our hands. In fact, health-care costs will soon account for more than 20 percent of the gross domestic product of the United States. Eighty percent of these costs come from chronic *lifestyle* diseases. This is stuff we can prevent and turn around.

With the introduction of modern farming practices, stagnant lifestyles, and rampant toxicity, our bodies cannot cope with all the changes and are storing excess fat. Food used to look like one thing for millions of years, and now it is different. Let's dissect this out so we can wrap our brains around what the problem is. Once we're clear on that, the solutions are rather simple.

Modern Farming

After World War II, we decided to take the industrial machine we'd created for the war on Nazis and turn it on our society for the betterment of all. It was a noble idea but has gone overboard in many ways. The chemical and petroleum companies started to look at farming practices and how they could enhance yields. We started overtilling the soil and using toxic chemicals to kill off pests. Fertilizers came into the mix and so did genetic engineering. We went wild with it, getting more output from the land and showing the world how the marvels of science can fix all our problems. We were able to silo grains and offset famine. We were able to help countries in need and provide humanitarian support. It was certainly not all bad, but we went too far and are now paying for it.

By overfarming the land, we deplete the soil of essential minerals that our plants need. Our brains ask us to go out and get nutrients, so we experience hunger. Normally, the food we'd eat would satisfy the brain by bringing in the needed elements. Because today's food is depleted of nutrients, however, we just keep eating and eating without the intended benefit of receiving the stuff we need. We keep loading up on empty calories without a "stop" signal from the brain because it is still starving for what it requires.

Our ancestors would rotate in certain crops (like legumes) to fix nitrogen back into the soil and help replenish it. They would let plants rot in the soil, and the other species that grew alongside helped create diversity, balance the bacteria, and oftentimes ward off the pests. The animals lived on the same land, and they ate the pests. Their manure helped fertilize the crops. They ate the weeds and coexisted on the land. But when we split the plants and animals into huge industrial farms, we upset this balance. The soil has been stripped of nutrients and, hence, so has our food. The animals now swim in feces, and the plants are drowning in poison to ward off the pests.

Yes, pests are a nuisance, but nuking them with pesticides has proven to be an overzealous approach filled with hubris and folly. Using pesticides to kill everything in the soil leaves it open to major fungal overgrowth and also to other resistant bacteria that don't support our healthy farming needs. These also seep into our foods and poison us. Look at DDT. That was a bad idea that has left its scar on a few generations. Just because someone in a chemical lab can come up with a new compound that shows promise in a test tube doesn't mean we should rush out and spray it on our food.

We're now recoiling from this trend toward insanity and realizing that countless people are sick from overexposure to all the bullshit we've been pumping into our food and our environment. This is a far cry from the world of our ancestors where things were pure, natural, organic by default, and fresh. If you look at our departure from this link to nature and the sudden rise of a flood of modern diseases, the correlations are staggering.

In the early days of cancer research, some "rogue" doctors came out to suggest that cigarettes could potentially be leading to the rising cancer rates. They were ridiculed and ostracized. A famous quote from the era by a leading doctor was that the rise in cancer was just as likely to be caused by nylon stockings, which had also just flooded the market around the same time as the rise in cigarette use (and cancer). Since so many people were smoking, it was hard to isolate it and find causality. As more and more research began to come in, though, the researchers had a huge "uh-oh" moment, and now everyone knows that smoking causes lung cancer.

I believe we're in a similar era with all of the chemical poisons we've introduced into our environment. There's so much of this shit out there that it's hard to isolate *what exactly* is causing this huge rise in cancer, autoimmune disease, autism, and maybe even some cases of diabetes. If you look at the trends, they line up with our industrial era and our "better living through chemistry" ideology. What if the cumulative effect of all these toxins was causing our rise in disease? What if 20 years from now we look back and ask, "What the hell were we thinking by putting all that shit in our food?"

The Urban Monk steps out in front of this and is a part of the solution and not the problem. We don't wait for the ship to sink. This is *our* planet. We owe it to our children.

Sugar Is a Drug

One of the darkest hours in our history was the era of slavery. It was a booming and robust part of the economy of the New World, and most of the Old World players were on the gravy train. Labor was needed to exploit the bountiful riches and resources of the New World, and thanks to some assholes, ships filled with African slaves started to arrive to provide workers for the plantations.

One of the major cash crops that drove the slave trade economy was sugar. The Old World elites had gotten a taste of it and were hooked (literally). This drove an enormous demand for more and more sugar cane and pulled more people into slavery. In fact, that addiction to sugar (and tobacco) in Europe was much of the driving force for a continuous stream of people being taken from their homes and sent to work on plantations.

We can say that sugar drove the demand for slaves, but the fallout is that we *all* became slaves to sugar. Long after the scars of slavery started to heal (and there's still plenty more healing left to do), the addiction to sugar we've developed as a society has overwhelmed our medical system. It turns out that sugar is 10 times more addictive than cocaine and that it lights up pleasure centers in our brain that drive us to want more. We're totally hooked on the stuff, and the fallout of this is just starting to become apparent. It tweaks our blood sugar, lowers our immunity, triggers us to store fat, and feeds the bad bacteria in our guts.

When you think about sugar, don't just think of the white stuff. The development of high-fructose corn syrup allowed Big Food to take a monocrop that our tax dollars subsidize and refine it into a *super sugar*. Food manufacturers put that crap into everything, and it is making us fat. Because of years of misinformation and confusion, we all thought that it was the fat in our diets that was the problem. In fact, according to my friend Mark Hyman, MD, a big problem we have is the word *fat*. The stuff we eat and the stuff we store are not the same, and this misuse of the word has led to lots of confusion about weight loss. It is also refined sugar that causes weight gain. It quickly gets stored as fat because the body often can't handle the blast of calories sugar provides. Good saturated fats are needed for the brain and for hormone synthesis. They get burned and are fine for most people. Sugar, and especially fructose, converts to body fat very easily, and that's where we've gotten into trouble.

Carbohydrates to Feed the World

Sugar is a carbohydrate, which is a macronutrient that we use as one of our primary sources of energy. One of the big things we fell for was that a calorie was a calorie, and if we were able to get high yields of wheat, soy, and corn, we'd produce enough calories to feed the world—problem solved. What we didn't account for is that these monocrops would strip the land, feed us empty calories that can get stored as fat, and destroy biodiversity.

Complex carbohydrates break down well and help feed much-needed energy to our cells. They are tempered by natural fiber and aren't engineered to be loaded with more sugar than we can handle. Still, too much of a good thing *isn't* healthy. Just because complex carbs are fuel, it doesn't mean our bodies can drink them from a fire hose. Slow and steady is the name of the game with biology, and that's how we've adapted to consuming calories from carbs. The occasional treat of honey or a sweet fruit was tempered by fiber, protein, fat, and water in our diets. Treats were rare, and that's what made them special. Today, people can effectively eat a mega dessert for lunch and think nothing of it.

So the food from Big Agriculture has fewer nutrients each year and more calories. Our brains signal us to go out and get nutrients, and if they are not in our food, no matter how much empty bullshit we eat, we still feel unsatisfied and hungry.

Toxic Exposure and How the Body Deals

Around 70 percent of our immunity lines our guts because this is the primary interface between "us" and the outside world. Over millennia, our bodies have evolved and adapted to deal with natural substances. When something is recognized as friendly, it is shuttled in and used in the body as fuel or a nutritional resource. When it is deemed a threat, then the immune system mobilizes and attacks to get it out at all costs. If the toxin rings the bell and our troops mobilize, enormous energy reserves are drawn upon. We are, in effect, at war and sending troops to fight the invading army. Once in a while, this is okay, but with repeated exposure, this wears away at our immune system and exhausts our energy reserves. A tired army is more likely to draw friendly fire. It is more likely to turn on its own. We're now seeing an enormous rise in autoimmune diseases, and it's likely that this exhaustion of the immune system is the cause. There are so many new toxins hitting us that our systems get edgy and turn on our healthy tissue.

The other side of this equation is when the immune system doesn't get triggered by a foreign substance, so it's able to fly under the radar. This happens with mercury, arsenic, lead, and some other heavy metals. The body often recognizes that they don't belong, but instead of mounting an attack, it decides to put them away somewhere so they don't cause any harm. The go-to places to store things out of the way in our bodies are our fat cells, our bones, and our brains.

When we store toxins and metals in our fat cells, the cells insulate them and hide them from the daily operations of our physiology. This works okay until we wake up one day and decide we're too fat. We then starve ourselves, do a boot camp, or go on some other crash diet and start to call on the stored fat for energy. Then the metals and toxins get out of jail and are released back into the bloodstream. The body recognizes what's happening and signals the thyroid gland to slow down our metabolism so we can store more fat and lock up the bad guys again. They can't roam the streets, so we have no choice but to lock them away in fat cells again. Welcome to the rebound weight gain we've all experienced. Later, we'll talk about how to get the toxins out so we can avoid this roller coaster.

The other place the toxins and metals get stored is bone. Usually we don't notice this until later in life when our hormones change and we start to draw on the bones for our deficit in calcium. This is when we unlock the bad stuff, suddenly feel like crap, and wonder why. Again, toxins get released and the body can't have it, so it has few choices other than to store the toxins away in fat or bone again to avoid further damage to the body. Sometimes these dislodged toxins end up in our brains instead and that spells trouble.

The Microbiome

One of the ways we've been able to modulate our immunity, insulate ourselves from toxins, absorb foods better, and crowd out nasty invaders is by having a symbiotic relationship with certain healthy strains of bacteria in and on our bodies. The microbiome isn't just in the gut. It's in our noses, throats, urinary tracts, and genitals, on our skin, and through our entire digestive system from mouth to anus. We have trillions of good bacteria all around us that help support our life processes.

These bacteria work with our bodies to help life along. We live together to thrive and adapt. Our friend Ann never got properly seeded with this "gift of life" because of the way she came into the world, so, without the web of bacterial life to support her, she had room for other opportunistic bugs to take root and start running the show. These bad bacteria often feed off sugar and drive Ann's cravings. The fascinating thing we're learning about the microbiome is that much of genetic expression comes from bacterial DNA. This opens the door to a conversation about who we are, since what we consider "me" is mostly coding from the other life inside of us. In fact, the concept of Karma is alive and well through this transference. Dad kisses mom and they share common gut bacteria. Then baby is born through mom's vaginal canal (optimally) and is exposed to this "bouquet" of life that is unique to them. The good, the bad, and the ugly get transferred generationally this way. It opens the door to a larger conversation about prenatal medicine and our role in taking care of ourselves long before baby arrives.

Dealing with healthy bacteria in our lives is critical, and our ability to find a healthy balance between the good guys and the pathogens is really what determines our overall health. How well can we coexist with the life all around us? Do we snuff it out, or do we work with it?

It turns out that high-starch carbs and sugary foods feed a lot of the unhealthy colonies. Yeast and candida love sugar. So does cancer. The problem with the standard American diet is that it feeds the beasts, and then we take antacids and antibiotics every time the body sends us a sign of this imbalance. The antibiotics keep pressing reset by killing everything in their path, and because we don't have a diet rich in fermented foods, we simply leave space for bad guys to settle in again. The good news is that we can turn this around with what and how we eat. The body is resilient and dynamic. I'll share some dietary strategies to rehabilitate the gut with you later in this chapter.

Leaky Gut

Leaky gut is a syndrome where the lining of our intestines becomes compromised. This happens when we eat foods that cause inflammation or trigger food allergies, or when we inadvertently consume toxins that damage our cell walls. Essentially, most of us have some degree of leaky gut because of all the bullshit we've been eating. Wheat, corn, soy, dairy, peanuts, and alcohol negatively affect many people, and we've seen an explosion of food allergies and sensitivities to these foods. You may eat healthy now, but did you since day one? If so, then good for you and thank your parents. For the rest of us, we've had our share of chips, cheeseburgers, and sodas before we realized those foods weren't working for us.

Leaky gut syndrome begins when little gaps start to form in the intestines that allow food particles to sneak through into the bloodstream. This causes the immune system to go crazy and attack, resulting in more inflammation and an all-out war. The body notices substances that don't belong on the wrong side of the fence and mounts an immune response to defend the realm. This triggers the synthesis of antibodies to the various particles that make it through and explains the rise in food allergies we see in the West. We first feel it as gas, bloating, fatigue after meals, and indigestion before it goes further south from there. A food coma (when you feel extremely lethargic after eating) is a sign of illness. Food cravings are not your natural state. Food shouldn't punish; it should energize you.

URBAN MONK WISDOM

There is far more empty space within our bodies than matter. We're so focused on matter all the time that we don't really allow for the deeper understanding of what it really is in the first place—simply a *state*. We have so little actual "stuff" compared to empty space, in fact, that most of the waves, currents, fields, and fluctuations of the universe simply move *through* us. Even the parts of us we feel are so real, say our hands, in actuality don't touch things; what we feel is the repulsion of the electrons around our hands against other electrons of the objects or people we encounter. What we see and feel as "material" is a state of vibration of certain atoms in our universe. Some exist in gas, some in liquid, and some in plasma form. They come and go, *as do we*. They bond with others and were formed in the fusion reaction of stars.

Every atom in our bodies—all the stuff we consider "us"—has come from stars. We're way more interesting than we think, and the way of the Urban Monk is to delve into the mystery of life itself.

Look at it this way: You've already lost thousands of pounds in your life and added back thousands more. Cells are born and others die every day. In fact, you have replaced trillions of cells and continue to do so. You burn plenty of fat and store plenty more. It's a question of burn rate. Are you storing slightly more than you are burning?

Have you gained 10 pounds over the last year? If so, then the good news is that out of the thousands of pounds you've gained in the past few months, you were able to burn off almost all of it; you just missed by 10. That's not so bad at all. Maybe that's 10 plus the 40 you've stacked up from the last 4 years, but that's still not much in the grand scheme of things. It simply becomes an issue of adjusting your burn rate *of matter*. Before we can understand this, though, let's jump into a few key questions:

Who is burning the fat in the first place?

Who are you anyhow, and what are you doing here?

What's this all about, and what's the meaning of life?

This has been the essential missing ingredient in the weight-loss conversation for the most part. We're so fixated on the number, the waist size, and how we look that we've forgotten to check in with how we feel, and more important, *who we are.*

The Urban Monk digs deep to find himself first. This is the only real game in town when it comes to managing your weight, and everything else is a distraction. What does it mean to be born of the stars? What did the ancients mean when they spoke of eternity? How do we fit into the grand scheme of all this, and can we even understand our role? These are the primary questions.

Once these questions have been answered, the secondary issues of how we eat, move, play, and burn energy can be addressed. Without meaning and purpose, we're spinning and trying random shit all the time. With no real center, there's no frame of reference and no real reason to *care* about losing, gaining, maintaining, or carrying the weight. After all, why should we bother?

Eat Like a Monk

Reverence is the key concept when discussing the way an Urban Monk eats. It is reverence for what is in front of you and where it came from.

After all, our plates are the sacrificial altars where we lay *life* to ingest for our own benefit. It's heavy. The plant, fruit, animal, fish, or whatever else has *died for you.* We take on this life, break it down, turn it into energy and nutrients, and feed the machine that carries us forward. This is why it's so important to eat things that are or were recently alive and eat only natural things that come from the earth. They carry much more life force.

The central theme of all monastic practices around food is thankfulness. Are you grateful for the life that laid itself down in front of you? Why is your life more valuable than the one you're eating? What makes you so special, and *most important,* what are you going to do with your life to deserve it?

If the web of life and love that surrounds us is supporting you and your growth, how are you feeding back into it? What's your role in nature, and how are you helping further support the ecosystem that sustains and supports you?

In the West, our entire culture has departed from this understanding. Without connection to life, meaning, purpose, and our place in the grand scheme of all of it, we are capable of throwing our chewing gum out the window and driving off. We're more willing to get the Styrofoam cup despite how bad it is for the environment because we're late and don't have a mug. We're happy to buy the cheaper eggs from tortured chickens because we don't have to see their anguish or abysmal living conditions.

Waking up to food is waking up to life.

The way of the Urban Monk is to give pause and breathe before each bite. It's to give thanks for the food that we have in front of us *and really mean it.* The Urban Monk feels utter gratitude for what's been provided to her, and she never takes life for granted. She commits to doing something valuable with her life to *deserve* the right to take other life, and still, she remains humble and thankful. We don't know why we've been chosen to keep going on, and tomorrow we can be hit by a bus and be gone, so what's today about? How are you committed to living your life fully?

We departed from the core wisdom around eating when we started to see food as simply calories in and out. Food should be the cornerstone of the *rituals* you build into your life. If you are what you eat, start by cleaning up the quality of the food you purchase and ingest. Slow down and give thanks with each bite, and really savor the experience of eating. Another major piece to this is chewing. That's where we do a fair amount of work to "predigest" our food, and it serves a valuable role in the whole process. Not slowing down to eat also means not chewing enough. This gives your gut more work to do and makes you more sluggish, less efficient, and less mindful of the process.

In the monasteries, the act of dining serves as one of the most powerful tools for bringing awareness and mindfulness to our lives because food is where we fall asleep so readily. After all, we've been doing it since birth and have taken the act for granted. Becoming

PERSONAL JOURNEYS

When I was a monk, I would go on mini sabbaticals to places all over the world. One time I went into Waimea Canyon on the island of Kauai. Here I fasted on water for 5 days and performed my qigong and meditation practices. The first couple of days were not easy because my blood sugar was unstable and my body was detoxing. But then the magic started to happen. I started burning fat and experienced exceptional clarity. I felt lighter by the hour and began to see some of the places in my life where I was avoiding some harsh realities. I faced many demons and cleared lots of stagnant qi. Upon return, everybody noticed. My energy field was lit up, and I was glowing. Why? Because I cleared out the old by spending several days drinking from the sun and allowing my body to rid itself of impurities. I was clean, light, happy, and enthusiastic. *This state is our birthright.*

conscious and aware around food is a critical step to waking up and becoming aware in life.

Eating Builds Your Qi; Qi Feeds Your Spirit

The quality of the food we eat leads to the quality of the energy we have in our system. Note that I said *quality* and not *quantity* here. We're so caught up in the "more is better" mentality of capitalism that we have forgotten about an essential component to the makeup of our life force. Namely, the quality of the energy we take on from nature leads to the refinement of said energy into a brighter and clearer spirit. It is important to know that energy comes in variant frequencies. The higher the vibration, the lighter and brighter we are. Things that resonate closer to the purity of the sun and natural systems simply carry a cleaner vibration. This is the essence of the ancient alchemical traditions and is an understanding that's been lost in the modern world. Life emits light and we are that light. The consumption of food helps keep our light burning, but not all fuel is the same. Without reverence and respect for the life we've just taken, we create a spiritual malady that infects our very being. When you learn to take "you are what you eat" to the ultimate level, you know that everything we consume becomes a part of us.

Fasting

A central practice of most monastic settings is fasting. This gives us an opportunity to take a break from solid food to heal the gut, clean the blood, and think about life with more clarity. By slowing down the workload of the digestive system, we give it a chance to clean up a bit. When we fast, we divert some of the energy we spend on breaking down food into repairing the gut lining. We give our immune systems a break by cutting the barrage of challenges, and we allow our pancreas and stomach cells to rejuvenate by cutting off the need for them to create a steady flow of digestive enzymes. When we fast properly, we take on teas or fluids to help nudge the bowels along so the fasting process also helps our detoxification pathways.

Not only is this good for our health and well-being, but it also helps us simplify life. Not having a steady flow of food makes us appreciate it more. It helps us think about what we eat and miss it. The constant panging hunger makes us more aware of our body and its needs.

There's another important thing that happens when we fast: Our bodies start to break down stored fat cells in a process called ketosis. This is an extremely efficient way of providing energy to the brain, and the exceptional clarity people report while fasting can be attributed to it. In fact, the ancients understood this and found that they could dive into far deeper meditation while fasting. Think about it: Jesus, Moses, Buddha, Muhammad, Gandhi, and so many more famous people reported deep mystical experiences *while fasting*. It's a tried-and-true spiritual tradition and has lasted the test of time for a reason: It works.

Fasting helps us turn things down a notch and take a day to contemplate life and distill things back to the meaningful nuggets. It helps us keep it real and not get caught up in the noise that has distracted us away from life, nature, love, and truth. The key is to take the day to slow down and do some personal spiritual practice. Don't fast on a regular workday with deadlines and bullets flying at you. You'll miss the whole point. Make it a ritual and slow down. I concurrently take a vow of silence on days I fast. I conserve my breath and pull my energy in.

George Bernard Shaw said, "Every fool can fast, but only the wise man knows how to break a fast." This is a major issue I see with modern people trying to play with ancient practices, and it has caused lots of harm. If you're going to fast on water for a day, you need to ease back slowly into eating food, starting with a broth, then a blended soup, then steamed vegetables, and then eventually solids the next day. The key practice is to ease back into foods and, on a spiritual level, really connect with the food that you're breaking your fast with on a profound level. Giving thanks for the life energy you're letting back in to the Source from which it came is a powerful way to reconnect with nature and meaning. Missing this part is foolish; you may as well not fast if you won't do it right.

Soups

As mentioned in Chapter 3, our ability to extract energy and nutrients from food sources was greatly enhanced by the use of fire. In fact, looking at human skulls throughout history, we see that the size of our brains increased dramatically after we learned to unlock nutrition with cooking. It led to a quantum leap in our development and nudged us along. In fact, the Kabbalah states that all animals have access to the elements, but *fire* is the domain of humans and that has set us apart. This is to be taken with reverence and not hubris, as many of our species are quick to do. I've included a couple of soup recipes for you in the Resources section of this book. Having easy-to-digest foods that are high in nutrients and low in body burden is incredibly helpful. Soups help restore vitality and give us the energy we need to live life fully.

EASTERN PRACTICES
Get in the Dirt

The gut is the root of our being, and that's where our nutrients are absorbed. It is where we interact with all sorts of life all around us and connect with Mother Nature in a powerful way. Nothing brings us closer than getting involved in the growing process of our own food. Whether you have a kitchen counter or several acres in the back, learning to connect with food by growing some of it yourself is incredibly rewarding and therapeutic. You can get a CSA (Community Supported Agriculture) to deliver the majority of your vegetables or go to the farmers' market weekly, but supplementing with *something* you grow yourself is a way to see the cycle of life and take part in it. Of course, use organic processes and get some earthworms to help you out. Once you start, you'll see how amazing it feels to eat produce you've grown. I've seen kids overcome severe food aversions by kindling a relationship with a plant and bringing something to harvest. It is deep, meaningful, and important. You'll slow down to eat what you've grown and think twice about how you prepare it. The friendly bacteria that comes with organic soil and good cultivation will help nourish you, and what you do with your organic scraps will change how you view trash.

This practice is a must for anyone serious about getting back in a right relationship with food. Besides, what kind of stupid animal forgets how to survive in the environment it evolved in? If the shit hits the fan, can you produce food to feed your family? An Urban Monk sure can. Here's a guide to home gardening: well.org/homegardening.

Steam Your Vegetables

We spoke earlier about how cooking can unlock nutrients and help digestion. This is a key factor in getting healthy and staying that way. Make it easy for your body to break your food down, and your body will reward you with more energy. Steaming veggies lightly keeps the nutrients available while doing some of the "pre-chewing" for you.

Steamed veggies carry lots of water and fiber, which help blunt blood sugar and cortisol spikes. They help fill you up with good stuff that doesn't make you fat. The staple food item in the Urban Monk diet is lots of vegetables, mostly lightly steamed, in soups, or raw if you can handle it.

Speaking of vegetables, get yourself some organic cabbage (or better yet, grow some) and then ferment it into sauerkraut. I've included a recipe for you in the Resources section.

Rice

We can't talk about a monk's diet without discussing rice. Simple rice dishes with vegetables are a staple of the diet in many monasteries. Rice is a staple crop in many parts of the world and has a much lower allergy risk than other grains such as wheat. In fact, the Chinese symbol for qi is rice. It gives energy. In a world where life was a lot of work, eating rice provided the carbohydrate base to keep going. In the modern world, we often consume more calories than we need, so eating rice can be a challenge when we're trying to lose weight. There's also growing concern that certain rice crops are high in arsenic so it's important to be sure you get rice from a clean source. Limit your rice to two servings per meal in the evenings (one to three nights per week) with veggies and lean meats (if you eat meat) and you'll be fine. Don't eat meats with just rice, as this doesn't provide enough fiber and moisture to move it through your digestive system well. You can get gassy and belch a lot as a sign that your body isn't happy with this combo. If you still need to drop more weight, cut rice out of your diet until your metabolism is fired back up; then you can use rice as your staple grain with quinoa and amaranth. Essentially, grains provide easy access to energy as they've fed civilization and kept us going. Some people do end up inflamed on them, though, so see how you feel on them and take everything in balance.

Mindful Eating

The Urban Monk turns food into a ritual again; it becomes an opportunity to connect with time, breath, food, people, and life. Hack your calendar and start carving out more time for meals. I block mealtimes off in my calendar and hold the time that way. If you don't plan for lunch, you'll scarf it down in a hurry between events, and that will scatter your mind and your soul. Planning a simpler life around gardening, meal preparation, dining, cleaning up, and nice conversation is how we used to do it.

The culture of food convenience pushed by the food industry expelled us from the house and put us out of our bodies and our minds. *Bring it back.* Make food fun and make it sacred again.

Enjoying good food and savoring meals also helps us digest and assimilate. Learning to be thankful for *everything* in your life is a huge part of liberating your consciousness from the delusion of separation, and food is a great place to start. After all, we eat a few times a day and usually do so consistently, so it's a great place to build rituals; you can jump on something that's already a routine and add a life-enhancing hack to it. Bring friends around and eat together with laughter and good times. Being reverent doesn't mean being boring or too serious. You don't have to get weird or make people uncomfortable; saying something like this is fine: "I'd like to give thanks for this wonderful meal we are enjoying with great friends."

Understand that whatever it is that's going into your mouth is going to *be you* in the next few days and weeks. You are literally becoming what you eat, so realizing this will not only help deter you from choosing unhealthy meals, but it'll also help you stoke a relationship with your food, friends, and family to see more clearly into the cycle of life of which we're all a part.

Fasting Done Right

Fasting without deep contemplation is a risky proposition. Trying to run your day at the same velocity while depriving your body of food is stupid. The ancients fasted but spent their time praying and meditating. Don't mix metaphors. If you're going to take a day to fast and drink only water, then take the day to write, relax, and think about life. Sundays are good for this.

If you're part of the Paleo Movement and simply wait to take your first meal, then just be mindful of your exertion levels in the morning. The key is to make sure your adrenals are healthy enough to sustain a blood sugar dip. Young, healthy people can get away with this, but I've seen many a 45-year-old come in with major problems after trying things that were not suitable for them.

A good way to do a fast is to go sunup to sunup the next day as you set aside ample time for silent contemplation. If your blood sugar is stable, a water fast is great. If you have challenges there, certain other recipes may work better for you. There's a guide to fasting you can use on well.org/fasting.

MODERN HACKS

Satiety

Learning ways to curb your appetite is key to winning the battle against weight. Using fiber, water, and healthy fat to do so really helps in the battle of the bulge. Sugar is the devil, and making sure that we temper any sugar we eat (including simple carbohydrates) with fiber and good fats like avocados or coconut oil ensures slower transit time and a blunted insulin release. Also, learning to eat protein and fat preferentially when we're hungry helps us to get out of the sugar addiction and start to burn cleaner fuel.

In fact, in functional medicine, we tell patients that they should consume 1 gram of protein for every kilogram of body weight per day. So if you're 160 pounds, that's roughly 73 kilograms, so you should be getting about 75 grams of protein per day. In my experience, most people fall way short of this number, which is the *baseline* to run the shop that is your body. If you're lifting weights or sick, you may need more. If you're having three meals per day, that means each meal should contain an average of 25 grams of protein (in this example; calculate it for your own weight). In my experience, most people will fall short at breakfast and not hit the total number by nightfall, which puts the body into stress. Not getting enough protein in the morning makes us hungry earlier in the day, and we usually reach for carbs at that point. A simple solution is to use a good protein powder and make sure you get close to one-third of your protein needs each morning. Taking medium-chain triglycerides (MCT) is also a powerful way to stimulate leptin in the brain, which triggers satiety. MCT oil is commercially available, and I like the one at bulletproofexec.com.

For lunch, have some lean turkey with steamed broccoli topped with coconut oil. You could have steamed vegetables with paprika, brown rice, and fish for dinner. There are lots of ways to eat well and get out of the sugar trap. The key is to have lots of vegetables, some lean meats (if you choose to), legumes, and plenty of monounsaturated fatty acids (MUFAs). The fructose in fruit is very fattening, and the body doesn't metabolize it well. Grains should be used sparingly if you're overweight and can be used as quick fuel for athletes. I've included a list of the MUFAs in the Resources section.

Digestive Enzymes

If you're having trouble breaking down food, some enzymes can help. Identify which foods give you trouble and take the appropriate enzyme combo. Starches get broken down differently than proteins. If you have a hard time digesting meats, you may be low in hydrochloric acid. A good functional doctor can really help with this and jump-start your system. You'll find more information on digestive enzymes in the Resources section.

Cortisol

If you don't have a well-rounded approach to weight loss, food alone won't cut it. Go back to Chapters 1 and 4 and make sure you resolve any issues you have with stress and sleep. Modern medicine compartmentalizes too much. The way of the future is to have an integrative approach to your health with lifestyle as the key. An Urban Monk understands how things are interrelated and is a master of life because of this.

ANN'S ACTION PLAN

Ann had a lot of bad habits that were resolved in a few hacks. First off, she never really did the breakfast thing. We were able to provide her with a recipe for a fresh green smoothie with protein that she would create in her blender each morning. Some clean produce with coconut milk, MCT oil, protein, and whatever fresh stuff the CSA dropped off set the tone for her day. This kept her full and happy through lunch. If she needed a snack, some almonds did the trick.

Ann never stopped to eat, and this was our biggest challenge. We had to work with her husband and kids to wrestle time back for meals. It took a couple of months but finally clicked in. We booked in a family dinner each week where they made more than they needed so they could take food to work and school the next day. They started a little garden, and the kids loved it. It gave Ann some time outside with her family that she really began to enjoy.

Changing Ann's diet and especially sugar intake was not all that hard. As soon as she started to eat only real food, she felt a positive change. Her skin cleared up and her energy surged. Her mood started to improve, and she became more active. This felt great, but her weight was still a lingering problem.

We took a look at her urine with an EDTA challenge and found all kinds of toxins. I directed her to a local clinic where she underwent a chelation program, which helped leach heavy metals out of her body. This took 3 months and was a bit of a ride. We took the time to fix her gut lining and support healthy liver function. A few weeks later, something shifted. She started to drop a couple of pounds a week, and they were staying off. It was as if a switch was turned on.

An important lesson in Ann's case is that even with a complete lifestyle change, we sometimes need the help of a good doctor to clean up our past. Once we cleared her food Karma, her weight problem went away and her new diet didn't insult her biology anymore.

Ann enjoys parties again. She takes MCT oil and adds it to veggies before the tempting foods come out. Being satisfied, she doesn't struggle to resist the unhealthy food and can drink her sparkling water and enjoy conversation. Losing the weight was not hard when her frame of reference shifted. Now, this is simply how she lives. Ann realizes now that she's more than just her appearance, and she's reading lots of great books and enjoying good conversation with interesting people at the parties. She no longer cares what she looks like because she's full of life and feels great.

CHAPTER 7

No Connection with Nature or Things That Are Real

ETHAN GREW UP IN Brooklyn, New York. He played on the sidewalk and rode his bike everywhere. If he didn't get home before supper, there'd be hell to pay, but otherwise, he was free to roam. Mom usually made spaghetti or pizza for the kids, and then it was homework time. He'd have to wash his hands before they ate, and all kinds of black stuff would come off from playing handball or basketball on the streets all the time.

There were some trees lining the roads where Ethan grew up, but he never really thought anything of them. They were ornamental at best, and at worst, they were an annoyance because he'd have to fetch his kite out of them every so often.

Ethan's mom was deathly afraid of the outdoors. She thought everything was out to get her. From street dogs to the bears and wolves she'd see on TV, nature was a dangerous place, and she tried her best to shelter her cubs from the wild monsters out there. His dad was too busy working to give a shit. Instead of counterbalancing mom's phobias, dad would unwind with a beer and watch the game. He would yell if the kids got bad grades but certainly wasn't a model scout leader.

Ethan grew up with an unconscious fear of nature and the dangers of the wilderness. Playing on the streets was cool, but the back woods were scary. He is now a marketing consultant in Manhattan who meets his friends for drinks and goes to music festivals for fun. The festivals are often in remote places, and he can't get over his discomfort with how "dirty" it is. Camping is not his thing, but his friends and his new girlfriend love the stuff. Ethan feels like a wimp and is trying to suck it up and enjoy the concerts despite their rough venues.

He goes to the gym routinely and likes to sweat but only showers at home because he doesn't trust the tile floors there. He uses hand sanitizer regularly and takes medications for his allergies. He applies sunblock daily and travels with his own pillow. He's the guy who triple lines the toilet at work with sanitary covers and wipes the bottom of his laptop bag after having to put it on the ground at a restaurant.

It's not easy being Ethan. After all, everything is out to get him.

THE PROBLEM

We all suffer from what Richard Louv, author of *Last Child in the Woods,* calls "Nature-Deficit Disorder." Two to three generations ago, we lived much closer to nature. Our agrarian roots were preceded by millennia of hunting, gathering, herding, and fishing. All of these activities required an innate connection with the natural environment. We needed to understand the birdsongs, read the clouds, know the direction of the wind, follow the currents, identify invasive insects, and tend to a sick cow. Our very survival was tied to this knowledge, and our ancestors rose up the food chain by mastering these valuable skills. They had a deep and profound respect for nature because they understood the thread of life-sustaining nourishment that came from it.

Our genetic memory and lineage had us all closer to the grasses, the trees, the soil, and the elements. Getting enough rain was a matter of life or death. We conserved water because someone had to hike 2 miles to fetch it earlier that morning. When we found food, we rejoiced and gave thanks. If it fell on the floor, we'd dust it off and eat it. There was no room for waste. Scraps went to compost, and bones went to the dogs who protected our land and helped us hunt; even they had purpose and direction.

Today, many of us live in areas where the earth is paved over and our only real access to it is in the "nature zoos" we call parks. From local parks to national forests, we've cordoned Mother Nature off in an attempt to preserve and protect her from ourselves. We encroach . . . we destroy . . . we pollute. We've come to know ourselves as the one animal that walks through the Garden and wrecks it. In the span of just a couple of generations, we developed technologies and synthetic chemicals that have allowed us to isolate ourselves from the natural world and disconnect from this thread of life. We kill off germs with antibiotics; we have air-conditioning in our fast-moving cars; we burn natural gas that comes from faraway lands instead of chopping wood to keep our houses warm, and our food is produced in labs and manufactured in plants.

We used to eat plants.
Now we eat crap that's made in plants.

All of this is taking a physical and psychological toll on us.

Now we have guys like Ethan who walk around big cities drinking fancy beverages that make him thirstier and eating bars wrapped in plastic. We fight wars to secure the oil that makes that plastic, and we fight the cancer that comes from eating the fake food that comes inside that plastic. Then we complain of being tired, fat, sick, and depressed and wonder what doctor or guru has the secret to unlock our problems when all the while we should be looking backward.

We forget where we come from.

We've lost connection with the source of all the life and nutrition we derive, and that's creating a gap in our ability to heal ourselves and connect with the life around us. Losing the connection between our bodies and the food we eat has been a powerful wedge that's splintered humanity into a mob of hungry ghosts stumbling through life looking for cars, purses, diets, pills, or mates to make them feel happy and whole.

It All Starts with the Soil

The environment in which a seed grows is where this story begins. The soil has harbored life for millions of years. Within this rich environment of minerals, nutrients, microbes, worms, and decaying organic matter, we have a glimpse at the miracle of life itself. This is where certain bacteria help convert inorganic matter into the building blocks of life as we know it. It's really at the nodes of certain plants where the good bacteria in the soil help kick-start this party and make everything work for us. The plants grow and prosper under the right conditions, and we eat them for food. We may eat the animals that eat these plants, but the baseline remains the same: pure organic life springing from pure soil where friendly bacteria (and some fungal elements) help seeds grow in the presence of water and sunlight. That's the real stuff. That's the essence of where we come from.

Now? Well, we've gone nuts with our "better living through chemistry" hubris. Farmers roll plastic over their fields and pump methyl bromide into the soil to kill everything 18 inches deep. It is now policy to wipe out life so we can grow food that's also dead. We eat this shit and wonder why we don't feel well. It carries less nutrition, no healthy bacterial cohorts, and certainly no real life force.

We've lost the wisdom of the family farm where the animals and plants coexist on the same land. The chickens would eat the insects, and the goats would eat the weeds. Manure came from animals and not petroleum. The dead plants would compost for next year's harvest, and the animals had names and were honored if they were to be slaughtered.

Dead Food Feeds Dead Souls

Food that doesn't come from natural growth provides us with far less nourishment. Yeah, we can get calories out of it, but is that all there is to life? There's something happening in our modern times that we can all feel but can't put our fingers on. Something is wrong. We scratch our heads and wonder why everyone is tired, sick, unhappy, and out of energy. We do this while we eat a processed muffin, drink dairy from a sick cow, take mood drugs, breathe in lead as we cross the street, and slather on creams that are filled with chemicals we can't pronounce.

The Body Recognizes Nature

For millions of years, our bodies have evolved to become very sensitized to natural compounds. We can determine friend from foe and mount an immune attack on something that doesn't belong in the realm. Now, we have so much bullshit hitting the immigration line that doesn't belong in our bodies that our border patrol agents are pulling their hair out. We're constantly under attack, and our bodies are in rebellion. It took millions of years to evolve into what we are, but in just the span of a couple of generations, we've put so much stress on our systems that millions of people are simply unable to cope with the newly introduced chemicals in our world. What doesn't help is our recent breakup with our natural allies.

The Microbiome

The genius of nature can be witnessed all around us. There's a continuous circuit of life that we hadn't really seen or known to respect. This comes in the form of friendly bacteria that coexist with us and help us thrive. It really is the poetic basis for the word *symbiosis*, which by definition means an "interaction between two different organisms living in close physical association, typically to the advantage of both." Symbiosis is how we peacefully coexist with the life around us and inside of us.

As I mentioned earlier, it starts in the soil. These friendly bacteria help the plants extract minerals and nutrients from the soil in order to grow and become the life that feeds and sustains us. On a personal level, many of these same bacteria have taken up residence in our own bodies. They've been with us the whole way through. In fact, they were here long before we showed up. We developed and evolved *around* an existing system of life transference that was already well articulated.

These bacteria are passed on from mother to child at birth and continue to exchange colonies and information throughout our lives until they return to the soil with our rotting bodies. They are literally with us for the ride, and our relationship with them is so critically important that this is an emerging branch of serious study in medicine. It turns out that these bacteria in our bodies account for more genetic information and encoding than the DNA from our own cells. In fact, it's been suggested that, since there's an estimated 100 trillion cells of bacteria in our bowels alone, we're actually outnumbered.

There's more "not us" than "us" in what we refer to as our bodies.

These cells code for proteins that help us fight off bad bacteria, digest certain foods, produce certain critical vitamins, and much more. Recent studies with fecal grafting even show tremendous improvements in the psychological states of patients who wipe out their own colonies and start over with a seed colony borrowed from the bowels of a healthy person. In fact, all kinds of crazy health issues start to go away in these people. This has blown the lid wide open on the subject, and some really smart people are now looking at health in a dramatically different way. What if killing these friendly bacteria is what's been leading us to get sicker? By wiping out the good bacteria, we are making room for bad, opportunistic colonies to land and wreak havoc. By bombing our internal "soil," we're taking out the good guys and losing our ability to roll with the punches. It turns out good health looks more like a *partnership* with nature.

This is also where we lost the script.

Antibiotics save lives, and there's certainly a place for them, but the rampant overuse of these drugs over the past generation has created an environment where we've systematically wiped out the good with the bad in our guts and created an environment for bad bugs to flourish. Mix that with processed foods, lots of sugars, and no contact with healthy soil, and it's no wonder why so many people are ailing.

Probiotics are being used to combat this now, but the science is really new, and nobody really understands the complexity of the microbiome. Just throwing acidophilus at it seems to *kind of* help, but it is certainly not the answer. The closest thing to the answer we've got currently is getting back to nature and stopping the nonsense; we need to go back to what worked for generations.

In the cities, we are all but cut off from nature. Streets are lined with trees, but how often do we look at them? We have backyards, but we spend most of our time inside in front of the TV. We kill the bees and genetically modify our crops to resist the millions of tons of poison we spray on the earth—poison that chokes out the living biosphere we all live in.

Our kids grow up with colorful plastic toys made in China. We're careful to sanitize them when they come in contact with the dirt, yet we fail to realize that many have lead paint residues that poison us every time we come in contact with them. They can be far more dangerous than the sticks and rocks kids used to play with. We give our money to people who make unsafe toys for our kids to play with because we're too busy working indoors and need to lock them up inside so they don't go out and get hurt.

The kids want to go outside.

We live in a delusion that it's "man versus nature" and have forgotten that we, too, *are* nature. This is where Ethan has gone wrong. He has no relationship with the earth and feels disconnected from and afraid of the very environment from which he sprang. The something that's missing in his life is actually all around him, but he won't let it in. Why? Because his mom convinced him that germs were bad.

Public Health and the Black Death

There was certainly a time when the germs were winning, but we need to unpack the history of this a bit. Modern medicine loves to take credit for everything, but this victory belongs to the realm of public health and sanitation.

The first bubonic plague happened in the Byzantine Empire under Justinian I around the 6th century, and the nasty one that followed in Europe was in the late Middle Ages (1340–1400). The first one wiped out an estimated 25 to 50 million people, and the second one (the Black Death) killed one-third of the human population. This shit was no joke.

The disease was carried in fleas on small rodents, and it got around fast. The question is why and how did it get out of hand, and we know that answer.

We started to move to more urban settings and live within cities where there was very poor sanitation. People would dump feces out of their windows onto city streets, and the towns were disgusting. With shit everywhere, the rats were happy, and they carried the bad bugs that festered in this disgusting human soup. That's what was killing us.

Once we figured out that plumbing and clean water helped, things got way better. With better street cleaning, garbage pickup, and basic human hygiene, we came through it. An interesting note is that the occurrences in Jewish populations were far lower because it was in their religious tradition to wash their hands before meals; again, hygiene wins.

So the short story here is that bad bacteria fester in bad environments, and, yes, there's a need for good sanitation and drugs to combat outbreaks, but the genetic memory of death and pestilence that has been handed down in certain families is a bit untethered to the reality. The soil around the organic radish you just pulled up is not the same as the sewage that brought the plague. We're at a time in history where we're really looking at how much baby we've thrown out with the bathwater and finding a new balance in our relationship with the earth. Good bugs are our friends. They help us fight off the bad guys and also help us express our vitality. Rekindling our relationship with the web of life that surrounds us is really the next frontier in medicine. It's a new way of looking at health that respects the role of friendly microorganisms in the big picture of life, in a new model of personal and planetary health.

URBAN MONK WISDOM

The ancient Taoist sages learned everything from their keen observation of nature. They followed the changes in the seasons, the movement of animals, the properties of medicinal plants, and the patterns of weather in the sky. They knew that we are part of this grand symphony called nature and that it has a "way," or the Tao, as they called it.

The careful observation of the fluctuations of the signature of life *through nature* gives us tremendous insight into ourselves. After all, this is where we come from, and this is where an immense treasure of genetic memory and innate wisdom resides. Everything has an energetic signature, and the energy fields of living things are robust and beautiful. When we walk through a natural environment, we're bathed in the pure energy of the life all around us and can feel part of this web again. There's a symbiotic array of life blossoming, and we're swimming in it. My kung fu Grand Master taught us that, in nature, usually within 100 feet of where you are standing, you can find an herb or a plant that can help you with whatever you are ailing from. He demonstrated this to us many times.

Nature is like an encyclopedia of life that is all around us. When the anthropologist Jeremy Narby wanted to study the roots of medicinal wisdom in the Amazon, he encountered a perplexing dilemma. For years, researchers would go to the shamans and ask them what they had for certain ailments. The shamans would come up with some crazy concoction of several leaves, roots, and other plant parts, mix them up, and boil them. Amazingly, they worked. The researchers would take the brews, study and isolate the active ingredients, run off and patent them, make billions of dollars, and *maybe* say thanks.

What Narby noticed was that each time the shamans were asked how they knew what to mix out of the impossibly large number of combinations of plants in the jungles, their answer was typically the same: "The plants told us." This was usually the point where the scientists would shake their heads and walk away to make their fortunes on the jungle's back. Narby had the wisdom to stop and ask, "What if we were to take these shamans' statements at face value?" He went to the Amazon and asked them to explain this phenomenon, and once they sensed he was sincere, they proceeded to show him. Essentially, they would take a psychotropic brew called *ayahuasca* and enter into ceremony. In this altered state, the spirits of the plants would communicate with them and the wisdom was handed down. Being a good scientist, Narby decided to partake and see what they were talking about. He was not disappointed. Narby realized so much about the nonverbal communication between plants and humans in his journeys and wrote a fabulous book on the subject, *The Cosmic Serpent*. Narby postulates that there is a subtle language that our cells understand in the zipping and unzipping of our DNA strands that connects us with all other DNA. Somehow, there's a universal language of "Creation" through our common DNA that connects us with all life, and the shamans have learned to tap into this with their use of *ayahuasca*.

This was very impactful for me because my Taoist teacher taught us to sit in the woods and meditate and then use our Shen, or spiritual sight, to communicate with the plants and have very similar experiences. We had learned to meditate on a plant or a tree and connect with its life force. After a while, I began to experience subtle communication with the consciousness of the plant and was able to learn from it. There's nothing more profound than having an actual *experience* of this. Do not believe me: Later in this chapter, I'll show you how to try it and you can *see* for yourself.

Following Nature Is Key to Our Liberation from Delusion

Syncing up with nature calms us and shows us our own inner nature. The more we can harmonize with this, the clearer and calmer we are. The more we tie into this, the more the energy of nature can flow through us and the lighter our footsteps are. Our forefathers hunted in small packs, crept around slowly and quietly, and learned to listen to the wind and detect minute scents from miles away. Awareness led to survival, and it was all anchored in Nature. The plants called on us to eat them and use them for medicine, and the animals often became our allies in transportation, protection, and farming (in this case, not always voluntarily). Our smaller tribes usually had a shaman who would lead us to the plant wisdom and connect us with the spiritual nature of our experience. There was *sentience* that permeated our lives—trees, plants, animals, insects, and yes, even rocks.

Learning to meditate in nature helps us tap into this underlying sentience. It helps us understand that we're never alone in the sea of life that surrounds us. More important, it helps us connect to all other life and wake up to our true identity. The reason why people are lost is because they're disconnected from the thread of life force that is carried through nature, and specifically, from the deep spiritual connection we have with all the life around us. Once that is back in place, there is no emptiness. I'll share some powerful practices with you to help you do this later in this chapter.

Nature Carries Life Force

An Urban Monk is at one with nature. He understands how *all things* are alive, and he links up with the life force of the nature around him to draw energy, inspiration, and clarity. Many a monk in my tradition was tasked to go into the mountains and cultivate their qi. What does this mean? It means connecting with the mountain. It means learning to follow the language of nature and be led to food and shelter. It means silencing our monkey minds and learning to listen to the buzz of life all around us. From there, we learn of our internal universe and learn to move, gather, concentrate, and refine qi energy within our own bodies. We wake up our internal stars (or chakras) and breathe life force into them. We monks were not to come down until we'd found that inner power, and there is no way to touch it without knowing our place in the natural world. Once that's anchored in, we take it with us everywhere. We can be standing in the middle of a busy city and be anchored into the earth like a giant oak tree.

Is this necessary for the Urban Monk? Yes.

Getting into the wild and finding the silence, peace, health, and abundance of energy that comes from some concentrated time in nature is critical so we can *calibrate* back to our essential selves. I like to get out once a quarter for at least a couple of days without my phone or e-mail. I'll hike into the wilderness with my backpack and a couple days' worth of food. Occasionally, I'll even rent a small cabin and hang back with the family in the woods for a few days. The key with this is to have a home base and spend your days out in the wild. Just a quick reset can go a long way when you are immersed in nature. It helps us remember our roots and origins so we can have something to draw upon when we're back in the thick of it at home. We stretch our energetic roots back into the soil and remember to drink fully. Once our thirst is quenched, it's easier to remember that peace is only a few breaths away.

Bringing It Home

Modern society's onslaught of the natural world is fundamentally imbalanced and dangerous. This doesn't mean we need to abandon our cities; there are some wonderful movements springing up that tastefully leave room for nature to thrive and coexist with us in our buildings and development. Urban gardening, rooftop gardens, indoor plants, tree houses, and organic architecture are all wonderful movements to look at. Walking together with nature is the way forward, and we're seeing this in urban planning, solar panels, air plants, green walls, backyard gardens, EMF-shielded rooms, air-purified rooms, VOC-sinking plants, and so much more. This is the next frontier. Getting out into nature is great and highly recommended, but bringing it back to the cities is what's going to fundamentally shift our planet.

An Urban Monk brings nature home.

She surrounds herself with nature and purity and curates her environment to *include life* all around her. From household plants to vegetable gardens, we can have an amazing culture of coexistence with nature all around us. Instead of isolating ourselves from nature, we can honor her and bring her with us everywhere. This certainly doesn't take away from protecting vast swaths of land for animals to freely roam, but it definitely helps us bring balance to our modern lives.

Remember, an Urban Monk draws from a position of power and strength. People are easily leveraged if they are disconnected from the earth. No roots, no home, and no survival skills lead to slaves that'll do what you tell them for money. Look around you. They are everywhere: wage slaves who are miserable in jobs they can't afford to leave. They have forsaken their dreams and aspirations and are stuck being a pawn in someone else's vision. This comes directly from being uprooted from their power, their connection to nature. They are hungry and don't recognize the natural food and medicine growing out of the ground. Our job is to wake them up. First, we take care of ourselves and ignite our own energy flow, and then we can help our friends and family by leading by example. We never left the Garden; we were simply duped into forgetting how to live in the very environment from which we came. In fact, according to shamanic teacher Alberto Villoldo, PhD, we in the West are the only culture that sees itself outside of the Garden, ejected and cast into a life of punishment and guilt. All the other native traditions see themselves in coexistence with Nature and don't have the "ejection trauma" built into their narrative. This has arguably led us to tear through the Earth and treat her as an object over which we have dominion. It is now time to cut that bullshit and get real. That model is killing the planet, and we can choose a better way.

EASTERN PRACTICES
Root Down

One of the most powerful ways to connect with the energy of the earth and literally tap into it is by doing the "Tree" qigong practice. It is designed to connect our energy field up with the earth under our

PERSONAL JOURNEYS

When I was a monk, we did a fair amount of kung fu training that enhanced our awareness of energy fields. This helps us predict someone's intention and the nature of their possible attack, which is super helpful in a scuffle. I began to take this to the next level and spent a fair amount of time learning to see energy coming off of plants at night. Once my eyes had adjusted, I'd begin to walk and feel my way around a natural environment. With practice, I was able to run trails at night during a new moon without any light sources. It required meticulous attention and full presence because any slipup would mean my front teeth. It was badass, and I always walked off that mountain feeling very alive.

feet and to keep us drawing from this abundant source at all times. The best part is, once you get good at this one, you can do it anywhere at any time. Nobody knows that you're doing it, and yet you're drinking from Infinity and anchoring your power all the while. Here's the practice:

○ Stand with your feet shoulder-width apart.

○ Touch the tip of your tongue to the roof of your mouth.

○ Gently breathe in and out of your nose down to your lower dantian (three fingers below your navel).

○ Now on the next exhale, visualize imaginary roots that extend from your feet 2 to 3 feet down into the earth.

○ On the next inhale, visualize white light drawing up from the earth through your roots all the way up your legs, into your torso, down your arms, and to the top of your head.

○ Now on the exhale, project your roots another 2 to 3 feet down into the earth.

○ Inhale and repeat, drinking up the roots to the top of your head.

○ Keep this going for several breaths until you visualize your roots eventually tapping into the very core of the planet.

○ At this point, just chill out and breathe energy up your roots on the inhale and simply feel the core of the earth on the exhales.

○ This obviously doesn't need to go to scale or 2 to 3 feet per breath would take weeks to get to the core. Take several breaths and then project your roots to tap the core within 4 to 5 minutes.

○ When you are ready to move on, simply return your breathing to your lower dantian and go about your day; there's no need to disconnect from the earth. In fact, the more often you do this, the better your connection will be and the more rooted you'll feel in your daily life.

Silent Walking in Nature

This is a powerful exercise I learned as a tracker and also from both Native American wisdom and my Taoist teacher. Essentially, get out into a natural setting and start practicing "empty stepping." We've become big, clumsy animals for a variety of reasons. The first is that we eat too much and carry far too much weight on our torsos. Another is that we sit in unnatural positions too often and our hips don't work correctly anymore, making our steps clumsy. The third is that we've insulated ourselves from nature and survival enough to become woefully unaware of our own literal footprint. You can tell a lot about a person by their footprint, and any good tracker can see this. This was part of our genetic wisdom and is lost to most people, but not to an Urban Monk.

In this exercise, go outside and start walking very slowly and methodically. Inhale as you raise your one knee up and then slowly exhale as your foot rolls from heel to toe on the ground. Now repeat on the other side. The goal at first is to slow your gait and develop balance in your step. You should not be able to hear your footsteps at all.

At first, you'll feel shaky and awkward—that's the office chair talking. Once your hips start to fire correctly again, you will gain strength in your core, which will help you pull up from your dantian as you walk. This will connect your legs to your core and your breath again.

As you get better, start doing this in different areas and on different surfaces. Once you can do it on dry fall foliage and not hear yourself, you'll know you've arrived. To see what this looks like, check out the video at theurbanmonk.com/ch7/naturewalk.

Once you've honed this skill, apply the same time dilation and calm demeanor to observing the patterns of nature around you. Slowing down puts us in a position to learn from Mother Nature, the greatest teacher of all.

Stream Meditation

This is one of my favorite pastimes from my monk days and is still one of the most powerful forms of earth medicine I know. I would do this practice routinely over the years, and it did more for my sanity and personal growth than most things I read in books.

Get out into nature and find yourself a river or a flowing stream that you can sit next to for a few hours. Make sure you have some privacy so you can unwind into the practice. Typically, I'd go into the backcountry and spend a full day doing this practice in an isolated area with nobody around for miles. If you have that luxury, take it. If not, find something that'll work for now.

- Sit a few feet from the water and get comfortable. You're going to be there for a while. If you're not in an area where there is a risk of flash flooding, I'd consider finding a rock in the middle of the stream and sitting on it facing *upstream* so the water is coming at you all day, cleansing your energy field and washing away the layers of bad energy that have latched onto your field.

- Have a seat and have a sweater or jacket handy so you don't need to go anywhere for a while. Drinking water should be nearby. Basically, get ready to stay there for a few hours.

- Slowly breathe in and out of your nose to your lower dantian. Take a few minutes to drop into your breath and settle in.

- Now listen to the sound of the water and start breathing with it. Allow the sound to wash away all other thoughts. Tie your breath to it and spend a good 20 to 30 minutes locking into this state.

- Gently breathe in and out as the water flows by.

- You'll notice thoughts popping up. That's normal. Simply acknowledge them and allow the water to wash them away. Each time you notice that you've gotten caught in the eddy of a thought chain, simply breathe and return to listening to the stream. Release the thought to the water and see if it floats away. Eventually, you'll get the hang of this, and the noise will start to diminish as the sound of the water permeates your being.

This will take some practice, so you need to be patient with it. My rule was that I wouldn't get up until I felt cleansed and all I heard was the stream. You'll know it when you arrive because there'll be a moment when you disappear and the stream is all there is. That's a good thing. There are powerful lessons in this practice about who we really are. Enlisting Mother Nature in helping us tap into the state of eternal flow is good medicine. Some students get startled and feel like they are tumbling down the river when their ego checks back in, but that's normal. Once we let go of our insistence on being the person we pretend to be, we can have fun discovering who we really are. I've done this practice often and had amazing experiences where many of the wild animals didn't even notice me anymore. That's when you know you've done it, when the river has washed away all your "crazy" and you have totally blended in with the natural environment.

Communicating with Plant Spirits

As promised, here's the practice for communicating with plants. It doesn't start with stumbling into the wild and asking plants to talk with you, and although I am a fan of the therapeutic value of *ayahuasca,* I feel it's been terribly misused of late and taken by people who are not ready for that journey. That being said, under the guidance of a true shaman, it is great medicine.

Here's the practice:

○ Sit in a natural place with no distractions and take a book or app with you that'll help you identify the medicinal qualities of the plants in that region. In the old days, you'd ask a shaman or use trial and error. Today, we can Google things.

○ Pick a plant that you have an affinity toward and sit or stand across from it. Start breathing to your lower dantian for a few breaths and keep your gaze soft and slightly unfocused on a leaf, a trunk, or the whole plant. Just start to sync your breath up with the plant and connect with it. You can use your third eye or your heart to reach out. You will quickly find that each plant (or life form for that matter) has a distinct personality, so come in softly and introduce yourself respectfully. State your intentions and ask if you can learn from it. Most plants are very helpful and kind. Begin a nonverbal conversation with it and (I know this may sound crazy to some, but just roll with it) see what comes of it. Ask if it has any medicinal power it can share and what it could be used for.

○ Don't just go plucking leaves off of a life form; rule number one in wild crafting is to ask permission before you pick.

○ You may hear something and you may not. This may take a while to get. If you do get a hit, thank the plant and then go validate it in your book, by Google, or however else you can. If you have your phone with you, get your answer and then shut it off.

Don't just go eating random plants, as they may be poisonous. Once your intuition and prowess at plant communication are established and *validated,* then the fun begins. You will never be alone again once you realize that there's a symphony of life and wisdom surrounding you at all times.

MODERN HACKS
Learning Primitive Skills

One of the most valuable skills an Urban Monk can have is to learn how to survive in nature. This was a given for our species for millennia, and in my opinion, the lack of this knowledge is why so many people are lost today. What kind of dumb animal forgets how to survive in the very environment it evolved in? That's humanity.

Wilderness survival training is fun and very rewarding. The core essentials we need to live, as taught by my good friend and survival expert Cliff Hodges, are:

Learning to make fire

Learning to get clean water

Learning to get food

Learning to make shelter

Once you have those four, you're alive. Those are your needs and everything else becomes a "want." This is a powerful lesson because most people are suffering because of their "wants" in our society. Keeping it real and learning to go back to our roots, we learn to recalibrate our "stress bucket" and stop worrying about the bullshit.

An immense sense of ease and comfort comes when we learn how to survive on our own in the wild. It is like taking away a huge burden of existential angst that we carry and can't explain in the modern world. Urban Monks learn these skills and know they can handle themselves. Classes on the subject are taught all over the world. Learning how to create fire by friction is essential, and several clips online can show you how. However, doing it is a whole other story, so you must practice to get it right. Once you've nailed it, then you have something that nobody can take away from you—a life skill.

Volunteering

A great way to get out there and connect with nature is to align with a cause that already has activities going on in your area. The Sierra Club is one of many organizations that run these types of activities. State and national parks need volunteers all the time. Getting out there is powerful, and doing so with like-minded people who are *of service* to the world is really good stuff. You'll make friends, make a difference, and have a little crutch to help you feel more at ease out in the wild. Over time, this doesn't replace the need for some personal alone time in nature, so use it as an orientation into the wild and then grow your nature time from there. Many of these organizations will help train you on valuable skills and also connect you with resources that matter.

Backcountry Backpacking

This is one of my favorite things to do and has been amazingly therapeutic to everyone I've recommended it to, even if they don't feel that way at the time. Getting out into the wild and living out of a backpack is primal and pure. That's how we used to roll, and it taps into our genetic memory of this. Backpacking makes us really consider what "stuff" we actually need and what is superfluous. Why? Because you've got to carry the shit. A few miles into a trip, you really start to wonder what the hell is in that bag. Seasoned backpackers travel as light as they can. They are in sync with the survival principles we spoke of earlier. We need food, fire, water, and shelter—that's it. Getting back into the wild lets us roam freely and choose where to call home each night. It gives us the freedom to know that "home" is with us at all times and that we really have nowhere we need to run back to. We're good. We've got all our "stuff" and can relax into enjoying this lake, stream, or meadow.

Getting out in the fresh air, we can burn off some fat, get some sunshine, and reconnect with nature in a meaningful way. Getting out there with friends, family, dogs, and a good book is an amazing and inexpensive form of recreation. Make sure you take some personal quiet time while out there and don't squander your access to the purity of nature with just small talk.

Local Parks

If you live in an urban environment, chances are you have some public park or green belt within a few miles of your house. It's not quite the wilderness we've been talking about, but you should take what you can get and grow it out from there.

I walk my dogs to our local park daily and get some time running with them on the grass. It's not quite Yosemite, but I'll take it. It's like a mini nature shot in the arm in between bigger trips, but just enough to anchor the qi and connect with some trees and grass.

Nature is powerful. Think of the sprout that breaks through a crack in a concrete sidewalk in order to live. That's the energy of nature, and it resides inside of all of us. Find a place to tap into it in your area and frequent that place. Maybe bring a blanket and a book or take the kids. The moral of the story: It is free, it is healthy, and it is where you come from. Find a park.

Houseplants and Home Gardens

Bringing nature home is a key ingredient in our reconnection with life. Sure, getting into the wild is awesome, but let's face it: We've all got jobs and shit to do in town. Indoor plants are amazing. They help establish ambiance and calm us down, and many of them help act as carbon syncs for volatile organic compounds that are in the air. They also remind us about the basics of life—needing water, good soil, and sunlight.

As mentioned before, home gardens are also the way forward. Lawns just waste water. Gardens give us food and help us connect with it. Gardening helps us commune with nature on a regular basis and remember the important things in life—the fundamentals of life itself.

Probiotics and Prebiotic Diets

The complex mix of good bacteria found in healthy human guts is something we're just beginning to understand, but one thing is certain: Getting plenty of healthy prebiotic foods helps create the right environment for good bacteria, and eating lots of fermented (unpasteurized) foods helps establish and maintain those colonies. Prebiotic foods contain fibers that don't digest well, so they create an environment where good bacteria can thrive as they pass through us. Essentially, not all the food we eat is for us. Fibers like chicory root don't break down in our stomachs or small intestines very well. This means they arrive in the large intestine ready to feed the helpful bacteria we harbor there. We feed them and they take care of us. The fiber helps clean our intestines and also supports our bacterial friends.

Here's a list of good prebiotic foods:

Raw chicory root: 64.6 percent prebiotic fiber by weight

Raw Jerusalem artichoke: 31.5 percent prebiotics by weight

Raw dandelion greens: 24.3 percent prebiotic fiber by weight

Raw garlic: 17.5 percent prebiotics by weight

Raw leek: 11.7 percent prebiotic fiber by weight

Raw onion: 8.6 percent prebiotic fiber by weight

Cooked onion: 5 percent prebiotic fiber by weight

Raw asparagus: 5 percent prebiotic fiber by weight

Raw wheat bran: 5 percent prebiotic fiber by weight

Wheat flour, baked: 4.8 percent prebiotic fiber by weight

Raw banana: 1 percent prebiotic fiber by weight

Here's a list of foods high in good bacteria (probiotics):

Tempeh	Kefir
Miso	Kombucha
Sauerkraut	Kimchi
Yogurt	

Take a big spoonful of one of these probiotic foods per day, and you'll hedge your bet against bad bacterial overgrowth. Include the prebiotic ones in your recipes, and you've got the winning formula. Make sure you go big on these after antibiotic use to restore your colonies, but taking a little a day also helps offset the loss from those that die off due to minute amounts of antibiotics found in traditional meats, too.

ETHAN'S ACTION PLAN

Ethan, like Ann from the previous chapter, was also born in the C-section generation. His mom's doctor convinced her to have one, as it'd be so much easier and was a fad at the time. Both mom and Ethan went on antibiotics from day one of his life, and he never got a healthy dose of good bacteria to start his life journey. Having mom preach the fear of nature didn't help either.

We spent some time adjusting his diet to get some insoluble fiber, prebiotics, and good fermented foods in. He liked sauerkraut, so I turned him on to a resource where he learned to make his own. He enjoyed it, and the ritual of preparing his own "medicine" was a nice play for Ethan.

He joined a local hiking club and started to get out there. He found that he was good at rock climbing, so we encouraged him to get going with it. It took about a year or so for him to really start getting comfortable with tent camping on his trips, but the fear gradually started to fade into the background. It helps to not be surrounded by people who suck. His new friends helped him get over it and move on in life. They sat around campfires and enjoyed their evenings after a long day of climbing.

I sent him on a wilderness survival trip, and it changed his life. He really got it and realized how fearful he was around so many things. When he was able to strike fire for his first time, it was like a religious experience, a rite of passage. The scared little boy was now a self-sufficient young man.

He grew up washing "black stuff" off his filthy hands after playing on the streets of Brooklyn. Now, he climbs and eats trail mix with his dusty hands, and it doesn't freak him out.

The climbing gym replaced the weights while he was in town, and he took his weekends to play out in the hills as often as he could. Access was hard from Manhattan, but he got time in Central Park and also started kayaking some local rivers.

The concerts were more enjoyable now, but he started to prefer some quiet time in the woods. Ethan actually developed a nice meditation practice, and it really helped him calm down. He'd still jump when a bug would crawl on his leg, but he learned to smile and go back to silence; the instinct will take a while to reverse, but the charge around it has gone. Ethan is now much more relaxed and has really found a home in nature.

CHAPTER 8

Lonely despite Being Surrounded by People

MARK HAD NO IDEA how he ended up where he was in life. He had friends in high school and got along well with people. He had a few girlfriends over the years and was okay with the ladies. He almost got to ring shopping at one point, but things shifted and that didn't work out. She was a nice girl, but there was some family drama that broke the deal.

He's a personal trainer who takes good care of his appearance. His clients like him, and he's got a great physique. He commutes more than an hour to get to the gym and puts in long, hard days. Actually, he mostly stands around and counts reps, but somehow his clients need that. What his clients don't know is that he sneaks out during breaks to smoke. They are also unaware of the fact that, after work, he drives home, drinks a 12-pack of beer, and watches TV till about midnight every night. He visits family on weekends when he can, but mostly, when he's not working, Mark is sitting around watching TV and drinking in isolation.

He's not quite sure how his life ended up this way. A few disappointing social encounters may have started it, and his last breakup made him question the whole shitshow. He makes statements like "people suck" and "all the good girls are taken" routinely to his clients, and they laugh about it. What the clients don't realize is that

Mark actually believes this now. Or maybe he needs to believe it because the alternative explanation is too hard to accept—that he's slipped into depression and social isolation, that he's now an alcoholic and his social phobias are derailing his life.

After all, why would a good-looking, super-fit, personable guy lock himself in and waste the best years of his life watching bullshit TV? The answer is all around us. Mark is not alone, and that's the irony. Millions of people are not alone in *being alone*.

THE PROBLEM

Despite being surrounded by millions, many people feel totally alone and isolated in our world. Like Mark, they tolerate people as best they can during the day, only to retreat home to a lonely life in front of the TV or spending countless hours goofing off online. We're still looking for connection, but somehow the broadband digital use of this word isn't as fulfilling. Faster Internet isn't solving this connection problem.

You could have a thousand Facebook friends and yet have nobody you can call to talk about your day. You could have a large network of old friends in your hometown who have no idea how depressed and miserable you are. The conversations are superficial and idiotic. The time together revolves around sporting events, birthdays, and weddings. Millions rally around sports, throwing their passion behind the ups and downs of a team they superficially identify with.

What ever happened to playing sports?

We've become a culture of nonparticipants: We watch others play sports while we eat chips, drink beer, and are elated or depressed based on the outcome of these games. We have our teams and our favorite players, and our moods are dependent on their variant performances. We wear their jerseys and follow their lives, often closer than those of our own children. We watch dating and travel shows instead of getting out there, and we play apps in alternative realities instead of tending to our own lives.

Millions feel totally alone and isolated inside of their married lives. You may have a husband and three kids but be dying inside. You married early and the math penciled out then: Let's make some babies and start a life together. As time stretched on, shit got hard. The kids don't let you sleep, and you lost your personal time. Your spouse comes home and watches sports, and you want to talk about design, philosophy, or child rearing, or maybe you just want to make love and he's not getting your cues. Maybe you've gotten tired of having to ask for it. A whole industry makes romance novels to serve this need, but again, reading about it isn't quite the same.

Some people feel ashamed about where life has led them. Their dreams and vision for the future didn't quite pan out, and they are stuck in some whatever job doing menial work and feeling unfulfilled. They feel like they should have amounted to something by now and live in a state of dismay and regret over a series of bad decisions they made or failures they've experienced. They often get into rationalization about how they ended up here. Maybe there's a spouse to blame. Maybe an illness swept in and derailed those plans. It could be that those good times lasted too long, and the drugs and alcohol led to a hazy decade that pulled them out of the flow of life. It is all fun and games until it isn't.

A huge component of this problem lies in self-image. We have a false sense of what we "should" be like—what we should look like, how we should dress, what we should do, how we should have fun. Many feel guilty about the extra 50 pounds they are carrying around. The TV says we need to look a certain way, wear certain clothes, and be up on all things "cool," but the reality is that it is impossible for anyone to fit that mold. That's why so many Hollywood stars and supermodels get into drug problems. It's all bullshit, yet the majority of the civilized world aspires to look like and be like the facades they see on TV. People feel ugly, old, drained, and insecure when facing the option of going out there in the world. The beautiful people will judge you until their own wrinkles start to show. Then they pay doctors to fix their facades so they can keep pretending to be better than the rest of us.

I'm not sure what's more depressing: going to the mall or not going. When we get out there, it seems the public spaces are filled with crazy weird people with whom we have nothing in common. There's never parking, and it can get pretty aggravating waiting for someone to take your money so you can get this stuff home. Enter online shopping and further isolation. Staying home has never been easier. The UPS guy isn't really your friend. He's actually in a hurry to get you to sign so he can run his route and get home to catch the game.

Today, the circle is broken.

As hunter-gatherers we traveled in small groups, and there was neither time nor patience for isolation. Someone would come grab you and pull you into the circle. Attempts to connect us through nationalism, religion, team allegiance, or school spirit often miss the mark, and millions of people fall out, getting lonelier and more isolated. Our need to belong to something comes from earlier circuitry in our brains that connects us with other mammals. As we climb the ladder of evolution up from our "reptilian" brain, where we deal with survival and the basics, we move into the "animal" brain, where social order and belonging are important. We need to know our place in the herd. We need to know where we stand in the pecking order. Unfortunately, the media places us pretty low. From flashy rap stars to tours of billionaires' homes, we are told the score every day. *These* people matter and you really don't. The only way you can be a part is to buy the cheaply manufactured merchandise they've slapped their names on and be a fan. They are the stars, not you. The industry has plucked the stars out of the sky and planted them on Hollywood Boulevard: Here's who *we* say is important to follow.

The media tells us that the world is dangerous and that we need the police to protect us. Death and destruction also get better news ratings, it seems. We are shell-shocked as we lock our doors and open them only for the pizza guy or the FedEx lady bringing our latest shipment from Amazon Prime.

Our drive toward sex helps force us to get out there and meet people, but the problem is that nobody taught us how to authentically communicate. Online dating helps a bit, but eventually, we need to sit across from another human being and communicate, and that's gotten so awkward. New apps and dating sites make dating into a sex slot machine where we can use each other for physical needs and quickly go back into social isolation.

The older we get, the harder it seems to be to meet somebody as we get pickier and more set in our ways. We grow bitter, yet we crave connection. We busy ourselves, yet we long to connect. We long to be touched, heard, understood, and loved. We're lonely and can't figure our way out. Drugs, alcohol, porn, video games, serialized TV, and social media are all distractions for us. They layer on some noise to keep us distracted from what's really going on; the truth of the matter is too painful to see.

We are disconnected from our Eternal nature and are therefore terrified that this is it—that all our problems will keep getting heavier, and that, as time passes, things will get worse.

Feb 5/18
1:11 Thoughtof
SWM & Alex
email.

URBAN MONK WISDOM

The reality is that every single one of us is destined to be a star. By this I'm not referring to some status that the sociopaths in Hollywood and New York confer on us, but in the real sense of the word. How can we step into our destined path and live the life of our dreams? How can we tap into our purpose and align our personal ambitions with planetary good? How can we gain access to our inner wisdom and experience self-realization? The essence of alchemy is the ignition of spiritual centers within our bodies and the ignition of the Light that eternally flows from the Source of which we are part. It is said that Jesus was the Son of God. Well, in Hermetic wisdom, he is attributed to the sixth Sephiroth called Tiphareth, which is the Sun Center. He was in a real sense considered the "Sun" of God because he ignited his Light Body and showed that he could be a Light Unto Himself. Now whether you believe in Jesus or not, the story teaches us something important. From my Taoist lineage, to the Tibetans, to the Incan and Mayan shamans, to the Western traditions, there's a living body of wisdom that teaches us how to activate our Light Body and tap into the energy of the Eternal Will to Good. The halo depicted above the great Masters' heads was to illustrate what happens when we wake up and come to life. It was a depiction of what people actually

Halo

saw around the sages and is what practitioners can expect to attain with a spiritual practice.

The exoteric religions of the world have really limited our access to this wisdom because they've watered it down and distracted humanity from the truth. They've worked to leverage our "animal brain" need to belong and made religion much more about community than personal spiritual growth. They've run out the mystical and watered it down to a degree where people are leaving in droves. Why? Because people sense how empty it has become, how commercial and contrived. On dating sites, the number one designation now for "religion" is "spiritual but not religious." People are over it but still need something to tap into. People feel a connection with life and light that transcends the old stories of kings and homicidal brothers from the Bible. These tales held our society together for millennia, however, so we are in need of a new ethical code—a new narrative that supports a changing world.

Back to Our Roots

Our drive toward individuation has led us on a path of unchecked growth and advancement, which has also pulled the rug out from under us on the home front. Historically, we come from strong family traditions; our ancestors grew up in small tribes and had extended families that supported and cared for them. They lived in a symbiotic web of support for defense, foraging, hunting, and interconnection. The modern Western world has seen the destruction of the strong family unit.

In the New World, the original colonists had very zealous and extreme religious views that drove them away from the fabric of society. They left everything to start over and have the freedom to practice their beliefs. This helped them break away from oppressive regimes at home. It also helped them justify slaughtering the natives they found here and burning scores of women they accused of performing witchcraft. They were in a rough new world where there was room for rapid expansion for personal gain. So what if Mom and Pops are in Delaware? I hear there's plenty of land and opportunity in the West, so let's do this! The glue had come undone.

Yeah, families come with codependency and drama, but they also come with support, comfort, pooled resources, and people who care for you. The splintering of the Western family has been a tear in the fabric of our society. Now, kids can't wait to move out at 18, but they struggle to make ends meet. Instead of having the support of their family to get a better education, learn about the world, share costs, and cook collaboratively, they are driven to wait tables and work two other jobs in order to have their "freedom." This leaves no time or space for personal growth and creates a society filled with isolated people living in small apartments all wondering why the American Dream isn't panning out for them. If you look at immigrant families, many of them live under the same roof and work together to "make it" in the West. This happened with the Italians, Irish, Mexicans, Indians, Chinese, and pretty much every other Old World race that arrived in the New World. They work hard, get the kids into college, and build a future for themselves. The isolation comes a couple of generations later when the kids confuse freedom with debt slavery as they bite into the wrong "dream."

A Balanced Family Life

An Urban Monk finds balance between the invasive currents of family affairs and a culture of personal isolation; this balance revolves around *spiritual work*. What if we could grow together? How about gardening as a family? There are many ways we can hack our environment to instill healthy activities we can do with our loved ones. Taking walks, riding bikes, playing board games, listening to audio books, or cooking together are all great ways to hang out while doing something good for yourself.

If you live far from your loved ones, you can use Skype or Facetime to literally hang with each other in the room while you do things. The point is to be there for each other and know that there's no need to fill the silence with small talk. If you've got something to say, then say it. If not, enjoy being together and holding space. This is a lost art that you can bring back. If your family is hard to deal with, heal where you can and find a new "family" you can bond with on deeper levels. We need this connection deep down, and the loss of it causes anxiety and emptiness in our lives. Take it back!

When we connect deeply with others,
we are whole.

We can be there with our families and friends and be present. We can take a sip from Infinity and not feel thirsty all the time. Balancing the codependency of family life starts with learning to get what we need from the Source and not resenting others for not giving us that which they cannot give. They have their own stuff going on, and our job is to support one another and not blame our loved ones for getting in the way of our dreams.

Monks practice social isolation because they need the time to contemplate reality and cultivate their inner power. When they come down from the mountain, they are all smiles and are usually very approachable and kind. They have spent ample time taking care of themselves and are *full*. This allows them to be loving and caring toward others. Why? Because they took the time to dig in. They faced discomfort and are okay with being alone. After all, what is it about ourselves that we don't want to be left alone with? *That* is where the good stuff is. That is where an Urban Monk mines for spiritual gold and comes up with the real treasure.

As a householder, take what time you can get. A couple of hours on a Saturday is a great start. Take turns with your spouse if there are kids to tend to, but *cover each other* so you can both fill up your tanks and become whole. When this is communicated correctly, we can support each other's pursuits in life.

The irony is that every moment is an opportunity to tap into Infinity and drink from it. What we see as dead time, loneliness, and social isolation is actually an incredible gift. It means we actually *have the time* to develop a personal practice and dig into the good stuff. Just this shift in perspective will change your life forever.

Killing Time Is Killing Yourself

Time is the greatest gift we have, and if you find yourself trying to fill it with distractions, then the good news is you're rich. You've got right in front of you the only thing you need to drop in and figure out who you are. Instead of ingesting low-vibrational content on TV or the

Internet, you can read, listen to audio programs, watch meaningful stuff, grow personally, and cultivate your qi.

Every moment is an opportunity to wake up and tap into the Nectar. If you feel lonely and isolated, then you must know that the solution is an inside game. Don't look to fill the silence or emptiness with meaningless things to do or other people to waste time with. Fill it with yourself. Breathe into the moment and check in with how you feel. Sense the life force moving through you and notice where it gets stuck. That's your work. On the other side of that, you'll realize how great a gift time really is, and you'll never waste a moment again.

Grow into it.

When you do this, you'll find that the right people are drawn to you. You'll see clues that show up along your path that lead you to wonderful places. Opportunities will arise that will move you in directions that will light up your life. The first stop is always finding one's self and asking the key question: "Who am I?"

There's never really an answer to this—just more questions. Once you get used to that notion, you'll realize that life itself is a giant mystery and we're here to learn and explore.

This is the end of boredom
and the end of loneliness.

When you tap into the Source, happiness springs from within. Once you're internally content, then the right friends show up. You don't need each other, so you enjoy the company without all the codependent weirdness. You can enjoy silence together or even sit on the same sofa and read books and enjoy a fire.

Curating Your Experience

Finding yourself doesn't have to happen in isolation. Follow the bread crumbs of the things that have interested you in the past. Have you always wanted to try kayaking? Great, start doing that. Tennis? Cool. Find a club. How about seeing the Pyramids? Fantastic. Book a flight and get a hotel.

 An Urban Monk is never afraid of doing things alone. In fact, she

Yes!

looks forward to it. The greatest things in life happen when we're on our path. Some of my best friends in the world I've met in high Himalayan villages or on beaches in exotic lands. Why? Because they also untethered from their world of perceived limitations and were enjoying life. When you take the leap, all of the excuses and petty fears step

PERSONAL JOURNEYS

My kung fu master had me running around like a lunatic in my late twenties. I was taking 24 units at UCLA, running a summer camp for kids, and training more than 30 hours per week in kung fu, tai chi, qigong, and meditation. Every time I flinched and started to feel sorry for myself, he'd ask me to find a way and stay focused. I quickly realized that I was accustomed to zoning out in lectures, so I'd have to read all of the material over again at home. I realized that I didn't have time for this, so I became very attentive in class. I'd have the books out and be reading them during the lecture and take notes as the professors spoke. From there I realized that what I thought I needed as "downtime" wasn't nourishing me. Instead of an hour phone call or watching some brainless show, I'd go outside and do some tai chi. I'd come in with more energy and clarity. It was restorative and actually recharged my batteries and enthusiasm. As I started looking at all facets of my life, I began to carve out inefficiencies and got really good at getting shit done. I nailed straight A's that quarter and was on my game in all other areas. This taught me a powerful lesson in life, which was that my experience was my own to create. I simply stopped doing things that didn't serve me, and instead I went against the grain of cultural habits. Now, when I relax, I mean it, and when it's time to get shit done, I'm on it.

aside and life's adventure begins. When you're doing awesome things out there in the world, then you meet people worth hanging out with. If those people are not there, then you're just fine hanging alone.

Maybe you're not good at tennis yet. So what? Daddy's not watching you anymore, but it sure feels like it. We all start somewhere. Take some lessons and start to learn to have fun doing things for yourself. Nobody cares if you suck at it. All beginners do.

The key is to not care what people think and do things for the joy of doing them. At first this is difficult, but with practice, you'll learn to let go of the bullshit and start enjoying life without fear of judgment.

Then you are on the road to freedom.

A Life of Service

In a city of several million people, is it possible that *nobody* is interesting, or are you isolating yourself because your attempts at friendship and social connection have failed? It is easy to blame the world for our isolation, but we need to look at ourselves.

due to no desire for significant other relationship

+ Do we need to get better friends?

+ How can we make amends with our families?

+ What are our interests, and how can we move toward those?

+ How can we use our alone time to better ourselves and help us be lighter of heart?

When we take a close look at ourselves, we can appreciate people more and grow to be more loving. Even if you're the smartest and most interesting person in the room (and we all think we are), then make a commitment to *serve* the people around you and step out of your shell.

SWM

Through service to humanity, the best in us comes out, and we start to step out of the delusion of grandeur we may have and out of the illusion of separation. Through service we connect with people. Who the hell are you anyhow? Why does that identity matter? If your fabricated identity doesn't really matter, then why do you take your-self so seriously?

Finding yourself doesn't mean stepping into some exalted state. Everyone I talk to who's done a past-life regression says they were a king or a princess or something badass in a past life. We all think that's the answer, as if Hollywood has also infected our sense of spir-ituality. What if the essence of who you are is no different from the essence of all of the people around you? What if nobody was higher than anybody else, and we were all part of the same beautiful life force? How do you distinguish yourself? How do you rise to the top? You don't. Trying to place yourself above others is bullshit.

Humble service teaches us about our true nature. It helps us under-stand the universal plight of humanity and allows us to be an agent of change in service to all of life. Self-importance and self-righteous atti-tudes are a fast track to loneliness and isolation. After all, how can I hang out with those people? They are so beneath me . . . or those others are way too classy for my likes. As we judge, we isolate and suffer. This is a key piece to the notion of class and social status. Many people are bred with toxic memes from their families that teach them from an early age that they are different. They are taught that their families come from a higher place or that their race or skin color trumps that of those other people. They learn this so early that they assume it is true, simply the way things are. Undoing this program-ming and learning to be free of racism, sexism, class isolation, and any other generalized shittiness is important. This is a necessary part of personal growth that we must all go through.

It's important to remember that this growth goes both ways. Learning to forgive the perpetrators is also a challenge. We see this with whites in the South and the new generation of young Germans. At what point are they free from the sins of their predecessors?

Now—change it in your lifetime and stand on your own merits.

When can we stop hating each other? When we stop needing con-flict to define us. Our moms, dads, uncles, teachers, and various other adults all dumped opinions about others into our supple minds before we had a chance to be discerning. As adults, we can reexamine all of this and let go into something bigger.

When we dedicate our lives to service and the *why* becomes greater than the *my,* then we start to liberate from the delusion of separation. Stepping into a higher purpose means doing things for the greater good and helping people in need. It means serving your community and cleaning up the environment. It means connecting with people and selflessly serving their needs. When you tap into this, it is a fast track out of isolation. There's too much work to do and too many people to help. Get your ass up and join the party and stop taking yourself so seriously.

EASTERN PRACTICES
Heart-Centered Meditation

Learning to connect again to our heart chakra is a powerful way to step into transpersonal consciousness. It helps us get out of our egos and soften our personalities. This meditation is the core of many spiritual traditions and has helped people understand and support each other for millennia. Here's the practice:

○ Sit in a comfortable position and start breathing in and out through your nose to the lower dantian (three fingers below your navel).

○ Take a few minutes to settle your mind and anchor your breath down low.

○ From here, move your attention to your heart center (at the nipple line in the middle of your chest) and bring your hands into prayer position in front of your heart with palms together (fingertips facing up).

○ Have your breath come in and out of this area now for a few breaths.

○ Feel the area warming up as you breathe to it.

○ Now start to focus on a feeling of unconditional love in your

heart. Feel this for all of life: everything around you and everything and everyone you have ever known or will know.

○ Feel this love on each inhale, and on the exhale, project this love
out in all directions from your heart.

○ Feel it for everyone you know, love, hate, need to forgive, and have
yet to meet.

○ Do this for several breaths and really focus on expanding the
sphere of your heart with each exhale to grow and envelop everything you know.

○ Grow to engulf the Earth, the solar system, the galaxy, and finally
the entire Universe.

○ Sit with this for a few minutes and hold that love in your heart.

When you're ready to finish the practice, anchor this love in the
center of your heart and allow it to guide your decisions and influence
your interactions. With time, you'll see how valuable this practice is
for pulling you out of isolation.

Healing the Past

Learning to heal the wounds of our past is the only way to have a peaceful present. We all carry around tremendous burdens and judgments
from our past. Using the previous practice, once you're in an enhanced
loving state, you can isolate a feeling that has been haunting you and
apply this sphere of unconditional love to it. Wrap it and envelop it.
Bring white light to it and see its charge turn back to positive.

Once you've done so in the present, then trace back along the time
line into the past and try to find a triggering event that created this
polarity reversal. Go back in your mind's eye and heal the event in the
past. See the charge shift back to positive before you move on.

You may find several instances. Deal with them one by one and
work to heal each of them. Eventually, you'll find the original event
that triggered this energy in the first place, and you can heal that. See
the scenario and all of the people around you and it. Freeze time and
bring love to it. Wrap everyone in white light. Then, in that frozen
time, play out the scenario the way you'd rather it look. See it clearly

and imprint your consciousness with this vision. Anchor it in your heart and reinforce this rewrite and support it with love. Seeing it and feeling it are critical pieces. This is where anchoring our consciousness with emotions and visualization can really make magic happen.

Over time, this practice will change your life and free you from the heavy burden of emotions you've been dragging around. I learned this from Dr. Carl Totton (taoinstitute.com).

Dedicated Acts of Love

Donating your service and time to a local cause is a powerful practice in getting you out of isolation. Find a local cause that speaks to you and go volunteer your time. But don't stop there: Perform random acts of kindness and help people selflessly wherever you can. Do not expect accolades or recognition in return. Again, this isn't about you. Just be of service and get out of the way. After a while, you'll see how this softens your personality and gives you the space to be a part of something without all of the friction.

The Hebrew philosopher Maimonides spoke of the principle of giving freely and without need for accolades or recognition. When we do this, we tie into a Universal principle and take our ego out of the equation.

The Five Animals

A big part of the tradition of kung fu is the role of the Five Animals (Tiger, Leopard, Crane, Snake, and Dragon) along with several other animal forms that have been practiced and passed down over the years (Monkey, Bear, Eagle, Mantis, and many more). The ancient sages watched the mannerisms of different animals and saw the genius of how they fought and defended themselves. Each had a unique strength that they played to and used to exploit the weaknesses of the others. Each exuded a power that kung fu practitioners try to emulate.

A true martial artist *becomes* the animal they are "playing." Much like the art of drama, you get fully into character and tap into the spirit, the essence, and the power of the animal. In doing so, you tap into a pure archetype of something anchored in nature (and not some weird voodoo animism or dark practice). This allows you to step outside the "control drama" of the ego as you role-play something else.

Over time, we realize that this is fun and safe. In fact, it is therapeutic because each animal has its own emotional expression and we can use these practices to alchemically express and transform emotional energy. What this does is give us the space, permission, and the vehicle to change our mental and emotional state by tapping into something natural and pure. What it also does in a sneaky way is give us a little "playdate" away from under the thumb of the ego, or our manufactured identity. As we spend more time playing something else or wearing different masks, we start to realize that the one we wear every day is *also just a mask*. This is when the fun begins. When we stop pretending to be *that person,* we can finally get on with being who we truly are. Who is that? That's for each of us to find out on our own. It's a lot more fun to hang out with people who don't take themselves too seriously.

I've included a video of this in the Resources section.

Find Spirituality If Religion Has Failed You

If you come from a tradition where the nuns were too harsh, the people were too fake, or the priests did nasty things, or from one that simply made no sense to you, please understand that religion and spirituality are not the same. Organized religion has many merits and has held together the fabric of our cultures for millennia, but it has also messed a lot of things up. God didn't do that; people did—in the name of God. In fact, the best place for the Devil to hide himself is the House of God, and as a result, many people's trust has been severely violated with religion.

If this is you, please find a personal spiritual practice and find God yourself. Who's God? Don't let anyone tell you that. Go find out. Ask the big questions like "What was there *before* the Big Bang, and how did that get there?" There are wonderful books and works of saints you can read along the way.

That being said, I learned more about spirituality on the streets of India than I did in any ashram. Sometimes life experience is the greatest teacher, and we need to be open to receive lessons in whatever form they come. If you're off the God word, go Taoist, Buddhist, Shaman, or whatever else calls to you. These are just words trying to make sense of a common reality we share. The exploration of the essence of this reality is where they all come together. Don't accept dogma; instead, find the answers on your own. Then, the practice is yours and not something you blindly follow.

The trick is to commit to your enlightenment and really get to work on yourself. Everything else will work out from there. There's a lot of New Age bullshit out there that isn't tethered in anything real, either. My suggestion is to look at the tried-and-true traditions out there and go to the Source. If you are interested in Christianity, read what Jesus actually said. If your interests bring you to Buddhism, learn to meditate as the Buddha recommended (visit dhamma.org for help with this) and see what comes to you. If you want to explore shamanism, find someone with some real pedigree.

There's a world of parasites out there waiting to exploit the people coming off the "religion boat." Apply the practices you've learned in this book to check in with yourself and see what feels right. If it feels "cultish," run like hell. You don't need that shit.

MODERN HACKS
Farmers' Markets

Getting out to meet your farmer is the way forward in the food movement, but it also gives us back something that has been lost for a generation: the agora, or marketplace. This is historically a public area where citizens congregate and go about their business. The corporate takeover of America has created an environment in most cities (especially the new ones) where there really is no public square. There's no safe place to hang out that isn't private property, so we feel like we need to buy something or move on.

The emerging growth of farmers' markets in cities all over the world is a grassroots breath of fresh air. Here, you can mingle with people, listen to music, get fresh food, and simply hang around and people watch. It's a great way to get out of your shell and develop a ritual around good food and culture. Snapping out of isolation starts with getting out, and nothing can do this better than good old-fashioned hunger. This is another great way to meet over food, rejoice, tell jokes, and enjoy the company of real people in a public setting. Let's connect over food once again.

Local Groups

The Internet has recently given us a nice array of apps that help us get together and congregate. From local Facebook groups, Meetups, LinkedIn, and other social media to color races, mud runs, flash mobs, and more, the Internet is now reaching back and connecting people in real places doing real things that are fun. Start to look around and see what interests you, and then go for it. Meet people who, very much like yourself, are looking to meet others and branch out. You're not a freak; everyone is lonely and needing this. When you realize this, you let go of the bullshit and get to have fun with people again.

There's also a surging movement around specialty interests. Self-proclaimed nerds and geeks have outlets like WonderCon and Star Wars conventions. In fact, if you're into something, chances are thousands of others are as well, and gatherings are happening all over the place. If you like birds, there are bird-watching groups. If you like whales, there are boats that go out to view them. Basically, chances are you're not alone in your interests, and you can use the Internet to find like-minded folks and engage with them at events and conferences. A whole world of fun stuff is happening, and all we need to do is look and connect. People are awesome. They are quirky, weird, and interesting, just like you. It is time to find them and have some fun.

Cut the Cord

An emerging movement of cord cutters are moving away from cable TV and taking back their power in media and entertainment. There's really no reason to still be paying to get countless channels of garbage that push commercials and terrible content your way. Set-top boxes, subscription channels, YouTube, and iTunes are among the many new ways to get quality content that's enriching for you.

If you're interested in cutting the cord, several subscription services are popping up now. From Netflix and HBO to services like Hulu that aggregate content from major networks, there's less and less need now to pay for 500 channels you're never going to watch. You can subscribe to the sports network of your choice and drill down into content you actually care to consume. Podcasts are great, as are audiobooks and Vimeo feeds. There's some good and intelligent TV still out there for sure, and there'll be more to come, but that doesn't mean you need all those other channels. The moral of the story is that you have choices and should exercise them.

An Urban Monk curates the information she receives. Don't waste another minute sitting in front of your TV watching nonsense. Take your power back and cut the cord.

Better yet, get outside and start living again. Life isn't a spectator sport. You can just as easily listen to a podcast while hiking or biking and get the best of both worlds. Hell, you even stand a chance of meeting someone if you get out of the house.

Read Good Stuff

You are what you eat, so ingest the best stuff and wake up. This means taking some time to find books, films, shows, magazines, audiobooks, lectures, or whatever else you feel is going to help you grow. Use your valuable time to enhance your human experience and to learn new things. *Interesting people are way more fun to be around.* Develop a culture of self-betterment by committing your time to being a lifelong learner. Not only does this help us be more educated, worldly, and interesting, it also instills humility as we quickly realize that there's far too much for anyone to learn. This shakes off the arrogance that comes with thinking we know it all and also creates a personal culture that will help you better engage with people.

Here's the secret: *Everybody* has something to teach you. When you're interested in information and learning about life and reality itself, every single person you encounter has some valuable information about something for you. Whether you are asking a taxi driver about the town you're in, an old man about the ducks on the lawn, or a child about their favorite color, there's always something to learn, and the *inquiry* opens up dialogue. It allows us to empower someone with the noble task of teaching something. It honors them for something they know and makes them feel valued in society.

Always thank people for their wisdom and do so graciously. It is the ultimate icebreaker because it helps you connect with people in a noble way and keeps you in the culture of being a lifelong learner.

Good Psychotherapy Goes a Long Way

What happened and why did you go inward into isolation in the first place? The time line therapy in the "Healing the Past" section above is a powerful tool to help you unwind some of the stuck energy in your life, but many of us have histories of abuse and major trauma. We may need someone to help us move through it, and there are thousands of great therapists in our world whom we can enlist for help.

Now you may be thinking, "Dude, I already tried that," but just because you've tried it in the past doesn't mean that you should give up. Take what you've learned in this book and look for someone who will work *with you* in your quest to step out of your own way and be of greater service to humanity. Once you've locked in your intent as an Urban Monk, then you can recruit an ally in your pursuit of peace and happiness. There are lots of great doctors out there who can help you not go it alone.

Get Uncomfortable

Try a public speaking class if this terrifies you. Do things that pull you out of your shell. Improv comedy is amazing. They teach classes. (You can find some tips for locating classes in the Resources section.) What about dancing? Are you terrible at it? Great! Learn how to dance and step through this. It's okay to suck at things, because that gives us plenty of opportunity to get better and have fun doing so. Boredom comes from comfort and stagnation; neither of these have any place in the life of the Urban Monk.

Getting uncomfortable triggers our survival genes and wakes us up out of the humdrum, dreary reality that we've stagnated into. Shake it up and make some noise. Breaking through our fears is a powerful way of crushing habits that paralyze us and keep us down. Challenging ourselves in front of other people (especially strangers) makes us vulnerable and real. When we see that in each other, we find common ground in our mutual fears and concerns. When we see another person break through something we are terrified of, we develop respect and camaraderie. We then help each other through things. We bond. We connect. We come back together the way it used to be and should always be. We are in this together, and we simply need to remember this.

[handwritten: no late nights]

[handwritten: Change routine]
[handwritten: Exercise: Get up early to do hike (got a trainer together clients)]

MARK'S ACTION PLAN

Mark really didn't think he had a problem until I shared the definition of an alcoholic with him. It shocked him to realize that he was already pretty far down that road. What had started with a couple of beers had gotten out of hand. Why? Because something had to fill the void, and in the absence of anything real or interesting, alcohol steps right in.

We had Mark change his routine during the week. Instead of late nights in front of the TV, we got him hiking a local canyon every morning before work. This got him up earlier and made it too hard to justify staying up late. It cut out the beer, the TV, and the isolation at night. It wasn't easy at first. He'd smoke more often because his baseline anxiety was really bubbling up. He got another trainer to join him on the hikes, and within a month, there was a stable group of a few of them going, including some clients who wanted in. It became fun and healthy time. Over time, he needed less in the form of self-medication. Because he was getting up earlier, he couldn't stay up late and get in trouble. He still had moments when he craved a drink, though, so we put him through a detox and supported his brain chemistry with a combination of 5-HTP and L-tyrosine. These supplements really helped Mark along until he got back in the swing.

With a bit of positive energy back, Mark began reading his Bible again. He had grown up Catholic and took it seriously at one point. Now, I introduced him to Valentin Tomberg and a number of other influential writers from the Catholic tradition, and Mark found a refreshing body of work that was deep, meaningful, and relevant. He now had access to wisdom that gave him things to contemplate and drove him to ask the bigger questions.

He started reading books voraciously again and made friends with a few people through clients. They'd go hiking, camping, and have nights where they alternated cooking. I had to make sure Mark left enough time for himself once his new social life took on a life of its own. With balance and temperance, Mark left time for play, got in his workouts, and had nice people in his life to hang out with. Last I spoke with him, Mark was enthusiastically planning a trip with his buddies to Peru, where he'd hike the Inca trail, see Machu Picchu, and also volunteer at an orphanage for a few days. He now barely resembled the sallow closet smoker suffering from self-imposed isolation who he had been. Mark got his life back and was busy helping others whenever he could.

CHAPTER 9

Never Enough Money

NATALIE CAN'T REMEMBER A TIME when she wasn't stressed about money. She grew up in a house with four siblings, and her dad was out of work pretty often. Money was always tight, and this was tough on a little girl. Her brothers seemed to be okay wearing the same shoes to school, but by junior high, the girls were vicious and constantly ridiculed people who were not put together well. Natalie was always ashamed of her wardrobe. Things like school trips, summer camp, backpacks, and new shoes were always reminding her that her family didn't have enough money and somehow they were "less than."

As a young adult, Natalie got jobs as early as she could. She waited tables, answered phones, promoted a nightclub, and then started cutting hair. The money got better, and she was able to finally afford things in life. She would go on trips with her girlfriends and buy nice shoes, purses, clothes, and whatever else she thought she needed. She leased a nice car and got a bunch of great stuff for her apartment. Things looked pretty good on the outside.

Natalie's problem is that she is totally overextended.

The little girl who doesn't want to look poor is now playing a dangerous game of "show and tell" that is working her into the ground. She cuts hair 6 days a week and spends thousands of dollars treating her back at the chiropractor because it kills her to stand all day. Her heels don't help her back pain, yet fashion dictates that she suffer through it. She doesn't have any savings, doesn't own a house, and has no retirement plan; if she gets sick and can't work, there's no money coming in.

Natalie has stacked her life with the edifice of "stuff" to bolster her "I've got money" identity. There's always a new purse that she buys even though she can't afford it, and her car is now 2 years old, so she's eyeing the new model. A four-star hotel is not enough when her girlfriends are staying at a five-star and renting a limo for the party. She keeps throwing up plaster on the edifice of a facade she's living—namely, that she's got money and can roll with the "in crowd." Natalie is paying more than 20 percent interest on average for credit card debt she's stacked up, and she's almost maxed out. Her father offered to help her come up with a payment plan, but she bailed on the idea when a new boyfriend came along and she wanted to treat him to a spa weekend. They both *deserved* a break.

Natalie thinks that the solution to her problems is more money. She doesn't realize that *she* is at the center of a problem more money can't really solve.

THE PROBLEM

We live in a world that leverages us on our desires. Whatever we have, it's not enough. We are made to feel incomplete and isolated if we don't wear the latest fashion, drive the newest car, go to that new restaurant, or buy those new games for our kids. There's never enough, and we are incomplete without the latest and greatest in all things.

Natalie is no different from the people who make the lottery winner statistics. Research from the National Endowment for Financial Education estimates that 70 percent of people who had unexpectedly come into large sums of money ended up broke within 7 years. Why is this? Why do people who come into large sums of money end up broke again?

Poor Energy Economics

People don't understand the value of money as energy and are therefore in a rush to squander it. When we put it aside, it accumulates and grows. It takes on a life of its own and begins to generate abundance as its own vehicle. It can generate interest and fuel investment in our dreams. It becomes like a bank of potential energy that we have stored up and is available to us to use. Saving money requires a different psychological state that takes discipline and cultivation. It is a state of mind and a state of being.

PERSONAL JOURNEYS

When I was a child, we moved around a lot. My dad was in construction, and we went from house to house as he was flipping them and trying to feed his family. I landed in a suburban area without any friends just at the start of junior high school. I went from a comfortable kid who didn't care about what he wore or did to being ridiculed for not wearing the right clothes or watching the latest shows. It was awful. It was the first time in my life that I felt like an outsider, and I needed desperately to fit in. At the time, there were these Oakley Iridium glasses that were in. They were really expensive, and we didn't have much money. I begged my parents for weeks to get them for me. Being hardworking first-generation immigrants, they thought it was ridiculous, but I wore them down until they complied.

I had them! Finally I could flash my wares and fit in with the cool kids. Nope. They hardly noticed and had moved on to shaming each other over other ridiculous shit. I remember the look on my father's patient and understanding face when he saw how this played out. I was embarrassed. That was food off the table, and all for what? I was driven to coerce money out of my parents' pockets to ante up in an unwinnable game of bullshit.

Most people live in survival mode.

Like Natalie, most people are unconsciously playing out a childhood drama, and their lives are the storybook of their plight. Some want power. Others are trying to attract a mate. Never wanting to feel poor again is what has driven Natalie's actions for 3 decades. There are lots of reasons why we do the things we do, but money is the medium by which our imbalances often show up. You can tell a lot about a business by looking at its financials, and you can see into a person's life by looking at their personal finances. Why? Because money is energy, and financial statements record the *flow* of this energy in our lives. You can see money issues slobbering through all facets of a person's life.

Advertising

The economy *needs* consumers to spend money on stuff year in and year out. The term itself is degrading. Why are people called consumers? Because they feed a system that functions like a cancer which needs us to buy more things year in and year out while avoiding the fact that those things pollute the air, water, land, and cells of our bodies. We're willing to kill the Earth in order to perpetuate this nonsense because it is "our way of life." The advertising industry is built around human desire. Advertisers goad you to feel like you are not whole, happy, healthy, sexy, young, pretty, or secure if you don't have the product or service they're trying to sell you. Our entire society is built around this.

So how do advertisers get happy people to care about their products, and how do they get them to actually spend their hard-earned cash on this stuff?

Step 1: Get consumers to feel like shit. Make them feel unworthy and lacking in some way. Show them a skinny celebrity and keep reinforcing the idea that *this* is beauty. *This* is desirable. Over time, they will fall for it. They'll bite.

Then comes Step 2, which is putting something in front of them and tying it to the open loop of desire you created in Step 1. You are not sexy and she is. Now buy the face cream that she uses so you, too, can be sexy like her. *Ching* rings the cash register at makeup counters across the globe . . .

You want a truck? Well, this badass athlete real man hero drives *this one*. You should run out and get it, too . . .

It takes dozens of media impressions to make this work, so that's why we're bombarded with banner ads, TV spots, radio commercials, signs, flyers, spam, and whatever else advertisers can send at us. The subconscious mind needs to be overwhelmed by a barrage of messaging until we simply accept these fabricated memes as facts.

This is another reason why Urban Monks don't watch traditional media, by the way. There's no reason to take arrows all day because, in a weak moment, you'll bleed. It is like sitting in a room with people sneezing on you all day. Eventually, you, too, will start to have the sniffles.

Debt

We live in a debt-based economy where most of us don't actually own much: We have a mortgage on the house, leased cars, payment plans on appliances. In fact, most American families are 1 to 6 months away from rock bottom if they were to lose their jobs or have some catastrophic illness or injury. This is where Natalie lives and is the underlying reason why she's always stressed—because none of the shit she has is actually hers. She owes so much on credit cards that if she were to stop making minimum payments, they'd take the car and come seize her accounts. She's actually an indentured servant to her lifestyle, but like a typical junkie, she doesn't see a clear path out of the mess she's in.

In Natalie's mind, her social circle will ostracize her if they detect that she's broke, just like the girls in junior high did. Then she'll be alone and miserable. She holds this belief deep down and doesn't even know it's still running, yet it powers a large percentage of her daily decisions. The scary thing is that we're all crazy like this. The stuff right under the radar is driving our behavior more than we realize.

Debt is a powerful tool in capitalism to leverage one's business and scale rapidly. It has helped us finance good ideas and move power and energy around. Used correctly, it can vitalize a good idea or business and make it grow exponentially. Good businesspeople know how to use debt wisely and leverage it to get ahead in life. The problem is that most Americans are saddled with consumer debt, which is killing them. Swiping something on a credit card because you must have it now is okay if that something is food for your baby, but certainly not a stupid purse or another gun. Impulse buying on credit cards gets us to step out of our rational minds and spend money *we don't have* oftentimes on things *we don't actually need*. This then gets us locked into high interest rates and perpetual payments to the lenders, who are laughing all the way to their own banks.

This cycle keeps us in a "fight-or-flight" mentality. The walls are always caving in, and lenders can come and take away the house, the car, the stuff, and we'll be left with nothing. It is a primal trigger to our limbic system that challenges our very survival. We can never have enough money to deal with the unforeseen, so the stress is always there. It is the fundamental challenge a householder must face. The ascetic renounces all money and moves into the mountains. This lifts him from the burden of money and the world so he can practice freely and contemplate reality. We householders have no such luck. We need to deal with money daily and get good with it. The roof over your head, the power bill, tuition, and food all tie us into money, so we need to face this issue head-on.

Holding On to It

The misreading of spiritual scripture and ideals in their translation from East to West and ancient to present has confused this matter. Many people try to detach from money but find themselves stressing about it daily. I personally dealt with this and had to let it go. I hung with lots of hippies, religious folk, and New Age types for a good decade, and their thinking infected me. What thinking? Oh, that money is evil and that good people don't seek it. These were often the same people who were always broke and having to deal with a lack of money. It's stressful when you have bills you can't pay. When the power is shut off and the eviction notices appear, that's when focusing on money is a bit late. I finally understood the difference between being an ascetic (which is what many confused people try to be) and a householder (a responsible member of society who works to make the world a better place). If you have bills, you're a householder. This is a key understanding of an Urban Monk and will liberate you.

Even when we do have money, we're constantly in fear of losing it. We protect our assets and grow keenly aware of people who are out to scam us. We are on the defensive, much like a lion that stands guard over an antelope he can't eat by himself. Do you let it rot or share it with others? How do you trust people who approach you because they all seem to want your money? In fact, once you have a couple bucks, you become keenly aware of how parasitic the world can really be. People come from nowhere, and it seems they're all scheming to get your money. They latch and they suckle. They are suddenly your friends and are much nicer than the assholes you grew up with. The problem is, unlike your true friends, these guys disappear once you've run out of cheese or cut them off.

This leads to another malady, one of mistrust. I know lots of wealthy people who have been shell-shocked into being constantly on guard because they feel that everyone is out to get them and their money. They become paranoid and defensive, shut off and uncool to their fellow humans.

The common thread, ironically, is the same. Whether you lack money and are constantly trying to get some in the door, or you're sitting on a pile of it and are waving a stick at anyone who approaches, the essence of the issue points to *survival*.

Sink or Swim

We all stand in a panicked frenzy because tomorrow's headline may render us irrelevant. Who wants to be the next MySpace or Kodak? We don't want to be flash-in-the-pan successes who get a taste of the high life and then get knocked down to Earth by the next big thing. A little success doesn't leave us fulfilled; it just drives us to want more. Stonemasons are out of work due to faux-finished fake rock walls made in China. In today's competitive landscape, we're all one slipup away from being irrelevant, from being mulched by a newcomer.

Change is the alchemical Universal force that compels us to stay on our game and remain relevant.

You Can't Take It with You

The reality is that we're all going to die and can't take our money with us, no matter how big of a pyramid we build and how much gold we shove in there for our afterlife. This story isn't new. The biggest and baddest lion in the jungle is always facing challenges from young upstarts and knows he will eventually fade into old age and get taken down. This is why we start foundations and trusts. We try to have children and carry on our legacy. Keeping up with the Joneses is the toe into this insanity that distorts our vision of what's really important: our growth, our experiences, our Self-Realization, and our legacy.

Let's take a deeper look at money so we can peel back what this stress is really all about.

URBAN MONK WISDOM

Money is currency, and this implies a flow. Water and electricity also flow in currents, hence the term *currency*. Qi flows in currents, too. The dynamic movement of life force is tied with abundance and the life-giving qualities that come with it. Whether you believe in Creation or some Great Mystery, the fact that we're here and come from procreation is pretty amazing. Life grows, flourishes, and multiplies. This is one of the great miracles we have. If we tie into the flow of our life force and tap into the energy of abundance, then we're in the flow of that, too. Tributaries lead to rivers and then lakes. When we step into the natural flow of this energy, money flows through our life and fuels our dreams and travels. When we learn to direct some of that flow into vehicles where it can accumulate, we generate abundance and growth that's not tied to our labor, much like a garden that takes off on its own after our initial toils.

Some people have serious hang-ups with money, though. "Money is evil" is a principle that's infiltrated the psyche of humanity, and we are forced to reconcile our stance on this when we come of age. Once the bills start showing up, we feel like we've got to bite the bullet and get into the real world, which we believe is filled with assholes and cheats. Somehow we come to accept this as "reality" and stop questioning why it needs to be that way. Sociopaths love the money game because it gives them a common currency of power and control that helps feed their control dramas. It helps fill some emptiness in them.

Normal people usually work their nine to five and then go hang with friends and family. They have other things they care about more than money but are often stuck stressing about it more than they'd like to. Either we believe money is evil and avoid "touching" it energetically, which repels it from us, or we take on a "love of money" stance and go for the greed. That's the polarized view many take, and it's very primitive. How do we establish a healthy relationship with money, since we do live in this world? The ascetic monks were free of this, but as housholders, we are in a society that functions on money. Avoiding it and ignoring this matter doesn't resolve anything. Let's take a closer look at it.

The fact that we're all overwhelmed by debt means that we've fallen asleep to what money is supposed to be for us. Money is a means by which we can trade for value in our society, and it helps us have a common medium of exchange for simplicity. It should buy you food, shelter, water, and freedom to do as you please with your time.

Money is a medium of exchange.

It is a way we trade goods, services, and assets for an agreed-upon convention of transfer. The perceived value of a thing or service is determined by the market, so prices fluctuate based on supply, demand, consumer sentiment, and other factors.

The price I pay for a delicious organic apple will depend on a few things. Because it's a commodity, I can Google the average price of an organic apple and find that it is $2.34 per pound, as compared to a conventional one, which averages $1.57 per pound (a 49 percent difference). Many can argue that this price is steep, so what justifies it? Well, organic apples are not sprayed with harmful pesticides and poisons. They are not genetically modified, and they're grown in a sustainable fashion. This makes them healthier for our bodies and the environment. If my family is poor and I'm just trying to get food onto the table, I may argue that the value isn't there for me; my priorities are bringing home the most food that I can for the least amount of money that I can, so I'll just go conventional. Someone may argue with me and claim that the health risks could lead to greater costs down the line, but I can counter that my health care is covered by the state, so I'll kick that can down the road and get some food on the table for now.

I can walk down the road at my local farmers' market and see two stands selling apples that are similarly organic, but one costs more. Reason would dictate that I buy the cheaper one. But the guy selling the more expensive apples goes out there and prays with his trees every morning and takes care of orphans in Africa. He donates a percentage of his profits to charity and remembers my name when I walk by. Maybe I like the *story* and the *narrative* told by the more expensive farmer and, therefore, spend an extra dime and get his stuff. This is perceived value, and it determines pricing all over the place. This is how the market shifts. Now if I've already bought into the organic thing, there's also another "apples to apples" piece that's interesting.

You see, the value we assign to a given product or service will also help determine the cost. Essentially, the question is: What are we willing to pay and why? This transaction represents your beliefs, your values, and your priorities in life. The fact that we have better access to organic foods today is because certain people elected to pay more for the good stuff and helped support farmers to continue growing that way. Today, an enormous industry based on sustainable practices is emerging thanks to the values of the people who cared enough to take a stance on organics.

Money becomes the common currency of a language that calculates valuation and benefits. It is an idea that we agree to share so society can flow smoothly. It is our *energy* and power that are banked into these monetary units we swipe and throw down each day. How many real hours of your life went into that 100 bucks you just spent? How much value did you get out of those cute shoes you got to wear once at the party? How many breaths or beats of your heart earned that money that you just squandered on something you didn't need? No wonder you feel tired. If you live in the "time is money" economy, then squandering money is like squandering away your life force. You can actually track the hours of your life you just wasted on something.

Understanding what desire is and how we react to it is our way out of the crazy cycle of dependence on money to satisfy abstract needs. We're so far down the rabbit hole that we often don't recognize the difference between our needs and our wants. Let's go back to the concept of "needs" versus "wants" we talked about in Chapter 7. What we *need* is food, shelter, water, and fire. Everything else is a *want*.

We *need* food and shelter.

We *want* steak and mansions.

The Human Soap Opera

Fancy cars and mansions give us cultural capital in another game we play: the game of status, class, and human social positioning. We do it to jockey and position ourselves in the global tribe. We do it to belong and establish our place in the pecking order. We do it to attract a desirable mate. We do it to show those punks from high school that we *did* make it. We have primitive instincts that are satisfied with some of these basic impulses. In Paleolithic times, the hunter who took down an animal was rewarded with the finest cut (the fillet) and the fur or skin of the animal. He would then be able to gift the skin to a mate and share the meat with her. Steak and a fur coat, anyone? Some things have not really changed. The desire to be able to show you have wealth and can take care of a mate is a powerful and primal instinct that comes from ancient times. It means you are likely to survive. We understand this on a core level and respect this culturally; it is unspoken but always there.

The desire to buy random things to show off your affluence can stem from one of these primitive instincts. If you can easily afford the stuff after putting money aside for retirement and supporting a cause that matters, then fine: Enjoy the fruits of your labor and parade around like a proud peacock. That's your prerogative. But if you can't and you're buying shit to bolster a facade, then you're in big trouble.

Purchasing things you cannot afford makes no sense, yet many of us do it. Why? Because the advertising industry has learned to find out our pain points and leverage us on our desires, as discussed earlier. Our friend Natalie buys stuff to fit in and not feel poor. She goes to expensive shows and keeps herself distracted with the illusion of some sort of status she derives from owning expensive shit. She has fallen asleep to what brings real satisfaction and meaning in life and has chased the shiny objects all the way to the poorhouse. The advertisers have gotten very good at this game, and we are often unaware of how easily manipulated we are. In fact, teams of neuroscientists study behavior and impulse buying. They work to trigger the pleasure centers in our brains and test their strategies with MRI scans to make sure they've nailed it. Why?

Because we are asleep and impressionable.

We stumble through life looking for solutions outside ourselves to our problems, instead of looking within.

+ What face cream is going to make me look young?

+ What car is going to attract the ladies?

+ What *things* do I need in order for people to like/want/respect me?

+ Who is out there who can help me?

+ Who or what program can make me happy?

This is where the Urban Monk steps in. She understands how to detach her ego from "wants" and understands what she actually *needs*. When we disconnect our sense of self from material things, cultural accolades, compliments, and old emotional dramas, we are free. When we are free from the bullshit, we can think clearly and allocate our money appropriately. We no longer squander it like a kid wasting his summer vacation away because he's bored. We learn the value of it and invest it wisely.

So where should our money go?

+ Into things that enhance our health and vitality

+ Into useful products that are free of poisons and toxic chemicals

+ Into a sustainable future for ourselves and our families

+ Into companies that are giving back to communities

+ Into causes that help protect nature and our collective future

The Dawn of the New Economy

We stand at a crossroads in human history, and there's an amazing thing happening right now under our noses. Thousands of well-intentioned people are directing their companies to serve as agents for change. People are getting tired of the consumption economy. The Ferrari didn't buy happiness, and neither did the Prozac. The time for a fundamental rethinking is here. From benefit corporations, to non-governmental organizations, to sustainable co-ops, companies and groups are emerging around the planet that essentially practice the Buddhist precept of "right livelihood." This means that what we do for money should also benefit our communities and our world. The old patronage model is falling away because we're realizing that most nonprofits spend a high percentage of their time chasing after money and donors instead of doing their work. Now, well-intentioned companies are working to allocate profits and sales to causes in a way that creates *vehicles* for money to flow so this steady stream of energy can keep the flow going. Companies can make money, do good work, and be a part of the solution. This is built into the fabric of who they are, and they can be proud of it. They can collectively be righteous and full of integrity.

So Where Do You Spend Your Money?

The Urban Monk redirects his retirement money to a sustainable fund. He is an informed consumer and doesn't buy products from companies that are known polluters or sponsors of lobbies that push for dirty energy. He helps support his local economy and supports art, culture, education, and other investments that make positive and lasting contributions to his own life and to his community.

The Urban Monk doesn't buy bullshit he doesn't need.

He sees that his hard-earned money is *energy*. He invests this energy in people, causes, trips, courses, investments, and products that help make him better and simultaneously make the world better.

This is the mark of the new economy. It is an ecosystem in which we all live and interact. The old one was predicated on people remaining asleep and stumbling around buying what they were told to buy. This has kept the status quo and lined the pockets of douchebags who've bought our politicians and influenced the direction of the world toward pollution, war, and distress. Enough is enough.

Money is energy, and stepping into this understanding means we learn to understand the flow of this energy.

The essential question is: Who am I in the first place?

Then ask:

+ Why am I spending this money?

+ What is driving me?

+ Do I need this, or is it feeding some emotional pain?

+ Is it a habit or a need?

+ Will it actually make me happy?

+ Why and how will it do so?

Money makes the economy go around, and there's nothing wrong with keeping it flowing, but there's a key component here to highlight.

We vote with our money.

We are giving power, energy, and influence to the people to whom we give money. Be very clear about this flow and start to control it on your end. If you want to see a better world, vote in that direction. Spend in that direction.

If you find yourself like Natalie and you're stuck in the "money is tight game," it's time to clean up your act. There's a saying that the best things in life come for free, and aside from food and shelter, that's pretty true. It is incredibly empowering to redirect your money toward a savings account, paying off a high-interest credit card, or giving to a charity instead of the usual shit it flies out for. That's the first half of the equation: Cut the losses and stop spending money frivolously.

The other side to this is getting into the flow of money. An Urban Monk can comfortably pursue financial success because it means being a better householder in the classical sense. Using money and influence for good is the way of the future. Altruism and authenticity are woven into the fabric of how an Urban Monk engages in business and commerce, and he leaves the world a better place at every turn. Therefore, the more money he makes and generates, the more good he can do for the world around him. Remember, people assign value to products and services and will part with their money accordingly. Where are you in the value chain? What do you need to do in order to improve your value, your offerings, your rate, or your prices? How can you get more customers and generate abundance in your world? There are lots of powerful tools out there now that can teach you this. The Internet has revolutionized how we do commerce, and *anyone* can be a millionaire now with an online busi ness. The only thing in your way is *you*. Even if you have to haul yourself down to a public library and grow your online business from there, you can do it. The key is in understanding what value you're generating and for whom. Who is your audience and how are you helping them? If you're in a brick-and-mortar business or in professional services, the same principles apply. You can have a side gig that sells your handicraft online and grow it into a blossoming company. You can create a blog that extends your voice out there and builds you a following. Tribes are formed around nurses, teachers, poets, and anyone else today.

The economy is just an idea, and so is money. Once you become clear on this, you are unbound and can craft the life of your dreams. If you're spending money on some identity drama, cut that shit out and get with the times. You are better than that, and the world needs you on the right side of the line. Bring your energy to the party and work with like-minded people to generate abundance, wealth, and positive change for generations to come.

EASTERN PRACTICES
Checking-In Meditation

You can do a very simple and powerful exercise at the point of any purchase. Simply ask yourself as you pull out your wallet, credit card, or phone, "Is this a need or a want?"

This seemingly simple practice will bring up lots of interesting data. You'll find that you'll be arguing with yourself over certain items. You will feel like you need certain things or that they qualify as needs because they are technically "food." This doesn't mean that you shouldn't get them; it simply means that you should *think about it* and see how often this happens. We rationalize our impulse buys and then stress about money. We think we deserve things and then curse our luck when that work deal falls through because we actually needed that commission to make rent.

This exercise is a simple accounting practice that'll save you thousands of dollars if you do it right. It is also in line with the Buddhist concept of right livelihood, where you can ask whether this purchase is harming anyone or the planet. If so, then don't be a part of it.

Here's the second part.

Take note of each item you were going to buy and write down the price. At day's end, transfer that amount into your savings account and lock it down. Leave this money out of reach so your impulsive old habits don't claw into it. Walk away, and if you really still want it after a week, take money from your current budget and buy it when you can without tapping into your savings. Soon, you'll start to see your money begin to increase, and you'll realize that you've gone on just fine without the thing you withstood buying.

Investing the savings into things that will yield profits and support your future will then change your life. It all starts with snapping out of the spell and stopping the impulsive behavior at the time of purchase.

Spending Fast

In this exercise, you stop all unnecessary expenditures for 1 month. Each time you come to spend, you ask, "Do I actually *need* this?" Unlike the first exercise, which is a good practice to use throughout your life, this one is set to be temporary so you know you'll live through it. Be 100 percent strict with it for 1 month. Take every penny you were going to spend and put it into a savings account. This includes going out to dinner, buying toys for your dog, upgrading your phone, or even getting coffee out of the house. At the end of the month, you can pay off some debt, invest it, or even buy yourself something you've always wanted. The goal of the exercise is to learn how to refrain and see how it's really not that terrible. What's terrible is worrying about money all the time. When you step out of that slavery, you're free to enjoy your time and relax without the survival genes kicking in.

"Get in the Flow" Exercise

The previous exercises are designed to stop the bleeding. This one is designed to increase the flow and actually generate more cash.

Visualization of energy and money coming into your life is an important practice to keep you in the flow of the qi of the Universe. The mind needs a framework or a vision for the energy to assemble around. This practice is designed to help align you with wealth and attract abundance.

○ Sit up comfortably with your spine straight.

○ Start breathing to your lower dantian (three fingers below your navel) to calm your mind.

○ Breathe in and out of your nose for a couple of minutes and settle into your body.

○ From here, put your hands in prayer position in front of your heart (fingertips up and palms together).

○ Start breathing in and out of the heart center.

○ Put a big smile on your face and feel your heart warming up.

○ Now see your heart center as a bright yellow shining sun emitting light in all directions.

○ From here, visualize a warm rain pouring down from the sky on and around you.

○ As the rain hits the ground all around you, visualize flowers and plants springing forth.

○ See the life energy growing as the rain falls and notice that it's the sun in the center of your heart that's igniting this whole process. *The sun in the center of your being is activating the life all around you.*

○ Sit and revel in this for several breaths and then direct this visualization to some part in your life where you're stuck.

○ See the circumstance and bring it into your garden. Have the rain pour down to nurture it and shine the light of your heart sun on it.

○ See life growing all around it, and let the energy of life unlock wherever it is stuck.

You can go back to this visualization anytime, and I recommend doing it with all aspects of your business.

Over time, you'll see all kinds of wonderful things unlock for you. You can also apply this visualization to past events and memories and bring healing and the flow of abundance back to them. In fact, many of our blockages in life are trapped somewhere in our past, and the use of this exercise to go back and clean up the energy around a problematic event is very powerful.

Benevolence Leads to Abundance

One way to unlock your abundance is to stop making it conditional. Volunteer your time and help people to understand where true wealth comes from. When we learn to get out of the way and become an *agent* for abundance, we live a life of service. When we do so, things magically start to open up for us. Abundance needs to move through us, and what better way to achieve that than to *get out of the way?* The less you have anything to do with it, the easier it flows. Yes, your feet do the walking, but the energy is always working through us. When what you're doing is bigger than you, there's room for good things to happen.

After all, if you have food, fire, shelter, and water, shouldn't you be ecstatic? Imagine all the people who don't even have those basics.

Here we are suffering over things *beyond* our basic needs when there are people who don't even have those. This realization helps remind us of what's important and also keeps our desires in check.

MODERN HACKS
Do You Have a Budget?

Are you watching the flow of your money? A lot of people love to look away here. Money is evil, they believe. It is stressful and dirty. Ascetics can get away with this stance, but householders cannot. Avoiding money as an issue doesn't work because rent is due on a regular basis, so we need to face it.

Setting a budget gives you structure and order in life. It helps build discipline and gives you a framework to say "no" to items that are not in the plan. Remember, negation is the key to mastery. It comes from the prefrontal cortex and is a function of higher cortical reasoning. This is also lined up with the third eye from spiritual traditions. Working to cultivate this center (and this part of the brain) is a *must* in life mastery. An Urban Monk doesn't play "spiritual" and avoid material reality. Stepping up and dealing with reality head-on is a huge step in our homecoming.

Setting a budget starts with your needs. Those include rent or mortgage, water, gas, electric, cars, taxes, and the like. Once you've isolated these, go back and see where you can trim them. Can you stop watering your lawn? Are you leaving lights on in other rooms? From there, you can list out all your other expenses and look at what they do for you. How do they serve you? What is unnecessary? Start there and then keep cutting. Once you've identified the money in versus what money goes out each month, you can start separating the "needs" versus the "wants." Cleaning up the wants is usually not the hard part. Taking a cold hard look at the "needs" can unearth some juicy stuff. Perhaps you stop leasing brand-new cars and buy a 3-year-old car that'll last you a while. Maybe you carpool to work and save on gas. Maybe you downsize the house you're living in now that the kids have moved out.

If this feels like the last thing you want to do, then it is probably the *first thing* you should do. Stop avoiding reality.

The Richest Man in Babylon

George Clason's classic book, *The Richest Man in Babylon,* teaches a powerful practice that can change your life forever. Once you've set a budget and are paying attention to your in- and outflows, the key to success is to allocate 10 percent of your income to savings *forever.* Let it grow and see what happens. The magic of this is that money also takes on a life of its own, and when left to grow, it will start generating energy. Capital is a powerful thing. It can fund ideas, generate interest, be used to qualify for bigger loans, and much more. The key is to let your money grow and pay it forward for generations to come. This is a key piece of wisdom that's been lost in many families in the West as we've fallen prey to the advertisers and gotten into consumer debt. Real freedom comes when you can walk away from your shit job and know you can eat for a (long) while. You can fund your dreams, buy some land, and invest in a brighter future for your kids with money, but how will you ever accumulate it if you don't save?

Start now. Take 10 percent of all the money that comes into your life and sock it away in a CD or high-yield bank account. As it grows, you can speak with advisers and move it into funds that have a higher yield, but don't worry about that yet—just start saving. If you really want to be good about this, make that 10 percent come off *on top of* your retirement contribution. You'll need to work that much harder to trim your lifestyle and spend less in your day-to-day living. The rationale here is that your retirement money is to live off of when you've reached a certain age, but the 10 percent savings helps fuel investments and capital growth, which will liberate you from the time-is-money hamster wheel.

If you combine this with the previous exercises taught in this chapter, you can add on top of this 10 percent all the monies you were going to spend on bullshit and put those funds away, too. Soon, a couple grand will turn into some real money, and you'll find yourself acting like an investor. It really does change the game.

Invest in the Future

Another key piece to being a part of the solution is investing only in funds that are dedicated green and sustainable. All kinds of vehicles for positive investment are springing up now, and they often have very competitive yields. There are people who have decided to be a part of the solution and have already blazed trails for us to follow suit. The good guys are out there, and we can help them help the world. There is no way we can individually fix the entire world, but together, we've got a bright future at hand. An Urban Monk puts his money where his mouth is. Remember, you vote with your dollars. I've included links to some of these funds in the Resources section.

Release the Old

Marie Kondo's best-selling book *The Life-Changing Magic of Tidying Up* has made an enormous impact by teaching us to declutter our lives. I think the point is good but misses something big. Sure, sell off or give away the things you don't need and get organized, but also *stop buying more bullshit*. We accumulate so much stuff over the years, and most of it just sits there. That's why I love backcountry backpacking. It begets simplicity. Go through your stuff and see what qualifies as a need or a want. Pictures and family heirlooms are cool, but what about that tennis racket you've saved since college? Are you really ever going to swing that again? Clutter acts like stagnant qi that's lodged in your system. It doesn't help and gets in the way. The garage could be turned into a dance studio or a gym if all that shit wasn't in it. Why are you paying for all that square footage to hold junk you don't need? Sell it off in a garage sale or on eBay, or donate it and write it off. Unload the extra stuff and declutter your life. Out with it! The money you get from unloading it will just be a bonus.

A key to this practice is the powerful lesson we learn in the process. Dealing with the boxes and crates of junk we've accumulated over the years makes us also think twice when we want some trinket the next time we're out. Look into the future and see yourself selling the item at a garage sale. How did you feel about it? Was it worth your money and your life force? If so, get it. This is another way of creating a step where reason could intercept an impulsive purchase.

Don't Buy Depreciating Assets

Once you've cleaned out the garbage and seen how little you got for all the junk, you'll learn a powerful lesson. That is that depreciating assets suck, and you should avoid buying them as much as possible. A new car will depreciate as much as 11 percent in value as soon as you drive off the lot. For a $30,000 car, that's more than $3,000 you just lost, and it's downhill from there. On the other hand, home values rise on average year after year. Jewelry, antiques, guns, nice musical instruments, and land all tend to go up in value, whereas the millions of tons of plastic garbage coming over on ships from China are basically junk once they're bought. This isn't always the case, however. Collector's items can increase in value and are good investments.

The point here is to always look at your expenditures as an investment. Of course, be a conscious consumer and buy things that are sustainably produced and help make the world a better place. The more we align with the value we invest in, the more clarity we have. Remember, your money is your energy and is not to be squandered chaotically. Pay it forward into the dream world you are creating and watch the magic happen.

Level Up

Once you've stopped the bleeding, the next step is to improve your craft, message, or sales to upgrade your income. More water into leaky pipes creates a bigger mess, but once you've managed to set a budget and have a good sense of what's important, turning up the volume is awesome. This means having a framework for more success. If you could be content with your lifestyle once you've dialed it in, what would more money do?

This is where you can allocate a higher percentage of the new flow into investments and fun. I like to put 5 percent of my income into a vacation fund and make sure we spend it each year. I also allocate 30 percent into investments, growing the company on that end and also investing in things I believe in on the personal side. Donating to charity is a powerful channel for this money as well. Once you have it flowing in, you'll see how much more potent you can be in society.

It's one thing to talk about changing the world; Urban Monks get their houses in order and actually put their money where their mouths are. We make good things happen and are a part of a global solution.

So how do you increase the flow? It depends on where you're at in life right now. If you're in a salaried job, start looking at how to get bonuses. You should *always* be reading, learning, training, and up-leveling your skills in whatever profession you're in. Look to get a promotion, get that bonus, or train to move to another position if the company you're in doesn't offer any good opportunities.

If you are self-employed or on commission, you already know that your bandwidth is usually the limitation. Learn better management skills and learn to delegate. Get help where you need it, and get better at everything you do. This starts with your vitality. Practice qigong and increase your energy. Being strong and fit makes us more productive. Eat right and move your body. Get better sleep. You can invest the added qi into your career. You can read those books, make those calls, go to that event, or do whatever it takes to get ahead.

Once you increase your personal vitality, you have more to invest into your career and build energy there. Again, money is a form of energy, and it fuels the economy. With it, you can hire help, increase your advertising budget, or get that machine or warehouse that'll get you unstuck, and away you go.

An Urban Monk kicks ass because she knows how much good she will do with that money. A good householder is a community leader who can employ thousands of people and fund several charities. Money isn't an object for her because she's mastered it and uses it as a vehicle for good.

NATALIE'S ACTION PLAN

Natalie had a lot of bad habits but was easy to work with because her back was already against the wall. The credit card payments were killing her, and when we peeled back the layers, she was aghast at how much of that money was just interest. Natalie was paying a full third of her income in interest each month. I connected her with a debt specialist, and they negotiated payment plans with each bank, and she found a sane way out. The discipline was painful at first. We had to cut up her credit cards and shake up her lifestyle a bit. No more expensive trips and no more new shoes. In fact, she sold off more than 40 pairs of shoes she wasn't even wearing.

Running off a debit card, Natalie started to see how expensive her ways were. The $6 she spent at Starbucks each morning was reabsorbed by getting some good coffee at home and brewing it before she left. The bagel that went along with it was replaced by some organic eggs from her fridge. She started to cook at home with friends more often, and some of her crew moved on. Good riddance. Her real friends were people who could simply hang out, chat, go for walks, and watch movies together.

As Natalie got into some yoga, read some real books, and started journaling, she came to understand how her childhood was driving a lot of her financial chaos. This helped her become more aware of her emotional states and impulsive decisions. With some reminder cards placed in her wallet, a limit on her debit card, and a bracelet that anchored her down to her personal mantra, Natalie got pretty good at saying "no" to things. She stopped going to the mall for fun and went to places where she could enjoy life without spending money she didn't have. The park, hikes, museums, and friends' houses became mainstays.

The yoga and better food helped her with her back pain, and that saved the ton of money she was giving to the chiropractor each week. He helped her with some home exercises, and this time, she listened and started doing them. It turns out compliant patients get better.

It took Natalie two years to get out of debt, and then something powerful happened. She so liked her new lifestyle better than her old that, when the debt was paid off, she kept putting the same amount of money into a savings account for her future. She knew she couldn't keep going at the same pace in her job, so she needed an exit strategy. She started looking into nontoxic hair dyes and found some cool stuff. At night, she took some courses on Internet marketing and started a Web site. With her debt gone, she invested a percentage of the money she was putting aside into her new Web business, and within a few months, money was coming in from sales. She became "the nontoxic hair dye girl" and business started to take off.

She eventually left her day job and is doing great as a business owner. She's careful about how she spends and is saving money each month. Natalie is proud of herself, and she should be. She donates money to orphans in Bolivia and also works with preteen girls on developing a positive self-image.

CHAPTER 10

Living a Life with Purpose

VERONICA WOKE UP ONE day and realized she was lost. She was 4 months into the promotion she had been gunning for, and she still felt the same. For 3 years she pushed to get this position. She stayed up late, didn't take lunch breaks, Skyped with the teams in Asia well after hours, and always went the extra mile. Now, her hours are just as long, and she has more responsibility. The pay jump also put her in a higher tax bracket, so she isn't taking home as much as she anticipated. A new car and a country club membership later, here she was sweating bills again.

Her push to get the promotion left her adrenals tired, and her hormones were starting to mess with her. She was gaining weight, feeling anxious, and having trouble sleeping. Her husband still snored, and the kids were getting into trouble at school. Now she had the same number of headaches and even less time to deal with any of life's problems.

This wasn't the first time Veronica felt this way. Earlier in life, she and her husband were having some issues, and her resolution at the time was to have a baby. Her mom convinced her that this would take care of the problem. She was wrong. The baby brought sleepless nights and numerous battles over whose turn it was to "deal with" the kid. After the initial buzz of having a new baby had worn off, Veronica was back to work and resenting the nanny who got to hang out in her house and watch her daughter grow up. One day, she came home from work, and the baby cried to go back to the nanny's arms. This tore Veronica apart. Baby number two brought more of the same.

What the hell was going on, and why was any of this worth it? She was unhappy and unfulfilled, and despite a strong work ethic and lofty career goals, she was hitting her targets but still not getting the emotional payout. What was missing?

THE PROBLEM

We live in a culture where meaning is lost. We look for it in places it can't be found. The hero's journey is not in front of us. The old tales that were told around the fire have been replaced by sitcoms and reality shows. We used to be inspired by great people who did the right thing and were honorable. King Arthur, Robin Hood, Luke Skywalker, Florence Nightingale, and Rosa Parks all stood for something. They offered us insight into the human condition and helped us understand ourselves better. Today, we live in a humdrum reality where nothing is really that interesting, so we crave something else. We search for meaning but come up empty or only partially satisfied. We bought into a worldview that was put in front of us, but it has failed to deliver.

Since the dawn of time, people have been trying to influence the thoughts and emotions of others. Our culture took *yet another* turn toward something unreal after the Second World War, and we've been trying to make sense of it ever since. A fair amount of thinking went into fabricating our identity after the war because we had to identify our ethos in contrast to the philosophies of communism and socialism, which had created our new nemesis. The Soviet Union was built on these principles, and they were expanding their sphere of influence all over the world. The frontal attack on capitalism, religion, and "our way of life" created a need for the West to draw up a narrative we could all get behind, something to bind us and make it all worth fighting for. What we got was *Leave It to Beaver* and *Father Knows Best*. TV and movies were being used to help paint a picture of who we should be and how we should fit into this thing called society. It was contrived, sexist, and far too limiting. It didn't take long for a counterculture to emerge as people innately felt how the whole thing was devoid of life. We have been dealing with this fallout ever since and are seeing it profoundly in the younger generations.

They know it is bullshit.

They know it doesn't work and causes suffering, but the problem is that there's no great alternative they know of. They watched Mom and Dad slave away at work and still get a divorce. They saw the dream job also lead to a heart attack. They watched cancer take it all away in families close to them. They know money doesn't solve all of this, but money pays for food, and we need jobs to make that money. If you want a job, you have to go to school or at least dress a certain way and toe the line. Oil and gas are dirty, but your job is 30 miles away and the bus lines don't get you there. The fashion industry is insane, but you actually do need a jacket this winter.

We know there's a better way and look for it, but somehow there's no cohesion. Something is terribly wrong, and we hear of icecaps melting and Arab cities being overrun by lunatics every day. We go to work, make the commute, contribute to society (maybe), pay taxes, witness wars and atrocities, read the headlines, and come home to TV and microwaved food. There's no spark.

We looked for it at church but came up unsatisfied. We tried drugs and had some fun but didn't really find answers, just more questions and maybe a misdemeanor on our record. Maybe we had a glimpse of what it feels like to be free during those days, but we saw what it did to a couple of our friends. We can't afford to be on the wrong side of the law, and now that we've got kids, that shit is off the table.

We thought it was all about getting married and starting a family, but that's a lot of work, and those obnoxious cartoons in the background are giving us a headache. The never-ending parade of play-dates, soccer games, ride shares, tutors, trips to the urgent care, and those damn flus they keep bringing home is exhausting. We love our kids and want the best for them. We'd do anything for them but feel we're losing our grasp. Every day, they come home with some new idea or sassy attitude from the kids at school. We feel out of control, as if we've handed our most precious assets to complete strangers who are too busy pushing paper to care about our kids' individual needs. We may be heavier and a bit bitter. After all, we thought we'd be better off or happier by now. Life gets in the way of many dreams, and as the clock ticks, we feel more uneasy.

Where do we look? Who are we, and what are we doing? How'd we get here, and has life always been this drab and meaningless?

We may be interested in many things but not excited about much at all. We try to get pumped up for things, but deep down, we don't really feel it. Things are all a bit gray; we feel closed down and disconnected from that sense of pure joy we felt for things when we were kids. What went missing?

Why get out of bed at all? What is worth fighting for? We see people dying in Africa and the Middle East every day—hundreds of them going through hell on earth. What can we do? We already invaded and tried to help, but that didn't work out. How does any of this make sense? Why is this shit *our* fault?

The world is a strange place. The average citizen in the West has grown up with layers of guilt that have been bolted on from our predecessors. From racism to slavery, imperialism, economic inequality, resource depletion, and global pollution, we've all had a healthy dose of "it's your fault" energy. Now, if you've actively played a part in this stuff, that's one thing, but most people in the West grew up, went to school, got a job, and have been trying to get by and do the right thing. Their daddies don't own oil companies and have never been to an African diamond mine. That being said, maybe they have bought diamonds, drive an SUV, and still carry toxic racist memes that got passed down by Grandpa. Do modern Westerners need to carry the load and pay reparations to the rest of the world and shoulder climate change all alone, or is this unfair? These are the questions of our time. We all want to pay for the sins of our fathers, but most of us don't know how. We want to imbue our lives with meaning and purpose, but we don't have role models for doing that. We want to give back to our communities, but we don't know who our community is or what it needs.

Getting Back On the Horse

In the last nine chapters, we've explored the landscape of many of the lifestyle issues that are tapping our life force and draining our vitality. We've taken a deep dive into each of them to unlock your personal power through exercises, hacks, and a better understanding of how to navigate the choppy waters. How do these impact the subject of meaning and purpose? They help us regain our connection with *life itself* and, therefore, put us back in the flow of the Universe. Let's look at each quickly here.

Stress

Being saddled by too much stress impacts the immune system and the nervous system, and it messes with our metabolism. It cuts flow to the frontal part of the brain, which is the part associated with higher moral reasoning and the critical thinking capacity that makes us human. Being locked out of this part of the brain keeps us in the animal brain of fight or flight and needing to belong. Looking for meaning when stuck in the primal stuff is almost impossible. We have to clear the path for the brain to fire and activate our higher spiritual faculties. Then we don't look for meaning; it presents itself to us from within.

Time

Time connects us to all the power in the Universe. Our better understanding of what it is and how we can exist within the flow of it will liberate us in ways we can't even imagine. Time is one of our greatest teachers and an ally in life. It is the anchor of our being; when we squander time, we waste our life force. Because we are disconnected from our essential selves, we spend it frivolously and speak of being bored. The Urban Monk masters his interface with time and finds meaning and purpose once he's met his essential self outside of linear time. Stopping time and finding eternity is the daily practice we must master.

Energy

This is the currency of life. As you may recall, qi energy can be cultivated into Shen (or Spirit). This becomes the juicy stuff that helps us connect with the life all around us. It is the fabric of consciousness that we share with all the life around us, and it is something we can enhance and refine with our practice. The baseline is having a robust, healthy system that flows with qi. Getting out of our own way and then refining our energy into spirit is the way of alchemy and one of the missing pieces to the "lack of purpose" dilemma we face in the West. A flickering lightbulb won't cut it. We must come to life.

Sleep

What goes up must come down, and sleep is where we heal on the soul level. It's where our subconscious minds connect with the collective unconscious and where we derive meaning from our day's events. Most of us are so far behind in sleep debt that we always feel like something's missing. Correcting this and connecting with our daily "small death" helps us tap into the web of life. When we have adequately slept, our baseline anxiety starts to go away, and we regain the focus and perspective to find answers for ourselves. We feel great, and our life force radiates a sense of comfort and ease. We must sleep to be full.

Stagnant Lifestyle

Sitting around pondering our existence was one part of a monk's life. The rest of it was fetching water and chopping wood daily. Life was active and the hills were steep. Life required us to move our bodies, sweat out in the sun, brave the elements, and lift heavy things. This has been the case since our species stumbled out of the first ice age. Now is the first time in human history that we've become so stagnant, sitting around most of the day. Many of us are lost and disconnected from our primal roots. Getting moving is essential to unlocking our vital energy and activating key genes that code for growth and longevity. When the body doesn't move, it signals a shutdown and makes the mind dull, leading to a sense of disconnection and unease. Purpose doesn't always hit you over the head. It comes naturally once we've turned our lights back on by getting back in the flow of movement.

Diet

Good food powers the brain and activates higher spiritual centers to wake us up. Bad food does the opposite; it lulls us to sleep and messes with our energy flow. Getting on the right side of this equation is critical. You can't eat junk and expect to find some higher purpose in life. You are what you eat on all levels, which include physical, mental, psychological, spiritual, energetic, and more. An Urban Monk curates her experience of life to ingest good stuff and avoid stuff that'll slow her down and burden her system on any level. You become what you ingest and use that fuel to further awaken.

Nature

As the shamanic teacher Alberto Villoldo says, in the West, we are the only people who see ourselves *outside of* the Garden. The perception that we were evicted from a natural paradise has cut us off from the profound respect for the natural world that is bred into so many cultures. We tear through forests, mine through mountains, pollute rivers, and fill the earth with plastic shit we didn't really need. Disconnecting from nature pulls us from the umbilical cord of the universe and separates us from all the other life to which we are bound. We do this and then go to workshops at mountain retreats trying to find meaning and purpose when the first stop should be reconnecting with the natural world in our own backyards.

Loneliness

There is no such thing as loneliness when we find God, Truth, or whatever you need to call It. When we're disconnected from our essential selves, we feel isolated and confused. Tapping into our childhood passions and understanding that we've all got bullshit we're carrying around is the first stop. We can then find meaning in each other.

We can understand our common plight and see ourselves in others. As we take care of ourselves and vitalize our own lives, we can support others and tap into the energy of service. Here, we get out of the way and let our Higher Selves work through us. Here, we understand better who we truly are.

Money

I know lots of wealthy people who lack meaning in life. They go on expensive retreats, wear the nicest yoga clothes, buy lots of massages, and are still miserable. Money doesn't buy meaning if you've bought into the false promise of conspicuous consumption. Use money to fuel your dreams and lead you on a life of adventure and inquiry. Use it to help others and make the world a better place. Meaning isn't bought. It is home grown. An Urban Monk doesn't confuse these matters. If you're stuck trying to identify yourself through various cultural memes or trying to buy your way into a higher society, you're lost. Understanding our needs versus our wants is key to freeing ourselves from the money trap. Distill things down to the essentials and build your worldview back up from there.

Peeling back on why we lack meaning, we see that it is inextricably linked to our connection with life itself. The problem isn't that we've yet to encounter the right philosophy or self-help book and then we'll suddenly have meaning. That's absurd. Much of this has been mistranslated over from Christian and Zen lore where the master suddenly imparts enlightenment on the student. Our culture can be summed up by the image of the mob boss going to church asking for forgiveness for whacking people all week. A few Hail Marys later and he's absolved and ready to sin again. A sudden flash and "pow" makes for a great story, but this isn't how reality works. We connect to life daily. We pray to God daily. We sit in meditation and find peace, meaning, and purpose through our practice. The Urban Monk practices what she preaches and walks the walk daily. She is an agent of life itself and serves the life around her. Through this and her daily practice, there comes connection, meaning, and purpose. Come back to life, and meaning is all around you.

URBAN MONK WISDOM

We live in a culture of proclamations instead of self-inquiry. What this means is that, at the ripe age of 17 or 18, we have to decide what we want to be for the rest of our lives and somehow announce that to the world. "I'm going to be a doctor, lawyer, programmer, teacher . . ." We end up making a proclamation about who we are based on what our whimsical interests were in our late teens and are oftentimes stuck with this decision for the rest of our lives. Suppose we decided to be a lawyer because we wanted job security and were good at reading; we then find ourselves surrounded by other lawyers for much of our lives. If we then decide to practice criminal law, we could then find ourselves with clients who may not be too savory. Doctors are surrounded by sick people and other doctors. Teachers are saddled with politics and crowded class-rooms. Essentially, if we are what we eat, the decisions we make early in life oftentimes surround us with the types of people we'll engage with for decades. This isn't inherently bad, but what it does is serve us with a worldview that reinforces a fabricated identity. Who we think we are is compounded by who buys into that mask.

All of this happens at a time in life when we should be asking an important question instead:

Who am I?

In Eastern culture, there was a strong emphasis on finding your strengths and pursuing your destiny. Who are you, and what makes you happy? How can you walk a path that's in alignment with what makes you happy? How do you discover yourself and walk a personal path that will be fulfilling and noble?

We avoid these questions in Western culture and are often lost. As teens, we proclaim a career that often defines us, and we are stuck bolstering the edifice of this facade for the rest of our lives. No matter how much mortar we apply to the cracking walls, what's inside is bursting out. Our true selves are lonely and are waiting to shine. We get pinned down and then spend the rest of our lives looking for ways to feel better. We look for distractions, cures for our anxiety, self-help books, and spa vacations to take the edge off of this underlying feeling, but somehow it's still there. What if we're not asking big-enough questions?

We Are All Heroes

Deep down, we long to be the people we read about in the classic tales. Movies, books, fantasy games, video games, or whatever else we can use to evoke these feelings are great, but in the end, watching Luke Skywalker wield a lightsaber is not quite the same as learning kendo and being a badass yourself. Cheering for Spiderman as he swings across a cityscape is not nearly as cool as swinging from a vine in the Amazon on your next trip. Watching dancing on TV and actually dancing are in different leagues. Dancing is fun, yet we've relegated it to a sport we observe on a screen rather than an activity that fills us with joy.

The problem with the modern world is that the "stars" get to have all the fun. You don't need to be an Olympian to take a gymnastics course and learn to do a back bend. We've lost sight of this fact, and millions of people have given up and been relegated to passively watching shit on TV. You don't have to be at the pro level in things to start doing them. Lots of people swim and enjoy it without holding world records. Maybe they simply enjoy the water.

They found their switch. Where's ours?

As we identify the connections to our inner selves, we tap into a wave of energy that is contagious. You can recognize it in people immediately. We can see when someone is activated, and we are drawn to them. Some people are jealous of them, as witnessed in corporations and families around the world. Either way, we notice signs of life, and we then weigh that insight against our self-image and have a reaction. Either we're impressed, influenced, repulsed, offended, or motivated by people who are vibrantly alive. They rub off on us and remind us of something we long to be, or we resent them for being what we feel we cannot.

What do you enjoy?

What's that switch that turns us on? Where do we find the spark that can ignite our spirit? The answer comes with cleaning up the items discussed in the first nine chapters of this book and taking the time to get to know ourselves again. When we're flowing with vitality again, we can taste life, and people can see it in our eyes. We don't need to go searching for meaning or purpose because our life's direction starts to become self-evident. We follow the bread crumbs and realize that we're part of something far bigger than ourselves. We help move society, art, culture, math, science, philosophy, or whatever else we touch *forward*. We aid and abet life itself to make it better for generations to come because we see our immortal selves in the future of all of life, and we understand this at a deep level.

Finding our true personality is the key to finding meaning and purpose. An undeveloped personality is like a radio without a clear signal so the perfect sound is distorted. Clearing the channels so we can resonate with the harmonic symphony of the entire Universe is the key. This means getting out of our own way. Happiness is the by-product of self-realization and the ignition of our vitality. When we tap into the essence of who we are through our qigong, meditation, prayer, exercise, diet, sleep habits, relationships, and whatever else we do, there's no perplexing question that keeps us up at night. We sleep with a smile on our face because we've had yet another awesome, full day.

EASTERN PRACTICES
The Big Picture Exercise

A powerful way to frame a transformation in your life is to change your current circumstances in a hypothetical scenario and play it out. Ask yourself: If time, money, and place were not a consideration, what would I *love* to do with my time? Then ask yourself the following questions.

+ Why?

+ What can I do to go there?

+ What stands in my way?

+ Is it a real or a perceived limitation?

+ How can I transform these obstacles?

+ How can I change my current lifestyle to accommodate this and move toward the goal?

These are simple yet difficult questions. Many of us have kids, bills, older parents, nine-to-five jobs, and other obligations that are real roadblocks to getting up and leaving our worlds, and that's okay. Many of us have spent so much time training ourselves to think inside the compromises and limitations of the life that we believe we're done. We don't remember what it's like to dream without limits. This exercise will unhinge that.

Stop running for the hills!

The Urban Monk is a householder. We live in society and have the lives that we have worked for. So now, how do we adjust the way we spend our time, money, and energy to make our lives work for us? Once you've liberated your energy through the practices we've learned in this book, you can reinvest it in optimizing the flow of your daily life. With more time and money available to put toward your dreams, you can begin to create a plan and make it happen. Start to curate a life that's fun to live and filled with good stuff every day. That way, you won't need to fantasize about bailing out all the time. Say, for instance, you've always wanted to see the pyramids in Egypt. Okay, that's a 1-week vacation. You don't need to upend your entire life to take a trip, even if it feels so distant and difficult to imagine because *your life is heavy* with responsibility. Levity is the opposite of gravity. Bringing more levity to your daily life will help you make a plan, set aside the time, save the money, and go have your trip. You'll have stories to tell and pictures to share, and now you're back. Hopefully, it's not to a life you hate. That's the moral of the story. The funny part is, once you've gotten good at living a full life at home, you'll have more energy, time, and money to also go on all the adventures you want in life. You'll know that you've arrived when your home life and your vacation time feel about the same. For the Urban Monk, life is a wondrous flow of experiences, lessons, adventures, and opportunities to spread goodness regardless of where you are.

Sabbatical

So how does an Urban Monk approach time off? Treat your vacation time as a mini sabbatical. Don't waste your valuable rejuvenation time on bus tours of yet another touristy town. Pick a place where you can be at ease and get into a book, a practice, or some personal work, or just catch up on sleep. Ask yourself what you need and allow yourself to drink from that fountain. One week should suffice for most people, and that's not too hard to get in today's world. If you have small kids, take turns with your spouse or a friend to watch them while you spend time rejuvenating. Take mini trips as often as you can, and make a plan for more extended time off when feasible. Waiting for an extended trip and not taking any small breaks can keep you in the rat race for years. Just know that these mini trips can really help reconnect you with the Source and give you the runway you need back in your daily life to stay clear and balanced.

On a micro level, I treat Sundays as my micro-sabbatical days. I do only what feels natural, and I try not to make any plans. This at least gives me some space to relax and let the day unfold. Because I have kids, the day still involves running around, but at least they can get some unstructured time to play and explore as well. Do it as a family and savor it. You can't get these years back, and the sense of peace that you will instill in your life is invaluable.

Ramana Maharshi's Essential Meditation

> "The thought 'Who am I?' will destroy all other thoughts, and, like a stick used for stirring the burning pyre, it will itself in the end get destroyed. Then there will arise Self-Realization."

—RAMANA MAHARSHI,

IN *THE SPIRITUAL TEACHING OF RAMANA MAHARSHI*

One of the great Indian saints of our time was Sri Ramana Maharshi. He was a no-nonsense man who didn't care to have a following, but people traveled from far-off lands to visit him. His simple and elegant approach to understanding reality didn't involve lots of breathing, cleaning, yoga postures, or donations to a temple. He simply taught us to ask very provocative questions that were designed to help us drill down to the essence of our being. They run as a constant scan of our consciousness, which probes the nature of our mind chatter and allows us a chance at insight into the nature of the "asker" of each question. This is a remarkably effective way to cut to the chase and dig into who we really are. Here's an example of his practice that I highly encourage you to play with:

- Sit quietly and listen to your thoughts.

- Once you've isolated a thought you've noticed, ask the question: "Who just had that thought?"

- The customary answer we tend to come up with is "I did" or "me." Then the game begins.

- Ask yourself, "Who am I?"

- From there, you may ask further, "Who just asked *that* question?"

- And then, "Who just asked that?"

This powerful practice enables us to drill deep down into our identity to help us unlock the layers of facades we've created as masks. As we start digging into the inquiry of who we are, we begin to encounter several of the facades or stories we've created about that identity. The more we delve, the more obvious it becomes that the whole shitshow has been built like a Brazilian shantytown, shaky foundations and all. The truth about who we are is profoundly deep and empowering, but here's the irony: You'll never find the answer, just more questions. Why? Because probing into something that's infinite leads you on an infinite quest. When we begin to explore our infinite nature, we realize that there are only more questions and that's okay. Welcome to the Great Mystery of life!

Chapters

Store# 00925 Chapters Regina
Southland Mall,
2625 Gordon Road
Regina, SK S4S 6H7
Phone: (306) 569-6060

YOUR FEEDBACK MATTERS
Tell us about your visit today
for a chance to win a $500 giftcard
Complete our survey at:
www.indigofeedback.com

Store# 00925 Term# 004 Trans# 785784
Operator: 955TK   12/10/2017 14:43
GIFT RECEIPT

****
URBAN MONK   IAA
9780999761120

****
A GIFT FOR YOU
****

Holiday refunds accepted until January
13, 2018 Items brought back with a gift
receipt and in store-bought condition
may be exchanged for a gift card for the
value of the item on the receipt
Store# 00925 Term# 004 Trans# 785784
GST Registration # R897152666

0092500407857842

Taoist Dantian Meditation

One of the most powerful Taoist practices I have pursued for years is designed to ignite the Vital Essence in the area called the lower dantian. We've been breathing to this area in various practices throughout this book, and now, in the final chapter, let's turn up the heat. This practice uses physical manipulation of the core to condense qi in the lower dantian and activate our personal power. You can also use this practice to enhance your athletic performance on all levels. I've helped many pro athletes with this technique and upped their games.

Once you feel this starting to work, the energy of life becomes abundant for you, and you'll find yourself filled with enthusiasm, new ideas, and energy to do awesome things in life. Here we go:

○ Sit in a comfortable position with your spine straight, or stand in *Wu Chi* position (with your feet shoulder-width apart).

○ Start breathing down to your lower dantian, three fingers below your navel and deep within the center of your body.

○ Inflate the area on the inhale and deflate it on the exhale.

○ Do this for a few breaths to anchor your mind and settle into the practice. If the following is too much for you, go back to regular dantian breathing and ease into this practice. It tends to raise qi to the head, and you may get dizzy at first, so don't push it!

○ On the next inhale, you are going to do four things simultaneously:

- Push down the air deep and low into your lower abdomen.

- Simultaneously pull your pubococcygeus (PC) muscle up. This is called a Kegel exercise, and it works the muscle between the genitals and the anus. With practice, you can draw this muscle up to help strengthen your pelvic floor.

- Once you've pulled your PC muscle up (this is all in the same breath), pull your navel in toward your spine.

- Finally, visualize pulling the back of your spine in toward your navel.

There's a lot going on here, but essentially, you're surrounding the breath and compressing it in from four sides, like four walls caving in on it. The top of the chamber is controlled by your breath, and you get to modulate how long you can hold this before you exhale (yes, this was all on the inhale). Over time, you'll start to feel the qi from this area getting more robust, and you'll have surges of energy rising up your spine and to your head.

As you learn to refine this into Shen (try the Taoist candle meditation in Chapter 2), you'll gain exceptional clarity and insight.

Dying to Your True Self

This Indian Shaivite meditation is powerful and unsettling. It really helps us disassociate from our bodies and our egos so we can gain further clarity on who we truly are. The Tibetan *Bon* tradition also uses this type of practice actively. The essential practice is to visualize your dead body (yes, you heard me). See your own corpse and see it falling apart. See the worms, the maggots, the flies, maybe the dogs and vultures, all eating away at your flesh. See yourself giving your body back to the cycle of life. See it decompose and settle into the earth, where it can feed flowers and plants in the soil. Don't balk; just let it go. What do you think happens anyhow? Facing death is a powerful practice that liberates us from the fear of it and allows us to fully live our lives.

See the flowers push up and the butterflies hovering all around the life that has sprung up from your contribution back to the great cycle of nature. Do this practice daily and feel the loss and the agony of the ego as it needs to hang on. See your loved ones mourning your loss. Feel it.

Why? Because it'll help you step back into real time and live your life fully *now*. It'll disengage the grasp of the ego and free you to learn, explore, and not take yourself so seriously. It'll unhinge you from the fear of death and put you in the flow of life again. Meaning and purpose come to those who stop pretending and understand their role in the miracle of life. Death happens. It is the opposite of birth. It is time to be okay with it.

Third Eye Meditation

As promised in Chapter 4, here's a practice to help open up your "spiritual eye" and help you develop your intuition. I've saved it until the last chapter to give you a chance to develop your lower dantian for a while. Hopefully, you've done some of the practices taught in this book as you've read along. They're designed to help you build a foundation that will ground your energy and help you stay balanced in your practice. Many Westerners make the error of going for the spiritual fireworks first. They mistake the experiences with true insight and get lost. Developing psychic awareness and seeing energy are side effects of opening the third eye, but doing this before anchoring the energy body in the lower dantian leads to scattering of the mind. Build a foundation on good solid practice and a healthy lifestyle, and then this stuff will fit into the right place.

Here's the practice:

○ Sit in a comfortable position and spend a couple of minutes breathing down to your lower dantian.

○ From here, inhale your hands up in front of you so that your palms face outward with your fingers pointing to the sky.

○ Now turn your wrists inward so that your hands create an arc between the finger tips and the *top* of that arc lines up with your third eye (in the middle of your forehead).

○ Soften your gaze and look at the space between your fingers while the tip of your tongue touches the roof of your mouth and you breathe in and out of your nose.

○ Stay here for as long as comfortable and simply observe the space in front of you.

○ When you're ready to close out, exhale out of your mouth as your hands settle back on your lap.

○ Take a few breaths down into your lower dantian before getting up.

With some practice, you'll begin to have deeper insights and perhaps some precognition or psychic awareness. This is a natural state of awakening. Your intuition will increase, and you will be able to tap into this inner guidance for better decision making in life. In fact, it'll open a whole new world to you that's been hiding in plain sight. I've shared a link to what this looks like in the Resources section.

MODERN HACKS
Daily Journaling

One of the most powerful ways to dig into our own psyches and get a better sense of how we tick and tock is to journal. This allows us the space to go through what's on our minds and also express our feelings and frustrations in a way that we often don't do verbally. Our sense of meaning and purpose will be buried in this noise. So many people drag resentment and anger around with them and take it out on the people around them because they harbor it right under the surface. If we don't know what's bothering us, how can we adequately communicate it to others? We're just being cranky bitches.

Journaling helps with this pressure release valve because it allows us to have a dialogue with ourselves. It helps the self and subconscious mind to reconcile differences, and it also helps direct our attention to themes that reemerge. Our world is so noisy, and we seldom take the time to check in with ourselves. This practice forces our hand and usually nets some interesting results. You may kick and scream at first and feel like you have nothing to write. That's fine; just start writing. It may take a week to get the good shit flowing, and you'll just need to be patient and keep writing what comes to mind. Eventually, you'll crack and you'll never look back. This process is so therapeutic that you may be amazed at how much better you feel after a couple of months. Soon, you'll see themes that emerge consistently. They oftentimes line up with our childhood dreams and aspirations. You may have pushed them aside, but as your clarity emerges, the path laid in front of you becomes clear. You start walking in that direction, and life's adventure takes off. Meaning and purpose radiate from within once you've tapped into this.

Dream Journals

Doing a dream journal is also a powerful way to capture messages coming through your subconscious and possibly from the collective unconscious. Some really good stuff can be captured here. The key is to have your dream journal by your bedside and reach for it immediately upon waking. If you wait even a minute, lots of the juicy stuff tends to get lost. Over time, you will start to see messages coming through to you from your dream state and can learn about yourself and your journey through this.

Whether it's a regular journal you write in daily (or nightly), a dream journal you keep upon waking, or a combo of the two, one

PERSONAL JOURNEYS

I grew up with a strict father for whom straight A's were never enough. I worked my ass off to make him proud, but it was seldom enough. When homework was done, I was to study something else; I never got a chance to goof off. I quickly developed a habit of looking busy at all times to keep the criticism down. It became an easy defense against Dad's criticism, but the unintended consequence was that it stuck. As I began to learn about myself and delve into the things that make me tick, I found this interesting virus in my programming and saw how much it affected different aspects of my life. I learned to re-parent myself and make space for the young boy to play again. I felt guilty doing it, and that's why I knew it was particularly good for me. Giving myself permission to goof off and do something other than work was very liberating for me. It helped me understand myself, my family, and all the wasted energy put into a facade that needn't be there.

important piece of this puzzle is to *go back and read it*. Many people skip this step and lose a treasure trove of valuable information that can help them. Go back periodically and see what you were tripping on. See where you were stuck and what was aggravating you. Getting this level of insight into your own inner psyche is priceless and a key entry point into the realms of meaning and purpose. Again, meaning isn't some abstract thing you find one day. It is a layered feeling and gnosis of your true self coupled with a deeper understanding of nature and how the universe works. Together, we find where we currently sit in this web of life and get a glimpse of our path. Very few people have a clue about where it'll all go and what it all means. That's not the point and, frankly, that takes all the fun out of it. The mystery and adventure life brings when we're on our path and enjoying the ride is really the fun part. You don't have to know where you're going so long as you *feel* you're on your path. The journal can help.

Re-Parenting

Learning to engage in dialogue with your inner child is a powerful way to access your inner joy. Many of us have stifled this voice as we've individuated to become the serious adults that we are. We stopped listening to our inner child and have kept a stiff upper lip and pushed through. Year after year we've done this, and where has it gotten us? Exhaustion and sadness are all around. The exuberance and enthusiasm of our childhood flame is flickering and seemingly lost. Learning to reconnect with our inner child is a powerful way of bringing this back. The first step is to connect deeply and lovingly with him or her. This means recapitulating. Your inner child probably doesn't feel safe. You've probably dragged your inner child through various uncomfortable situations and not protected his or her tender heart. You need to reach out and assure your inner child that you're here to connect and make friends. Ask your inner child how he or she feels and what is bothering him or her. It may take some time to develop trust, but keep working at this. Really visualize yourself standing along with your inner child and engaging in this dialogue. What does he or she want to do? Get ice cream? Great, go get ice cream for real and treat your inner child to this. Getting into the habit of listening to our inner child will help us do things that bring joy back into our lives. When we do this, our inner child doesn't rebel and drive us to eat the whole tub of ice cream. One cone and a nice walk or a day at the carnival would suffice.

The pent-up energy we contain when we repress the impulses of our inner child leads to a suffocating sadness in life. As you begin the dialogue and start to care for your inner child, you'll find a sense of freedom and elation return to your life. With that, meaning and purpose become self-evident. They are not something we seek so much as what emerges through our joy and fulfillment in life's purity and beauty.

Backcountry Adventures

In a throwback to Chapter 7, let's take another journey back into nature. Getting back to our roots and tapping into the realms of meaning and purpose all happen with more simplicity. We live in a world of complexity. We think more is better and that, since our minds are complex and overly stressed, our solution set needs to be some elaborate scheme dreamt up by some super professor team that's perfectly suited just for us. Hence we search and we shop for the person, program, diet, book, mate, or guru that's finally going to be the right fit.

What if the answers lie in the other direction? Maybe we've gotten too drawn out into abstract thinking and complicated reasoning. Maybe the beauty of watching a butterfly land on a flower in the glistening sunshine is exactly what we need. Perhaps getting back to the essentials of food, water, shelter, and fire can help us simplify and see what we have in common with that butterfly. Certainly understanding that our corpses will be pushing those flowers up soon enough can be a sobering thought, but maybe that's a dose of some good medicine. Sure, we can build monuments and great libraries for our names to last for generations, but then what? You're still going to pass, and did you enjoy the journey? Did you find peace and happiness in your short life, and were you able to walk the earth with a smile on your face? From there, we can move mountains and change economies, and Urban Monks are doing this around the world, but stop number one on this journey is a homecoming. Find your bliss in nature and tap into your essential self. Learn to appreciate the natural world we come from and share with all the life around us and use that as the active framework for all the work you do.

The Urban Monk draws inspiration from nature and returns to it frequently to rejuvenate and reconnect. Take the time to do so and go on ample trips where you can freely roam in the wilderness and walk in the fields. Once you develop this practice, you'll understand its significance, and it'll become a part of your rituals for the rest of your life. It'll remind you of what's worth fighting for.

We are part of the life all around us. It's time to rejoin the party.

VERONICA'S ACTION PLAN

Veronica had been chasing things outside of herself her whole life. She has the personal power and wherewithal to do it, but time after time, she'd get to the finish line and realize she was in the wrong race. We started with some journaling and got her to work from home 2 days per week. This gave her enough time with the kids and took away the mommy angst that was building up. From there, I taught her some qigong, and she really got into Ramana Maharshi's self-analysis meditations. Somehow her disposition really gravitated toward this line of inquiry, and it worked well for her. She started having some mystical experiences around this practice, and they helped soften her personality. After all, she'd spent so many years building up the edifice of this "person" she wanted to be, and the result sucked. Tearing it down was fun for Veronica.

She didn't like the death visualization but continued to do it at my request. Finally, she broke, and it really opened a door for her. She had been taking herself so seriously for so long that she was like an armored truck. She never wanted to think about her mortality or anything that pulled her off the rails. Seeing herself die and wondering whether it was all worth it became a powerful catalyst for Veronica. It really made her rethink how she was spending her time at work, at home, and with her loved ones.

Veronica used to love painting but basically gave it up after work got crazy after she had her second child. She hadn't done it in 8 years, and upon realizing this loss, she broke down and sobbed. It was a huge part of her life, but other shit had come in and crowded it out. We obviously got Veronica to start painting again in the evenings and on weekends. She'd go out to the local nature preserve and do some landscape painting. Her younger kid came with her sometimes, and it was a great way to connect and share in this thing she was so passionate about.

Over time, she was putting less time into work yet getting better results. She was happy and it showed. It got more clients in the door, and she landed some big deals. The company was happy just having her there as good things happened around her. More time with the kids made family life better, and the painting really lifted her spirits. She started reading again and has taken several courses on housing and environmental design. She quit the country club and saved a bundle of money.

She's now doing a cool blend of art meets urban living with plants all around. People love her work, and she's being featured all over the place. She travels and does shows, lectures, and studies cool things to bring back and inspire her own work.

Does she know where any of it is going or what the meaning of all of it is? No, but she's elated and enjoying the journey the whole way through.

NEXT STEPS

NOW LET'S ROLL UP our sleeves and get to work. Hopefully, you've been trying some of the practices as you've read through this book and have already unlocked some energy. This book was designed to address the major issues we are having in our hectic urbanized world and to help you get unstuck. Here's the rub, though: Reading alone won't do it. You need to jump in and do the practices.

HARD WORK

Again, the literal translation of the words *kung fu* is "hard work" or "eat bitter." So when a fellow martial artist asks me how my kung fu is, he isn't necessarily inquiring about my roundhouse kicks. It is a metaphor for life itself. The premise is that how you do one thing is how you do everything. Life is hard work, and when we apply ourselves to *mastery* of the items we choose to engage in, we do what it takes to be good at it. Whether you're an auto mechanic, tax planner, or athlete, the choice sits with you whether you actually apply yourself and master your craft. It is a frame of reference, *an attitude*. Once you adopt this attitude, it relates to everything else you do. We become good at things because we remain aware, alert, and present. Divided attention fragments us. It makes us anxious and wastes our energy. An Urban Monk is fully engaged in what he does and applies himself fully. When that task is over, he moves on to the next one. When he's tired, he rests fully and sleeps deeply. When it's time to play, he's enjoying the party. He's switched on and vibrantly alive.

Look at it this way: Life is going to be hard work either way. Either you're on top of it and living intentionally, or you're letting circumstances, weakness, drama, and poor decisions knock you off your perch. I think we've all seen and had enough examples of how life could suck. Let's try a better way. Let's step into our lives and make the necessary changes to bring up our energy, drop the dead weight, and get out of our own way.

MAKING A PLAN

Most people look at the heavy burden of all their problems and feel overwhelmed. There's no way to take on all of that shit at once. The very notion that you could is insane, and it's kept millions of people from even starting to walk down the right path. It takes time, and that's not something we're accustomed to dealing with in our culture. We've fallen for the "pill for an ill" or quick-fix mentality that's been sold to us, and, guess what, that's bullshit. Life is kung fu, and getting things back on track takes work. Those who do it kick ass. Those who don't, well, look around you.

The key to moving the needle and making lasting positive changes in your life is picking a couple of items where your energy is trapped and working through them first. With the liberated energy, you'll have more resources and personal power to keep going from there. After a few rounds of this, you'll have momentum and a track record to drive further growth and personal development.

The practice I recommend for this is called a Gong. It means a dedicated set of work you've committed to for an allotted period of time. The typical length of a Gong is 100 days. Yes, that's a fair amount of time, but studies show that it takes about 90 days to really rewire a habit. Doing something for 100 days straight builds it into your life as a new habit and serves as a pattern interrupt. I've been teaching this for years and have thousands of students who've fundamentally changed their lives with this practice. It works.

What do you do in a Gong? Well, that's for you to decide. You need to assess where you're lacking in clarity, vitality, and personal power and come up with a personal plan for yourself. This isn't me telling you what to do; it's you taking ownership of your life and doing what's best for you. Go through each of the chapters in this book and determine where you need help. Maybe your sleep sucks. Perhaps you've got too much stress. It may be that your career is in shambles. Make a list of where you think you're the most stuck and then pick one or two things you can do right now to address that issue. You can pick from the hacks at the end of each chapter and also check out the additional suggestions I've included for you in the Resources section. The point is to identify where you feel you need the most help and then pick *actionable items* you can do daily that'll help you move in the right direction.

An example would be poor dietary habits. Your Gong may be to get a solid breakfast with at least 20 grams of protein each morning for 100 days. If you miss a day, you start over. Another example would be adding one of the many meditations you learned here in this book to your daily routine. A typical Gong would include one qigong set and 15 minutes of meditation daily for 100 days. That's a good start to get your qi flowing and get some mental clarity. You can layer on whatever else you think you need, but be careful not to overreach. The deal (with yourself) is to do each of the items you commit to every day without fail for 100 days straight. Over the years I've had several types of students, but one student type tends to overcommit and fall on their faces, and the other comes in too meekly and needs to step it up in their next Gong. The key is balance. Look at what you've got going on in the next 100 days and make sure what you're committing to is realistic. I travel a lot, so a Gong that requires me to swim daily is not happening. Pushups are another matter, though. I do those everywhere.

Stepping up and tapping into our personal power is the first stop on the journey to becoming an Urban Monk. From there, we rise to be beacons of light in our communities and strive to make a difference in our world. An Urban Monk is calm, present, friendly, helpful, abundant, and full of life. She gives freely of herself because she's taken the time to drink from the Fountain of Infinity.

Look to where you need the most help and get started on your personal practice immediately. It takes practice and discipline to develop better habits. Meditating in line at the grocery store doesn't work as well if you have not cultivated a practice at home. You need to know how to get in because it'll be harder when you're standing there pissed off.

As Urban Monks, we need to reshape our lives to be more efficient and include new habits and mini practices that will help us unlock our energy, lower stress, and get out of our own way. Life gets better. We improve with time, and things become easier as we're more adaptive and resilient. I'm honored that you took your precious time to read this book, and hopefully it woke something up in you, but *this is just the beginning.* You now need to do the work on yourself and in your own life. Nobody can do that part for you.

Let it drive you to get unstuck and find peace in your own body and in your own home. Take that peace with you and spread it across the globe. We don't need well-intentioned people fleeing society and running for the hills anymore. We need you here, and we need you to be present. Our children's children need this of us. Our planet needs it. All the life around us needs us back on the right side of this equation.

This starts with each and every one of us, and it starts now.

I respectfully bow to the Urban Monk in *you.*

Let's do this.

RESOURCES

CHAPTER 1

Video on Shaking It Out

It's important to see this one, so check out the video at:
theurbanmonk.com/resources/ch1

Boosting the Immune System and Vitality

There are lots of great herbs and tonics out there to help boost the immune system and help offset stress. Here are a few I like:

Reishi Mushrooms

Help modulate immunity and are adaptogenic

Eleuthero (Siberian Ginseng)

Helps boost energy and adapt to stress

Asian Ginseng

A bit warmer and more tonifying than the Siberian variety

American Ginseng

Cooler and more sedating than the other ginsengs, yet packs a punch to boost immunity

Astragalus

Helps raise qi and lengthen telomeres, leading to longevity

The above herbs and tonics can be cooked in with the Urban Monk Soup recipes mentioned in Chapters 3 and 6. I've included a couple of them here in the Chapter 6 Resources.

Places to Get Classic Chinese Formulas

Chinese formulas are fantastic medicine, but you want to make sure you get them from a reputable place. Lots of the stuff grown in Asia is unregulated and laden with nasty chemicals and heavy metals. Because this is an ever-changing landscape, I've included a list of places I like and will update this list as new companies come up and other ones fall off the wagon. Check it out here:

theurbanmonk.com/resources/ch1

Tai Chi Exercises

Here are a couple tai chi qigong videos for you:

theurbanmonk.com/resources/ch1/taichi

Caffeine Substitutes

Lemon Water

Often just a cup of hot water with a lemon slice in it will fulfill the ritual of getting in your cup of joe and will help detoxify the body.

Sparkling Water

You can't pound this stuff, and it's a nice drink to sip on all day.

Hot Apple Cider

Tasty and caffeine-free, this helps satisfy the tastebuds and gives us a bit of a treat.

Peppermint Tea

It helps move liver qi and stimulates our energy flow naturally without the jerky feeling we get from caffeine.

Heart Rate Variability (HRV)

This stuff has been around for a while now, and some smart people swear by it. The Heart Math Institute is doing lots of research, and many organizations have accepted HRV as an acceptable marker for stress and resilience. You can find out more at:

heartmath.com/

CHAPTER 2

Four-Count Breathing Meditation Track

I've included a bonus meditation track to support the practice I taught in this chapter. This track was recorded in a professional sound studio with some great engineers. Enjoy it!

theurbanmonk.com/resources/ch2

Time Dilation Qigong Practice on Video

This is another practice you'd probably want to see. Here's a video of me doing it so you can get a sense of speed, cadence, and depth of stances.

theurbanmonk.com/resources/ch2

Candle Meditation Video Demo

Again, a lot of these practices have been taught by direct transmission for millennia. Here's a video of me demonstrating the practice. I need you to nail this so your practice takes you places.

theurbanmonk.com/resources/ch2

Calendar and Productivity Apps

There are more of these coming daily, so I've created a page with up-to-date lists of apps I like for time management and productivity. With wearable devices and the Quantified Self movement flourishing, it's important to stay up on what's new here.

Check this resource out at:

theurbanmonk.com/resources/ch2

Brainwave Meditation Tracks

The two companies that have done great work in this space have both been around for a long time. In contrast, there have been many upstarts that have not withstood the test of time and lots of impostors in the space. Here are the two that I like:

The Monroe Institute

They kind of started this party and have been doing fantastic work for a long time. With immersion experiences and lots of powerful data behind them, these guys are great.

monroeinstitute.org/

Centerpointe Research

This company has also been around for years. I've personally used this stuff and recommended it to patients. It works and can really calm stress and build resilience.

centerpointe.com/

Here are some tracks I created for you at:

theurbanmonk.com/resources/ch2/braintracks

CHAPTER 3
Mold Resources

bulletproofexec.com/moldy-movie-toxic-mold-exposure-documentary/

Urban Monk Qigong Practices (Levels 1 and 2)

These are powerful exercises that will revitalize your qi, boost your Essence, and invigorate your Shen . . . no kidding. There is one condition, though: You have to do them! I've produced these videos just for my readers (you!) and hope you take advantage of them. Do Level 1 in the mornings and Level 2 in the evenings for best results. This will balance yin and yang and help set the tone for your circadian rhythm.

Here's the link to access them:

theurbanmonk.com/resources/ch3

Tonic Herbalism

Tonics have helped millions of people get their mojo back and can certainly help you. In Chapter 3, I listed the tonic herbs that I like. You can find a list of the companies I recommend for high-end tonics at:

theurbanmonk.com/resources/ch3

For soup recipes, see page 252.

Detox Guide

Well.org created a comprehensive detox guide that I'd like to share with you. There are lots of things to consider before jumping into a cleanse or a detoxification routine, and this guide can help walk you through them.

theurbanmonk.com/resources/ch3

Adrenal Reset: Dr. Alan Christianson

Dr. Alan Christianson has done some amazing work, and he's a hero. He's a fantastic natural medicine doctor and is great with toxicity and adrenal issues. You can visit his Web site at: drchristianson.com/

For other qualified practitioners, look at the Institute for Functional Medicine: functionalmedicine.org

Functional Fitness

I've got a couple of heroes doing great work in this realm and think you should check them out.

Dr. Tim Brown is amazing. He's been working with elite athletes for years and is really on the cutting edge of sports medicine. Here's his site:

intelliskin.net/

Dr. Eric Goodman has also made waves, and his Foundation Training is excellent. Check it out here:

foundationtraining.com/

Finally, some great work is being done by Pavel Kolar out of Prague. You need to check it out at:

rehabps.com/REHABILITATION/Home.html

CHAPTER 4

Coffee Swaps

In the resources for Chapter 1, I shared some caffeine substitutes, and here I'd like to recommend some swaps for coffee.

If you are going to drink coffee, I recommend Bulletproof:
bulletproofexec.com

The stuff is great and clean, and Dave Asprey is a stud. Most people do great with coffee, but this section is for people who can't sleep and need to tone down on caffeine.

Here are some swaps for coffee if you need a break:

Green tea: It has a nice balance of caffeine and L-theanine, which helps keep you calm and stimulated.

Yerba maté: Naturally stimulating, this stuff provides a good buzz and gets the job done.

Rooibos tea: This African red tea is rich and flavorful and is mildly stimulating.

EMF Resources

There are tons of resources online on this, but it's the Wild West out there for EMF products, so I won't put any links in print, as the science is still dicey and people are selling all kinds of questionable items. Check out my resource page for the latest information on this subject:

theurbanmonk.com/resources/ch4

This is an issue we'll have to keep dealing with in our culture, but there are lots of fear-mongering companies selling stuff that they claim is "quantum" yet has no real scientific background. I'll have my team do the homework and put the most reasonable articles and resources up on this subject.

Wall Shielding

lessemf.com/wiring.html/emfsafetystore.com

Calming Sleep Meditation

Here's a link to a track I created with Holosync technology in the background that's designed to help you sleep:

theurbanmonk.com/resources/ch4

Put on some headphones and have the track guide you gently to deeper, more relaxed brain states.

Faraday Cages

These block static and slow magnetic fields, creating an electricity-free zone inside. Used for science experiments and named after Michael Faraday, who invented them in 1836, these ideal hollow cages have recently been used by people trying to avoid exposure to EMFs. I've slept in an insulated room that had been "Faradayed out" and had one of the best nights of sleep I'd had in years. Worth a look.

Here's a blog on how to build your own:

thesurvivalistblog.net/build-your-own-faraday-cage-heres-how/

CHAPTER 5
Creeping and Crawling

We're learning that we go through certain developmental arcs as we grow from infant to toddler. In modern times, some of these developmental steps are being skipped as parents put their kids into "jumpers" and other props that help keep them from roaming. We're now seeing some developmental disorders emerge in kids (and adults) who skipped creeping and went straight to crawling or simply went straight from crawling to walking too soon. Some great facilities are dealing with this and getting remarkable results with learning disorders, balance issues, and behavioral stuff. The parents are also seeing benefits as they return to "3D" and have to use their bodies from the ground up again. Here's a great resource on it:

rehabps.com/REHABILITATION/Home.html

You can also find some additional facilities I like on the following resources page:

theurbanmonk.com/resources/ch5

Kung Fu Square Horse Stance

The main stance in Chinese kung fu is called the Square Horse stance, and it is the basis of much of the practice. This is a great stance to hang out in because it strengthens the legs and glutes, improves balance, takes pressure off the lower back, and helps generate more energy for the body.

To get into a Square Horse stance, start with your feet together and then open from your heels as far as you can turn out, then do the same from the balls of your feet. Do it one more time turning out from your heels, and then finally bring the balls of your feet halfway further to point the toes forward. This is the appropriate width for your stance. Now, settle into it by sinking down. Your weight should be balanced between the centers of your feet and your heels, and your pelvis should be neutral. This means your butt isn't sticking out behind you, nor is it tucked in. Sink and settle while breathing to the lower dantian. Here's a picture of the stance:

For more information, check out:
theurbanmonk.com/resources/ch5

Sitting Health Consequences

Amount of time spent in sedentary behavior in the US, 2003-2004. *American Journal of Epidemiology,* Volume 167 Number 4, 2008. Online:http://aje.oxfordjournals.org/content/167/7/875.full.pdf+html

Leisure time spent sitting in relation to total mortality in prospective cohort of US Adults, *American Journal of Epidemiology,* Volume 172 Number 4, 2010. Online: http://aje.oxfordjournals.org /content/ 172/4/419.full.pdf+html?sid=89f676d6-cad1-4552-9a16 -efb73ae68137

Pennington Biomedical Research Center (quote from Is Sitting a Lethal Activity?, *New York Times,* April 14, 2011.) Online: http:// www.nytimes.com/2011/04/17/magazine/mag-17sittingt.html

Interindividual variation in posture allocation: possible role in human obesity, *Science,* Volume 307 Number 5709, January 2005.

Online: www.sciencemag.org/content/307/5709/584.abstract?
sid=b27f80a3-1e62-4759-b104-b5171391c8f7

Calories Burned Standing vs Sitting, Livestrong Foundation, August
2011. Online: www.livestrong.com/article/73916- calories-burned-
standing-vs.-sitting/

Exercise physiology versus inactivity physiology: an essential concept
for understanding lipoprotein lipase regulation, *Exercise and
Sports Science Reviews,* Volume 32, Issue 4, October 2004.
Online: http://journals.lww.com/acsm-essr/Abstract/2004/10000/
Exercise_Physiology_versus_Inactivity_Physiology_.7.aspx

Desk Kung Fu Stances

Once you've got your Square Horse down, you can start with a number of other stances in a series that will work different leg muscles,

build qi, and bring more stability. I've put together a basic sequence that I teach at many of the companies we work with. Hang in each during your breaks for up to 5 minutes, and simply breathe down to your lower dantian. Here are a few to start you off, and you can also check out the video I created on this at:

theurbanmonk.com/resources/ch5

Desk Exercises

There's a great little circuit workout we created at Well.org for our corporate clients. It helps keep the day moving and fun, and it switches things up. Here's a link to a video on it:

theurbanmonk.com/resources/ch5

Earthing Pads

Clint Ober and Dr. Stephen Sinatra have created a pad that plugs into the grounding cable in your electrical outlet and helps ground your electrons into the earth. You can put these under your desk, bed, or wherever else you hang out a lot. Check them out here:

earthing.com/

Environmental Design

Setting up your environment to help optimally suit your needs for movement is critical. Make it so you need to get up and move. Sit on the ground and have useful toys around that make you better. Surround yourself with good food that's high in nutrition and low in empty calories. Stock your fridge with only good food. Use natural light and get fresh air. The Urban Monk looks at every aspect of his environment and makes moves to optimize them. How can you make your car more peaceful? What can you do to avoid collapsing your postural muscles on a flight?

No stone should be left unturned. Take the time and think through all the places you go and time you spend throughout your week, and see what you can optimize for better mood, performance, posture, and agility.

Bosu Ball Eyes Closed Exercise

This one may be hard to visualize, so I've included a demo video of it for you here:

theurbanmonk.com/resources/ch5

CHAPTER 6
Healthy Sauerkraut Recipe

1 head cabbage, cored and shredded to a fairly even texture

1 onion, chopped (this is a good source of prebiotics in the form of inulin)

Fresh dill (to taste), finely chopped

1 tablespoon caraway seeds

2 tablespoons noniodized salt

In a large bowl, combine the cabbage and onion. Add the dill, caraway seeds, and salt and stir to combine. Pack tightly into a large Mason jar (or series of them to get it all in), making sure to get any air bubbles out. Leave 1 to 1½" at the top of each jar. (One head of cabbage is enough for one large Mason jar.)

Leave the jar slightly open for a week to allow fermentation and then seal. You could eat the sauerkraut within a week, but it gets better with time. Three weeks is ideal.

Here's a video I did with Summer Bock on the subject: www.theurbanmonk.com/resources/ch6

Soups

The Urban Monk uses soups to restore qi and nourish the body. In the old days, we'd cook medicinal soups in clay herb pots, but today, we have slow cookers, which are awesome. In the following recipes, simply combine the ingredients in a slow cooker and let it cook for at least 6 hours. If you're adding big bones, I'd go a minimum of 24 hours and add a little vinegar to help break them down.

As for the herbs, here's a list of suppliers of clean culinary and medicinal herbs:

theurbanmonk.com/resources/ch6

Taoist Tonic Soup Recipe

Place dried legumes of your choice in a bowl with water and soak overnight. The next day, drain the legumes and set aside.

Choose either grass-fed beef (round roast) or a lamb shank and add it to a slow cooker. The meat has a warming quality and will juice up your yang qi, so add more as needed. If you don't need the "pow," cut a whole chicken into large pieces, leaving the bones in, and place in the slow cooker. If you're a vegetarian, simply add more beans.

Choose a fresh variety of vegetables that are seasonal (such as celery, broccoli, bell peppers, carrots, and peas) and chop into uniform pieces. Sweet potatoes are nice to add for flavor. Add the vegetables to the slow cooker along with the reserved soaked legumes and stir to combine.

Next, stir in the following herbs:

6 pieces jujube dates (These help build blood.)

6 grams astragalus (These are not edible but will enhance the soup and help you boost qi. You can leave them in the soup but don't eat them.)

6 grams ginseng (This is also a powerful qi tonic. If you slow cook them long enough, you can eat these.)

Finally, I like to add a cup of glutinous rice, which makes it more like a porridge.

Cook on high heat for 6 hours. Let it cool slightly and eat it warm.

Taoist Sex Tonic

Use a lamb shank with bones in this one and, again, seasonal vegetables of your choice. Add to the slow cooker along with the following herbs:

6 grams He Shou Wu (*Polygoni Multiflori Radix*) (This is a great tonic herb that builds vitality.)

3 grams Chen Pi (This is sun-dried tangerine peel [*Citri Leiocarpae Exoparpium*], and it helps move qi.)

1 handful wolfberries (Himalayan gogi, *Lycii Fructus*)

If you need more yang energy, you can also add 3 to 6 grams of Du Zhong (*Eucommiae Cortex*) to boost vitality.

Let this one cook for 8 hours (longer if you've included big bones) and drink hot.

Home Gardening Guide

Well.org has produced a fantastic home gardening guide for beginners. Check it out here:

well.org/homegardening

Fasting Done Right

Well.org also has a great fasting guide that can help you decide which type of fast is best for you. Grab it here:

well.org/fasting

MUFAs

Not all fats are unhealthy. Monounsaturated fatty acids (MUFAs) are a healthy type of fat. Replacing less-healthy fats, such as saturated fats and trans fats, with unsaturated fats, such as MUFAs and polyunsaturated fats, is a great way to go.

Consuming these may help lower your risk of heart disease by improving your risk factors. MUFAs may lower your total and low-density lipoprotein (LDL) cholesterol levels but maintain your high-density lipoprotein (HDL) cholesterol level.

Here's a list of foods rich in MUFAs:

Olive oil

Nuts, such as almonds, cashews, pecans, and macadamias

Canola oil

Avocados

Nut butters

Olives

Peanut oil

Digestive Enzymes

Different enzymes break down different types of food. You may have issues with a particular one that's deficient, or maybe your whole system is challenged by now. You can experiment with the right enzyme for the type of food that bothers you the most. Here's a list of the different types and what they break down:

Proteases and peptidases split proteins into small peptides and amino acids.

Lipases split fat into three fatty acids and a glycerol molecule.

Amylases split carbohydrates such as starch and sugars into simple sugars like glucose.

You can get a pill with all three main types or get them separately and see how they help with different foods. Getting to know your body better will yield some great wisdom.

CHAPTER 7

Silent Walking Video

This is a little funky, so let me show you what it looks like:
theurbanmonk.com/resources/ch7/naturewalk

Primitive Skills Course

Learning how to survive in the wild with our most primitive technology is empowering and beautiful. Cliff Hodges is the man. He's been doing this for a long time and isn't a weird cultish person like some others in the industry. Here's a link to his school:
adventureout.com/

There are others out there that people swear by, but I've sent lots of people to Cliff, and he's always delivered on education and overall experience.

Outdoor Adventure Schools

There are a couple of schools that have been taking kids out for years. As a parent, you want your kids to have this kind of experience, and both of the following groups have a good track record.

The National Outdoor Leadership School: nols.edu/

Outward Bound: outwardbound.org/

Here's a great directory for other schools: outdoored.com/.

CHAPTER 8
Heart-Centered Meditation

Again, let's show you what this looks like:

theurbanmonk.com/resources/ch8

The Five Animals Video

This is funky, so you'll need to see it. Here's a video walking you through each of them and how to "play" the animals:

theurbanmonk.com/resources/ch8

Professor Carl Totton

My main teacher. He's a genius and living treasure chest.

taoistinstitute.com

Getting Uncomfortable

There are some great ways to get out of your shell, make some friends, and confront some fears. I like public speaking and improvisational comedy.

Toastmasters has been doing this for a long time, and they have clubs all over the place. They help regular people face their fear of public speaking by giving them lots of practice at it. This changes lives.

Here's a link to them: toastmasters.org/.

For improv, you'll have to search for a local school. I have the benefit of being around Los Angeles, so there's a ton of this stuff. Most towns have a comedy club, though, so that's a great place to start. Find out if there's any formal training they offer or know of. You may be able to get into a local group and play at it. It'll be fun and help you not take yourself so seriously.

CHAPTER 9
Debt Counseling

Getting into debt is no joke, and too many people are saddled with this burden. You need a plan to get out and never get stuck under that weight again. It takes some discipline, but it is well worth it. Here's a resource for you to get started:

    nfcc.org/

Media Academy

Well.org has been helping small businesses step up and implement online business and media strategies with great success. Most entrepreneurs and small businesses know that they need to go online and have a presence but have been confused about where to start and what to do. Well.org created a comprehensive course that has been helping people with this. Check it out:

    media.well.org/

B Corporations

These are the way forward. Well-intentioned companies are moving in this direction, and there's a lot of buzz around this. If you're in business, I highly recommend you consider electing to become a Benefit Corporation and going through the credentialing process.

    bcorporation.net/

Game Changers 500

This company was founded by my friend Andrew Hewitt, and it is changing the game. Essentially, what are the top 500 companies that give a shit and are making a difference? How can we reshape value for a company, and what criteria do we use? It is a great contrast to the

Fortune 500, which is all about profits with no eye on sustainability.

Check out this awesome resource:

gamechangers500.com/

Sustainable Funds

There's been some great movement in conscious capital, and I've been keeping my finger on the pulse. We've created a resource with up-to-date information on funds that are aligning with sustainable practices and putting their money where their mouth is. This list will continue to evolve, so visit:

theurbanmonk.com/resources/ch9

Let's vote with our dollars and really drive the change we want to see in the world.

CHAPTER 10

Taoist Dantian Meditation Video

Let me show you what this one looks like when I do it:

theurbanmonk.com/resources/ch10

Third Eye Meditation

Again, let's make sure your hands are in the right position here. This video will walk you through this practice:

theurbanmonk.com/resources/ch10

Backcountry Companies

REI is a great company, and they can help you get equipped and out there. You'll need a stove, shelter depending on where you are, a water filter, and other gear. It doesn't have to cost a fortune. You can rent certain pieces and grow your kit from there. Get a weekender under your belt and then go farther and longer out from there. You can find organized hikes on their bulletin boards and can meet all sorts of interesting people at them.

Check out: rei.com/. They are a co-op and a great example of the many ways a sustainable business gives back.

Get out there and have fun!

ACKNOWLEDGMENTS

I WANT TO START by thanking my beloved wife. She's put up with so much over the years as I've been making films and traveling the world. She's been a rock in my life and has always been there with love, encouragement, and support. She's an angel.

My kids are the light of my life and I do this for them and their children.

My parents who worked so hard to start a new life and give us all the opportunities to get to where we are . . . thank you.

And more thanks to:

My sister who's been my buddy in all of this and believed in me the whole time.

My family—cousins, aunts, uncles, grandparents, in-laws, and extended tribe. They have made me who I am and have held me with love.

My friends who've always believed in me and joined me on so many crazy adventures in life. I love you all.

And a special heartfelt thanks to Dr. Carl Totton who's supported my training and education all along and also to my amazing Well.org team who work so hard to make the world a better place.

ABOUT THE AUTHOR

PEDRAM SHOJAI IS THE founder of Well.org, producer of the movies *Vitality* and *Origins,* and the host of *The Health Bridge* and *The Urban Monk* podcasts. He is also an acclaimed qigong master, master herbalist, and doctor of oriental medicine. Shojai conducts seminars and retreats around the world and is the founder of the Taoist Path School of Alchemy. He is also an ordained priest from the lineage of the Golden Dragon Temple in China. Shojai lives in Southern California.

INDEX

Underscored page references indicate sidebars. **Boldface** references indicate illustrations.

A

Abundance, from benevolence, 204–5
Active mental scanning, for stress
relief, 23–24
Activity. *See also* Exercise; Movement
ancient vs. modern-day, 98–99
bouldering as, 103
lack of (*see* Stagnant lifestyle)
Urban Monk Wisdom on, 100–106
Adaptogens, 63–64, 69
Adrenal glands, effect on sleep, 77, 78
Adrenaline, effect on sleep, 78
Adrenal reset
for energy restoration, 68–69
resources on, 244
Adventures
backcountry backpacking, 159–60,
207, 233–34
for overcoming isolation, 173–75
Adventure schools, outdoor, 253
Advertising, 190–91, 197, 198
Alcohol, sleep problems from, 77
Aloneness. *See* Loneliness
American ginseng, for immunity boost,
241
Amylases, in digestive enzymes, 253
Antibiotic use
bad bacteria from, 120, 127, 146
restoring good bacteria after, 162
Apple cider, as caffeine substitute, 242
Appreciation of assets, 208
Ascetics, xi, 192, 195, 205
Ashwagandha, as tonic herb, 64
Asian ginseng, for immunity boost, 241
Asprey, Dave, 245
Astragalus
for immunity boost, 241
as tonic herb, 64
Autoimmune diseases, 125
Ayahuasca, 149, 150, 157

B

Backcountry backpacking
for connecting with nature, 159–60
for finding meaning, 233–34
simplicity of, 207
Backcountry companies, 255–56
Bacteria
bad, 120–21, 127, 148, 162
healthy, 126–27, 145–46, 148,
161–62
in soil, 144
Barefoot walking
barefoot shoes for, 111
for connecting with qi, 104, 108
hazards of, 108, 111
Bench press, drawbacks of, 104–5
Benefit corporations, 199, 254–55
Benevolence, abundance from, 204–5
Big Picture exercise, for finding
purposeful life, 223–24
Black Death, 147–48
Blackout shades, for sleep
improvement, 94
Blood sugar levels
during fasting, 137
sleep and, 77–78, 90, 91
stress and, 5–6
Bosu ball eyes closed exercise, 113,
249
Bouldering, 103
Brain, prefrontal cortex of, 6–8, 9, 36,
82, 205
Brain engagement, activity and, 101,
102, 106
Brain fog, causes of, 78, 91
Brain function, stress reducing, 6–8,
217
Brainwave meditation tracks, 46, 92,
243
Breakfast, 138, 139, 239

Breath and breathing
  for analyzing time, 34–35
  in meditation (see Meditation)
  in qigong, 107–8, 108–9
  for sleep improvement, 88
  for stress relief, 15–16
Brown, Tim, 105, 244
Bubonic plague, 147–48
Budgeting money, 205–6
Burn rate, weight loss and, 128–29

C

Caffeine
  effect on blood sugar, 78
  substitutes for, 242
Caffeine avoidance or detox
  for adrenal reset, 69
  for sleep improvement, 77, 90,
    91–92
  for stress relief, 22–23
Calendar apps, 243
Calendar use, for time mastery, 44, 47
Calming sleep meditation, 245
Candlelight, for sleep improvement, 86
Candle meditation, for time mastery,
    41–42, 242–43
Carbohydrates
  bad bacteria and, 127
  overeating, 124–25
Careers, defining identity, 221
Chamomile, for sleep improvement, 89
Changes, Gongs for, 238–39
Checking-in meditation, for buying
    decisions, 201–2
Chinese formulas, resources on, 241
Christianson, Alan, 244
Chronic diseases, 121, 123
Circadian rhythms, planning activities
    around, 84–86, 85
Cities, bringing nature to, 152
Clason, George, 206
Clutter, eliminating, 207
Coffee swaps, 245. See also Caffeine;
    Caffeine avoidance or detox
Communication, inauthentic, 168–69
Consumerism, 190–91
Core, strengthening, 105, 110
Core engagement, for standing, 107
Corporate countermimicry, 60
Cortisol, negative effects of, 3, 4, 5, 6,
    78

Countermimicry
  examples of, 58–61
  rejecting, 61–62
Crawling, developmental importance
    of, 100, 101, 112, 246
Credit card debt, 188, 191, 192, 209–10
Creeping stage, developmental
    importance of, 100, 246
C-sections, 120, 162

D

Dancing, 184
Death meditation, 228, 234
Debt, 188, 191–92, 195, 209–10
Debt counseling, 254
Decluttering, 207
Depreciation of assets, 208
Desire. See also Wants, vs. needs
  as root of suffering, 10–11
Desk kung fu stances, 107, 248–49, **248**
Desks, standing, 101, 106–7, 109, 116
Detoxification
  for adrenal reset, 69
  caffeine, 22–23, 91–92
  for energy restoration, 67–68
  guide on, 244
Dietary changes. See also Eating; Foods
  for energy, 64–66
  for weight control
    Eastern practices for, 134–37
    modern hacks for, 137–38
    Urban Monk Wisdom on, 128–34
Digestive enzymes, 138, 252–53
Digestive Fasting, soups for, 66
Digestive system, stress weakening, 5
Dimethyltryptamine (DMT), 83
Dream journals, 231–32
Driving, hip imbalance from, 114–15

E

Earth, for connecting with qi, 102–4
Earth contours, effect on brain, 102
Earthing pads, 249
Eating. See also Dietary changes; Foods
  for meaning and purpose, 219
  mindful, 136–37
  Urban Monk Wisdom on, 128–32
Education, from lifelong learning,
    183–84

Electromagnetic fields (EMFs)
  resources on, 245–46
  sleep disruption from, 76, 94
Electronics, sleep problems from, 76, 86, 87
Eleuthero (Siberian ginseng), for immunity boost, 241
E-mail management, for time mastery, 45
EMFs. *See* Electromagnetic fields
Energy
  analogies about, 50, 51
  Eastern practices restoring
    dietary changes, 64–66
    qigong, 62–63
    rejuvenation practice, 66–67
    tonic herbs, 63–64
  factors depleting, 50–53
  for meaning and purpose, 218
  modern hacks restoring
    adrenal reset, 68–69
    detoxification, 67–68
    muscle building, 70
  money as, 188–90, 199, 200, 209
  stress relief from, 22
  Urban Monk Wisdom on, 54–62
  visualization of, 203–4
Energy fields, connecting with, 149, 153–54, 153
Entertainment sources, curating, 182–83
Environmental design, matching goals, 110–11
Epsom salt bath, for sleep improvement, 89
Erectile dysfunction, from high cortisol, 6
Exercise. *See also* Activity; Movement
  for adrenal reset, 69
  desk workout, 249
  functional movement training, 112–13
  recommended amount of, 99
  for stress relief, 24
  for time-compressed patient, 46–47
Exercise stations, at work, 110
Experiences, curating, 173–75, 174

F

Families
  connecting with, 171–72
  isolation from, 170, 171
Faraday cages, 245
Farmers' markets, for overcoming isolation, 181–82
Farming practices, modern, 121–23, 144
Fasting
  author's personal journey with, 131
  benefits of, 132–33
  guidelines for, 133, 137, 252
Fatigue
  author's personal journey about, 56
  contributors to, 50–53
  Eastern practices for overcoming
    dietary changes, 64–66
    qigong, 62–63
    rejuvenation practice, 66–67
    tonic herbs, 63–64
  modern hacks for overcoming
    adrenal reset, 68–69
    detoxification, 67–68
    muscle building, 70
  patient story about, 49–50, 70–71
  Urban Monk Wisdom on, 54–62
Fats, healthy, 90, 124, 137, 138, 252
Fat storage, from sugar, 124
Fears, activities challenging, 184–85
Fight or flight, 2–3, 4, 8, 192, 217
Fire
  for cooking, 65, 134
  learning to make, 158, 159
Five Animals, in kung fu, 104, 179–80, 253
Floor sitting, vs. chair sitting, 109–10
Flow, examples of, 194
Flow state, 34, 35
Foods. *See also* Dietary changes; Eating; *specific foods*
  energy-draining, 51, 54–55
  energy-producing, 51, 54, 55, 64–66, 70, 71
  for meaning and purpose, 219
  probiotic and prebiotic, 161–62
  reverence toward, 54, 129–30, 132, 134, 136
  for satiety, 137–38
Foot strengthening, 111–12
Foundation Training, 105, 244
Four-Count Breathing Meditation, for time mastery, 38–40, 242
Functional fitness, 70, 105–6, 244
Functional movement training, 112–13

G

Game Changers 500, 255
Gardening, home, 134–35, 160,
        252
"Get in the Flow" exercise, for
        attracting money, 203–4
Ginseng, as tonic herb, 63–64
Gongs, xiii, 84, 238–39
Goodman, Eric, 105, 244
Grains, 136, 138
Green tea, 20, 245
Group activities, for overcoming
        loneliness, 182

H

Hard work, life as, 100, 237
Healing work
    for overcoming isolation, 178–79
    for sleep improvement, 80–81
Health-care costs, 121
Heart-Centered Meditation, for
        overcoming isolation, 177–78,
        253
Heart rate variability (HRV), for stress
        relief, 24, 242
Herbs
    immune-boosting, 241
    for sleep improvement, 89–90
    for stress relief, 19–20
    suppliers of, 250
    tonic, 63–64, 66, 241, 244
Hewitt, Andrew, 255
Hip imbalance, from driving, 114–15
Hodges, Cliff, 158, 253
Holy basil (Tulsi), for stress relief, 19
Home gardening, 134–35, 160, 252
Home security, for sleep improvement,
        87–88
Householders, xi, 224
    money issues of, 192, 195, 200,
        205, 209
    responsibilities of, xii, 193, 209
Houseplants, for connecting with
        nature, 160
HRV, for stress relief, 24, 242
Hunger, from nutrient depletion,
        121–22, 125
Hydration, 90, 113
Hyman, Mark, 124

I

Identity
    careers defining, 221
    meditation practice for finding,
        226
Immune system
    herbs and tonics boosting, 241
    inflammation and, 128
    stress weakening, 4, 217
    toxic exposure and, 125
Improvisational comedy, 184, 254
Impulse control, meditation for, 36
Inactivity. See also Stagnant lifestyle
    negative effects of, x, 99, 106,
        107
Income, increasing, 208–9
Inflammation, 102–3, 127, 128
Information, curating sources of,
        11–12, 182–83
Inner child, re-parenting for engaging,
        232–33
Inner state, for changing outer world,
        13–14
Insomnia. See Sleep problems
Investments, 198, 202, 203, 207, 208
Irrelevance, fear of, 193

J

Journaling, 230–32

K

Kava
    for sleep improvement, 89
    for stress relief, 20
Ketosis, 133
Kolar, Pavel, 244
Kondo, Marie, 207
Kung fu
    energy and, 22, _153_
    for fitness, 105
    Five Animals in, 104, 179–80, 253
    as hard work, 100, 237
    stances
        performed at desk, 107, 248–49,
            248
        Square Horse, 101, 246, 247,
            247

L

Leaky gut syndrome, 127–28
Learning opportunities, for overcoming
    isolation, 183–84
Legacy, money-driven, 194
Lemon water, as caffeine substitute, 242
Letting go, for sleep improvement,
    79–80, 81–82
Lifelong learning, for overcoming
    isolation, 183–84
Light, preventing sleep, 75–76, 86, 94
Lipases, in digestive enzymes, 252
Local groups, for overcoming isolation,
    182
Loneliness
    causes of, 166–69
    Eastern practices for overcoming
        healing past wounds, 177–78
        Heart-Centered Meditation,
            177–78
        role-playing Five Animals, 179–80
        spirituality, 180–81
        volunteerism, 179
    modern hacks for overcoming
        curating media and entertainment
            sources, 182–83
        farmers' market visits, 181–82
        joining local groups, 182
        psychotherapy, 184
        seeking learning opportunities,
            183–84
        uncomfortable activities, 184–85
    overcoming, for meaning and
        purpose, 219–20
    patient story about, 165–66, 185–86
    Urban Monk Wisdom on, 169–77
Lottery winners, 188
Louv, Richard, 142
Lovemaking, for sleep improvement,
    88–89
Lung cancer, from smoking, 122–23

M

Magnesium, for sleep improvement, 89
MCT oil, 138, 139, 140
Meaningless life. See also Purposeful
    life
    alternative to (see Purposeful life)
    contributors to, 214–17

patient story about, 213–14, 234–35
    Urban Monk Wisdom on, 221–23
Media, countermimicry in, 60
Media academy, for small businesses,
    254
Media fasts, 42–44, 191
Media sources, curating, 182–83
Medicinal wisdom, of shamans,
    149–50
Medicine, countermimicry in, 59–60
Meditation(s)
    for achieving calm, 9–10
    for adrenal reset, 69
    fear of, 80
    Gong for starting, 239
    for impulse control, 36
    in nature, 150
    practices
        calming sleep meditation, 245
        candle meditation, 41–42, 242–43
        checking-in meditation, 201–2
        death visualization, 228
        Four-Count Breathing
            Meditation, 38–40, 242
        Heart-Centered Meditation,
            177–78, 253
        of Ramana Maharshi, 225–26,
            234
        Slow Walking Meditation, 109
        Stream Meditation, 155–57
        stress relief meditation, 15–17
        Taoist Dantian Meditation,
            227–28, 255
        Third Eye Meditation, 229–30,
            255
    for sleep improvement, 81, 88
    weekend, 94
Medium-chain triglycerides (MCT),
    138, 139, 140
Meetings, walking during, 115
Melatonin, effect on sleep, 75, 82, 83,
    89
Mental scanning, for stress relief,
    23–24
Microbiome, 126–27, 145–47
Mindful eating, 136–37
Mitochondria, 52, 66–67, 70
Modern problems, examples of, ix–x
Mold, 52, 243
Money
    as energy, 188–90, 199, 200, 209
    fear of losing, 192–93

Money (*cont.*)
  investing, 198, 202, 203, 206–7
  lack of meaning and, 220
  saving, 189, 202, 206
Money problems
  author's personal journey with, 189
  causes of, 188–94
  Eastern practices for solving
    checking-in meditation, 201–2
    "Get in the Flow" exercise, 203–4
    spending fast, 202–3
    volunteerism, 204–5
  modern hacks for solving
    allocating savings, 206
    avoiding depreciating assets, 208
    budgeting, 205
    decluttering, 207
    increasing income, 208–9
    investing, 206–7
  patient stories about, 11, 187–88,
    209–11
  Urban Monk Wisdom on, 194–201
Monunsaturated fatty acids (MUFAs),
  138, 252
Morning visualization, for stress relief,
  20–21
Movement. *See also* Activity; Exercise
  for energy, 52–53, 55–56
  environmental design for, 249
  lack of, 53
  for meaning and purpose, 218–19
Moving Qigong with Time Dilation
  Practice, 40–41, 242
MUFAs, 138, 252
Muscle building, for energy restoration,
  70
Muscle imbalance, injuries from, 105

N

Naps, for sleep improvement, 81–82, 87
Narby, Jeremy, 149–50
Nature
  disconnection from
    effects of, 143
    origin of, 142–48
    patient story about, 141–42, 147,
      162–63
  Eastern practices for connecting with
    communicating with plant spirits,
      157–58
    silent walking in nature, 155
    Stream Meditation, 155–57
    "Tree" qigong practice, 153–54
  energy from, 57–58
  former connection to, 142–43
  meaning and purpose from, 219
  modern hacks for connecting with
    backcountry backpacking,
      159–60, 233–34
    houseplants and home gardens,
      160
    probiotic and prebiotic foods,
      161–62
    visiting local parks, 160
    volunteerism, 159
    wilderness survival training,
      158–59
  Urban Monk Wisdom on, 149–53
Needs, vs. wants, 158, 197, 198, 201,
  205, 220
Negative self-image, patient story
  about, 119–20
News, curating sources of, 11–12
Nonreactive state, for calm, 10, 14
Nutrient depletion, hunger from,
  121–22, 125

O

Ober, Clint, 103, 249
Organic foods, 54, 71, 135, 195–96
Outdoor adventure schools, 253

P

Parasitic elements, energy-draining,
  58–62
Parks, for connecting with nature, 160
Past wounds, healing, 178–79
Peppermint, for stress relief, 20
Peppermint tea, as caffeine substitute,
  242
Peptidases, in digestive enzymes, 252
Personal time, importance of, 172
Pesticides, 122, 144
Phone calls, walking during, 115
Phone reminders, for movement, 113
Pineal gland, effect on sleep, 75, 82–83,
  94
Plagues, 147–48
Plants
  communicating with, 149–50, 157–58
  energy fields of, 153

Play time, weekend, 94
Politics, countermimicry in, 59
Prebiotic foods, 161, 162
Prefrontal cortex, 6–8, 9, 36, 82, 205
Present moment, being in, 33–34, 37
Primitive skills training, 158–59, 253
Probiotics, 146, 161–62
Productivity apps, 243
Proteases, in digestive enzymes, 252
Protein
    for blood sugar stability, 90
    breakfast, 239
    for satiety, 137–38
Psychotherapy, for overcoming
    isolation, 184
Public speaking, 184, 254
Purposeful life. *See also* Meaningless
    life
    Eastern practices for finding
        Big Picture exercise, 223–24
        death visualization, 228
        sabbaticals, 225–26
        Taoist Dantian Meditation,
           227–28, 255
        Third Eye Meditation, 229–30,
           255
    lifestyle issues and, 217–20
    modern hacks for finding
        backcountry adventures, 233–34
        daily journaling, 230
        dream journals, 231–32
        re-parenting, 232–33

Q

Qi
    clutter stagnating, 207
    from connection with nature, 151
    of earth, 102–4
    eating building, 132
    energy as, 50, 218
    flow of, 194
    moving, 107–8
    rejuvenation practices building,
        66–67
Qigong
    for adrenal reset, 69
    for energy, 62–63, 107–8
    Moving Qigong with Time Dilation
        Practice, 40–41, 242
    performing, 108–9
    for starting the day, 21

"Tree," for connecting with energy
    field, 153–54
videos on, 243–44

R

Ramana Maharshi, meditation of,
    225–26, 234
Random acts of kindness, for
    overcoming isolation, 179
REI backcountry equipment, 255–56
Reishi, as tonic herb, 64
Rejuvenation practices, for energy,
    66–67
Relaxation, for time-compressed
    patient, 47
Relevance, fear of losing, 193
Religion
    countermimicry in, 59
    dissatisfaction with, x, 170, 180
Re-parenting
    author's personal journey in, <u>231</u>
    for engaging inner child, 232–33
Rest, for energy, 56–57
Retirement savings, 199, 206
Reverence, toward food, 54, 129–30,
    132, 134, 136
Rhodiola, as tonic herb, 64
Rice, 135–36
"Right livelihood," 199
Ritual of the Moon, for sleep
    improvement, 83–84
Rooibos tea, as coffee swap, 245
Room temperature, for sleep
    improvement, 90–91, 94

S

Sabbaticals, 225
Salt baths, for energy, 66–67
Sanitation, for preventing plagues, 148
Satiety, foods for, 137–38
Sauerkraut, 135, 162, 250
Saving money, 189, 202, 206
Saying "no," for time mastery, 35–36
Scheduled breaks, for time mastery, 44,
    47
Self-defense, for stress relief, 21–22
Self-image, dissatisfaction with, 167
Serotonin, effect on sleep, 82, 89
Service organizations, for connecting
    with nature, 159

Service to others, 175–77. *See also*
    Volunteerism
Shaking it out exercise, for stress relief,
    17–19, 241
Shamans, plant medicine of, 19, 83,
    149–50, 157
Shoes, barefoot, 111
Sierra Club, 159
Silence vow, for energy restoration, 67
Silent walking in nature, 155, 253
Sinatra, Stephen, 103, 249
Sitting
    alternatives to, 106–7, 109–10
    health consequences of, 107, 247–48
Slave trade economy, sugar in, 123
Sleep. *See also* Sleep problems
    for adrenal reset, 69
    author's personal journey about, <u>87</u>
    for meaning and purpose, 218
Sleep apnea, 82
Sleep problems
    causes of, 75–78
    Eastern practices for relieving
        calming meditation, 88, 245
        herbs and minerals, 89–90
        lovemaking, 88–89
        observing personal rhythms,
            84–86, 85
        Ritual of the Moon, 83–84
        starlight, 88
        wind-down routine, 86–88
    effects of, 73, 74
    modern hacks for relieving
        basic sleep hygiene, 90
        blood sugar management, 91
        brainwave tracks, 92
        caffeine detox, 91–92
        environment adjustments, 94–95
        room temperature adjustment,
            90–91, 94
        time management, 92–94
    patient story about, 73–74, 95–96
    Urban Monk Wisdom on, 79–83
Slow cooker, for making soup, 250, 251
Slow Walking Meditation, for
    overcoming stagnation, 109
Small businesses, media academy for,
    254
Small death, sleep as, 81, 218
Smoking, lung cancer from, 122–23
Social isolation. *See* Loneliness
Social media, time wasted on, 43, 44
Social status, from possessions, 197–98

Soil
    depletion of, 121
    good bacteria in, 144, 145
    proper treatment of, 122, 144
Sound reduction, for sleep
        improvement, 94
Soups
    for adrenal reset, 69
    for energy restoration, 65–66
    as nutrient source, 134
    recipes for, 250–51
Sparkling water, as caffeine substitute,
    242
Spending fast, for saving money,
    202–3
Spiritual practice
    finding, 180–81
    for self-realization, 169–70
Sports, nonparticipation in, 166
Square Horse stance, in kung fu, 101,
    246–47, **247**
Stagnant lifestyle
    contributors to, 98–99
    Eastern practices for reversing
        qigong breaks, 107–8, 108–9
        Slow Walking Meditation, 109
        standing, 106–7
        walking barefoot, 108
    modern hacks for reversing
        alternative transportation to
            work, 114–15
        barefoot shoes, 111–12
        functional movement training,
            112–13
        phone reminders to move, 113
        sitting on the floor, 109–10
        telecommuting, 113–14
        walking at work, 115–16
        workout tools, 110, 111
    patient story about, 97–98, 99, 101,
        116–17
    Urban Monk Wisdom on, 100–106,
        116
Standing desks, 101, 106–7, 109, 116
Starlight, for sleep improvement, 88
Stillness, benefits of, 37
Strassman, Rick, 83
Stream Meditation, for connecting with
        nature, 155–57
Stress, 139
    acute, 2–3
    author's personal journey with, <u>7</u>
    chronic, negative effects of, 3–8

Eastern practices relieving
    morning visualization, 20–21
    relaxing herbs and teas, 19–20
    shaking it out, 17–19
    stress relief meditation, 15–17
    Urban Monk operating system,
        14–15
effect on meaning and purpose, 217
modern hacks relieving
    active mental scanning, 23–24
    brainwave meditation tracks, 46
    caffeine detox, 22–23
    exercise, 23–24
    heart rate variability, 24
    self-defense, 21–22
from money problems, 192
patient story about, 1–2, 25
reducing, for adrenal reset, 69
Urban Monk Wisdom on, 8–14
Stress bucket, recalibrating, 12–13, 158
Stress relief meditation, 15–17
Suan Zao Ren Wan, for sleep
        improvement, 89–90
Sugar
    addiction to, 123–24, 137
    bad bacteria and, 127
    eating less, 137, 138
Sunday, as micro-sabbatical, 225
Survival training, wilderness, 158–59,
        162, 253
Sustainable funds, 255

T

Tai chi, x, xi, 22, 29, 69, 108, 174
Taoist Dantian Meditation, 227–28,
        255
Taoist Sex Tonic, 251
Taoist Tonic Soup Recipe, 250–51
Teas
    as caffeine substitutes, 242, 245
    for stress relief, 19–20
Technology purge, for sleep
        improvement, 86, 87
Telecommuting, 113–14
Television
    avoiding, for time mastery, 43, 44,
        46
    curating sources of, 182–83
    negativity of, 43
Thankfulness, for food, 54, 130, 136
Third eye, 6, 9, 42, 82, 157, 205

Third Eye Meditation, 229–30, 255
Time Compression Syndrome
    author's personal journey with, 29
    causes and effects of, 28–32, 51
    example of, 35
    patient story about, 27–28, 46–47
    relieving (see Time mastery)
Time dilation, 32, 33
Time dilation practice, moving qigong
        with, 39–41, 242
Time management
    apps for, 243
    planning for, 83–84
    for sleep improvement, 92–94
Time mastery
    Eastern practices for
        candle meditation, 41–42
        Four-Count Breathing
            Meditation, 38–40
        moving qigong with time dilation
            practice, 40–41
    for meaning and purpose, 217
    modern hacks for
        brainwave meditation tracks, 46
        e-mail chunk time, 45
        media fast, 42–44
        scheduled breaks, 44
    for overcoming isolation, 172–73
    Urban Monk Wisdom on, 32–38
Time pollution, 38
Toastmasters, 254
Tomberg, Valentin, 185
Tonic herbs
    for energy restoration, 63–64, 66
    immune-boosting, 241
    resources on, 244
Toxic exposure
    effects of, 125–26
    from environment, 52, 67
Transportation alternatives, 114
"Tree" qigong practice, for connecting
        with energy field, 153–54
Tryptophan, effect on sleep, 82

U

Uncomfortable activities, for
        overcoming isolation, 184–85,
        254
Urban Monk, background of, xi–xii
Urban Monk, The, organization of,
        xii–xiii

Urban Monk operating system, for
    stress relief, 14–15
Urban Monk Qigong Practices, 63

V

Vacations, 32–33, 225
Value of goods, factors determining,
    196, 201
Vegetables
    homegrown, 134–35
    organic, 54
    for satiety, 138
    steamed, 135
Villoldo, Alberto, 153, 219
Visualization exercises
    death meditation, 228, 234
    morning, for stress relief, 20–21
    for saving money, 203–4
Vitality, for protection from stress, 8
Volunteerism
    for connecting with nature, 159
    for overcoming isolation, 179
    for unlocking abundance, 204–5
Vow of silence, for energy restoration,
    67

W

Walking
    barefoot, 104, 108, 111
    with dog, 117
    silent, in nature, 155, 253
    at work, 115–16
Walking Meditation, for overcoming
    stagnation, 109
Wall shielding, 88, 246
Wants, vs. needs, 158, 197, 198, 201,
    205, 220
Weekends, time management on, 93–94
Weight gain
    contributors to
        carbohydrates, 124–25
        inactivity, 106

leaky gut syndrome, 127–28
microbiome challenges, 127–28
modern farming practices,
    121–23
sugar addiction, 123–24
toxic exposure, 125–26
Eastern practices for managing
    eating rice, 135–36
    fasting, 137
    home gardening, 134–35
    mindful eating, 136–37
    steaming vegetables, 135
modern hacks for managing
    achieving satiety, 137–38
    digestive enzymes, 138
    stress and sleep management,
        138–39
patient stories about, 97, 119–21,
    139–40
Urban Monk Wisdom on, 128–34
Weight lifting, for energy restoration,
    70
Wilderness survival training, 253
    for connecting with nature, 158–59,
        162
Workdays, time management on, 93
Workout tools, in exercise stations,
    110, 111
Wrangham, Richard, 65
Wu Chi stance, 109, 227

X

Xiao Yao San, for stress relief, 20

Y

Yerba maté, as coffee swap, 245

Z

Zucker, Martin, 103

Dr. Mark Hyman Video   Jan 2018

Top Mitochondrial Nutrients
Acetyl-L-Carnitine
Alpha Lipoic Acid
Coenzyme Q10 (CoQ10)
NADH
D-Ribose
Magnesium
Riboflavin (B2)
Niacin (B3)
N-acetylcysteine (NAC)